Racial Politics and Robert Penn Warren's Poetry

Florida A&M University, Tallahassee
Florida Atlantic University, Boca Raton
Florida Gulf Coast University, Ft. Myers
Florida International University, Miami
Florida State University, Tallahassee
University of Central Florida, Orlando
University of Florida, Gainesville
University of North Florida, Jacksonville
University of South Florida, Tampa
University of West Florida, Pensacola

Racial Politics and
Robert Penn Warren's Poetry

Anthony Szczesiul

University Press of Florida

Gainesville · Tallahassee · Tampa · Boca Raton

Pensacola · Orlando · Miami · Jacksonville · Ft. Myers

Copyright 2002 by Anthony Szczesiul
Printed in the United States of America on acid-free,
TCF (totally chlorine-free) paper
All rights reserved

07 06 05 04 03 02   6 5 4 3 2 1

Library of Congress Cataloging-in-Publication Data
Szczesiul, Anthony.
Racial politics and Robert Penn Warren's poetry / Anthony Szczesiul.
p. cm.
Includes bibliographical references and index.
ISBN 0-8130-2585-0 (cloth: alk. paper)
1. Warren, Robert Penn, 1905—Political and social views. 2. Politics
and literature—United States—History—20th century. 3. Political
poetry, American—History and criticism. 4. Warren, Robert Penn,
1905—Views on race. 5. Southern States—In literature. 6. African
Americans in literature. 7. Race in literature. I. Title.
PS3545.A748 Z885 2003
813'.52—dc21   2002028934

The University Press of Florida is the scholarly publishing agency
for the State University System of Florida, comprising Florida A&M
University, Florida Atlantic University, Florida Gulf Coast University,
Florida International University, Florida State University, University
of Central Florida, University of Florida, University of North Florida,
University of South Florida, and University of West Florida.

University Press of Florida
15 Northwest 15th Street
Gainesville, FL 32611-2079
http://www.upf.com

In memory of my aunt,
Sister Christine Therese Schneider, S.S.J., T.O.S.F.

Contents

Acknowledgments ix

Abbreviations xi

Introduction: Robert Penn Warren's Political and Poetic
Transformations 1

1. The Racialized Order of Warren's "Pondy Woods" Sequence (1929) 8

2. Rereading "The Briar Patch" 26

3. The Conservative Modernist Aesthetic of Warren's Early Poetry,
   1923–1943 39

4. Racial Themes and Formal Transitions in Warren's Early Fiction 57

5. Confession and Complicity in *Brother to Dragons* (1953) 72

6. *Segregation:* The Inner Conflict in Robert Penn Warren 98

7. The Consolidation of Warren's Romantic Aesthetic, 1955–1966 111

8. Warren in Transition: *Who Speaks for the Negro?* and *A Plea in
   Mitigation* 134

9. Reinterpreting the Personal Past: Race in Warren's Later Poetry 153

10. Toward the Self as Fiction: Language, Time, and Identity in Warren's
    Poetry, 1966–1975 173

Conclusion: Warren at the "Inevitable Frontier" of Postmodernism,
1975–1985 199

Notes 217

Bibliography 239

Index 247

Acknowledgments

This book has been several years in the making and would not have been possible without the assistance and support of family, friends, colleagues, and institutions. I would like to thank my parents first, for their constant love and support. I owe a great debt to Keen Butterworth and to the late James Magner, under whose tutelage my appreciation for Warren's poetry developed. Keen was especially influential in the formulating of this book's premise and method, as were Bill Richey and Amittai Aviram. David Kramer and Mark Hama read early draft chapters and offered valuable advice and criticism. My work in earnest on this project began with the support of two generous research awards from the Professional Staff Congress of the City University of New York, while I was on faculty at York College, CUNY. For several years, members of the Robert Penn Warren Circle have provided essential advice and criticisms at the many conferences and conventions where I have had opportunities to air my thoughts on this subject.

Since coming to the University of Massachusetts, Lowell, I have enjoyed a collegial and supportive department—for that I'm truly grateful. Bill Roberts and Melissa Pennell have provided much-needed counsel and encouragement, and special thanks also go to Hilary Holladay and Mary Kramer. Hilary offered judicious advice on several key chapters, and Mary generously offered to proof the manuscript before I submitted it to the University Press of Florida. My wife, Stacy, also read the manuscript in all of its versions, and I am grateful for her patience and thoughtfulness in this regard—and for her uncanny ability to know exactly how much criticism I could bear at any given moment.

It has been a pleasure working with the University Press of Florida, and I am especially thankful to Amy Gorelick of the acquisitions department, for taking an early interest in and encouraging my work, and Gillian

Hillis of the editorial department, for guiding my manuscript through the production process. Thanks also to Ann Marlowe, who did a meticulous job of copyediting the manuscript for the press. John Burt of Brandeis University and Ernest Suarez of Catholic University reviewed the manuscript for the press, and their detailed and insightful responses proved invaluable as I revised the manuscript prior to publication.

Finally, my greatest debt of gratitude is owed to my family: to Stacy, for her love, friendship, and humor, and to our daughters, Adelaide and Zoe, for always reminding me that there were better things I could be doing with my time.

Chapter 3 first appeared in *Style* and is reprinted with permission. Portions of chapters 7 and 9 previously appeared in *Mississippi Quarterly* and are reprinted with permission. An earlier version of my conclusion first appeared in *rWp: An Annual of Robert Penn Warren Studies* and is reprinted by permission of Western Kentucky University and the Center for Robert Penn Warren Studies. Special thanks to John Burt, executor for the Warren literary estate, and the Beinecke Rare Book and Manuscript Library, for permission to quote from the Robert Penn Warren Papers in the Yale Collection of American Literature. Excerpts from the following works by Robert Penn Warren are reprinted by permission of the William Morris Agency, Inc., on behalf of the author: *Collected Poems of Robert Penn Warren,* copyright 1998 by Robert Penn Warren; *Brother to Dragons,* copyright 1953 by Robert Penn Warren; *Segregation: The Inner Conflict in the South,* copyright 1956 by Robert Penn Warren; and *Who Speaks for the Negro?,* copyright 1965 by Robert Penn Warren.

Abbreviations

I have cited my sources parenthetically in the text; endnotes have been used when additional explanation was warranted. For texts by Robert Penn Warren, I use the following abbreviations:

AKM	*All the King's Men*
BA	*Band of Angels*
BD	*Brother to Dragons* (1953)
CA	*The Circus in the Attic and Other Stories*
CP	*The Collected Poems of Robert Penn Warren*
DP	*Democracy and Poetry*
JB	*John Brown: The Making of a Martyr*
Seg	*Segregation: The Inner Conflict in the South*
WSN	*Who Speaks for the Negro?*

Introduction

Robert Penn Warren's Political and Poetic Transformations

You can't be a Southerner and not have the whole race question on your mind in one way or another. It's bound to be there.

Robert Penn Warren, 1967 interview

This is a book about Robert Penn Warren's poetry and politics. But while much of this study is devoted to the analysis of Warren's changing views on race, my discussions of his racial politics are undertaken primarily in an effort to acquire a deeper understanding of his poetry's ever-changing aesthetics and themes. Warren's poetry was not written in a political vacuum, and by reading his poetic canon within the context of his changing racial politics, we can begin to discern the extent to which his poetry engaged in an ongoing dialogue with its changing social and historical contexts and with his own changing political and aesthetic perspectives. Given his early alliance with the conservative Agrarian writers of the South, as well as his association with the New Criticism, some might dismiss Warren as a right-wing defender of the old guard of American poetry, but his career and his canon of poetry are much more complex than such a view allows. Politically, Warren made the dramatic transition from a segregationist to an integrationist position. Poetically, his career bridges—successfully, I think—the modern and the postmodern eras of twentieth-century American poetry. Over the course of this career, he continually reshaped himself as a poet, moving from the high modernist principles of Eliot and Pound through a more open, subjective, and Romantic aesthetic, and finally toward postmodernism. But while most critics have portrayed the changes that occur in Warren's poetic career as the natural consequences of artistic maturity and development, this study reveals that his poetic canon evolved instead through continual personal struggle and conflict, and through constant self-evaluation and self-revision.

These aesthetic conflicts become especially apparent when we consider his poetry alongside his racial politics. An individual does not develop naturally and inevitably from a segregationist to an integrationist position; nor does a poet develop naturally and inevitably from a modernist aesthetic to a neo-Romantic one. Instead, both of these transformations resulted from the complex process of self-evaluation and self-revision. Warren's views on race and poetry evolved in a parallel and complementary manner, and by grounding my discussion of his poetry within the context of his career-long engagement with racial politics, I expose the competing ideologies underlying his diverse canon and underscore the political implications of the radical changes that occur over the course of his career as a poet. This is not to say that Warren's changing views on race *caused* his poetry to change, or vice versa; nonetheless, Warren's poetry does reflect the political and ideological conflicts he experienced as a white Southerner living through the enormous changes that altered the landscape of racial politics in the twentieth century, both in the South and in the nation as a whole. Reading Warren's poetry within this context reveals that the complex transformations that occur over the course of his poetic career sprang from his own difficult negotiations with issues of self and identity, politics and aesthetics, individual will and social change, and race and cultural pluralism—issues that are central to the way we define an evolving democratic community in America.

In *Playing in the Dark*, Toni Morrison argues that there is a strong and undeniable "Africanist presence" which "informs in inescapable ways the textures of American literature" (46). The subject of race may be said to exert a similar influence over the career and canon of Robert Penn Warren, who arguably wrote more about race than any other white literary artist of his generation.[1] Warren engaged racial subjects, themes, and issues in all of his genres and in every decade of his career, from the 1920s to the 1980s. Most notably, the young Warren advocated racial segregation in his 1930 essay "The Briar Patch," published in the controversial Agrarian manifesto *I'll Take My Stand*. As Joseph Blotner remarks in his biography of Warren, "He could not have known how 'The Briar Patch' would haunt him, or how he would be judged a racist by people ignorant of his later repudiation of the 'separate but equal' doctrine" (113). This public repudiation of segregation came in the 1950s. Against the backdrop of the growing civil rights movement, Warren became an advocate of integration and in texts such as *Segregation: The Inner Conflict in the South* (1956) and *Who Speaks for the Negro?* (1965) was writing to exorcize himself of his past opinions. But Warren's engagement with the issue of race extends far beyond these more obvious texts, and as the epigraph above suggests, Warren himself acknowledged—perhaps somewhat ruefully—the extent to which race was inextricably tied to his consciousness as a Southerner. In *Playing in the Dark*, Toni Morrison called for increased critical inquiry into "the impact of racial hierarchy, racial exclusion, and racial vulnerability ... on nonblacks who held, resisted, explored, or altered these notions" (11). Warren's various and evolving views on race run the entire gamut listed by Morrison, moving from a general acceptance of racial hierarchies to a self-conscious exploration and alteration of these concepts. In light of Warren's numerous textual engagements with race, texts that span the entire course of his career, we may view race as a common denominator in his extensive canon. And as the single concrete social and political issue to which he returned over and over again, race can serve as a useful tool in developing our understanding of this canon.

My rationale for reassessing Warren's *poetry* in this manner is twofold. First, I believe Warren's lasting place in American literature will be determined more by his poetry than by his fiction, and that his extensive canon of poetry is deserving of critical inquiry on its own merit. Second, more so than his fiction, Warren's poetry readily lends itself to comparison with his politics. Warren on a number of occasions claimed that his poetry stood as a more accurate and complete record of the particular beliefs he held at various points of his career. In a 1977 interview with Peter Stitt, for instance, Warren was asked about the relationship between his poetry and fiction and responded: "I started as a poet and I will probably end as a poet. If I had to choose between my novels and my *Selected Poems*, I would keep the *Selected Poems* as representing me more fully, my vision and my self. I think poems are more *you*" (Watkins et al. 242). I use Warren's altering opinions on race—stated explicitly in texts such as "The Briar Patch" and *Segregation* and more implicitly in poems such as "Pondy Woods" and *Brother to Dragons*—to provide a touchstone for clarifying the varying positions he adopted as a poet over the course of his lengthy career. By locating and investigating points of intersection between Warren's changing views on race and his changing poetic theories, I delineate the political and ideological implications of his poetry's evolving aesthetic and thematic principles. A clearer and more concrete picture of Warren the poet materializes: we can detect the ways in which his poetry responds to the various historical and cultural moments of its production, and we can begin to discern not only how his poetry changed in form, subject, and theme, but also *why* it changed. Warren emerges in this study as an even more complex poet than has heretofore been imagined, as his poetry—like his various statements on race—begins to reveal a number of conflicts, contradictions, and reversals.

Warren's career as a poet covered more than sixty years and produced seventeen volumes of verse; clearly, a career so long must be richly complex and varied. Yet critics of Warren's poetry have often portrayed his canon as a unified whole. While they have generally agreed that there are different phases in Warren's career, they depict his canon as one that evolved gradually and organically as the poet matured from one phase to the next. For instance, Victor Strandberg, in one of the most complete studies of Warren's poetry, asserts, "A fundamental coherence unifies Warren's whole body of poetry, as though it constituted a single poem drawn out in a fugal pattern—somewhat like Pound's *Cantos* or Eliot's poetry, but more like Eliot's because its total design was not preplanned but simply 'exfoliated' . . . according to some deep rhythm of development in the artist's temperament" (*Poetic Vision* 33–34).[2] According to such formulations of continuous development, each new phase becomes the natural outgrowth or extension of earlier works; consequently, Warren's early poetic texts are often deemed apprentice works, and his later texts are described as his mature achievement. While such critical appraisals have proven extremely useful to our understanding of Warren's extensive canon of poetry, there is, nonetheless, a danger that they may obscure from our vision other, perhaps equally fruitful, avenues of inquiry.

The 1998 publication of *The Collected Poems of Robert Penn Warren*, edited by John Burt, allows us to reevaluate the scope and shape of Warren's poetic career, and instead of looking for consistent, unifying aspects of his canon, perhaps it is time to expose and investigate the cracks and fissures beneath its surface. By highlighting the intersections between Warren's politics and poetics, this study shows that, rather than being consistent and unified in its development, his poetic canon is marked by an abrupt break which resulted in conflicting poetic theories. More specifically, following the ten-year hiatus of 1943–53 during which he published no new poems, Warren essentially recreated himself as a poet with the publication of *Brother to Dragons*; here, he repudiated the high modernist aesthetic of his earlier poetry by adopting what may best be described as a Romantic aesthetic, an aesthetic that—in theory at least—is antithetical to the modernist aesthetic principles he had earlier espoused.[3] Significantly, this poetic transformation coincided with and was inextricably linked to his political transformation from conservative segregationist to liberal integrationist. It is important to emphasize that Warren's emerging Romantic aesthetic was not the natural outgrowth of his early views of poetry, as Lesa Carnes Corrigan has argued; to the contrary, it came about through a conscious effort by Warren to distance himself from his poetical *and* political past.[4] Critics have suggested that Warren's decade-long break from poetry was simply the result of his turning his attention to fiction, but Warren has explained that over this ten-year period he still frequently attempted to write short poems—he simply could not finish them.[5] Warren's break from poetry was the result of a deeper aesthetic crisis or conflict over the very nature and purpose of poetry. This study attempts to illuminate the complex nature of this conflict, a conflict that continued to inform and shape his aesthetic well after his midcareer poetical and political conversions. Indeed, just as Warren kept returning to the subject of race well after his conversion on the issue, he continued to question, alter, and modify his Romantic aesthetic, moving ever closer to his encounter with postmodernism.

The chapters of this study are arranged chronologically, and I have tried to locate texts as much as possible in their immediate cultural and historical moments; when I glance either ahead or backward to other periods in Warren's career, it is usually to emphasize the contrasts and differences in the periods, which in Warren's case are often quite startling and always revealing. The first three chapters of this study focus on Warren's conservative racial politics and modernist poetics from his early associations with the Fugitives and Agrarians up through the publication of *Selected Poems: 1923–1943*. Chapter 4 considers Warren's early fictional treatments of race, particularly during his decade-long break from publishing poetry. Chapters 5 through 7 focus on the political and poetic transformations that occur in Warren's work of the 1950s and early 1960s: his public adoption of an integrationist position and his shift to a more subjective Romantic aesthetic, wherein the self becomes the primary subject of its own inquiry. Chapters 8 through 10 focus on the last two decades of Warren's career, tracing the alterations in his thinking on race and his increasingly radical poetic inquiries into the nature of identity. In *Who Speaks for the Negro?* Warren repeatedly raises difficult and uncertain issues regarding the nature of self and identity which mark a departure from his poetry and criticism of the 1950s and a step toward postmodernism; these more radical views of self and identity also form a new thematic emphasis for his late poetry.

I should emphasize at the outset that in using terms such as "modernist," "Romantic," and "postmodern" to describe various periods of Warren's poetic career, I am not attempting to draw rigid distinctions between hard and fast natural categories. Rather, I employ these terms in a more heuristic fashion to describe various intellectual moments at play in Warren's career and thinking, as certain themes, ideas, and methods move to the foreground of his poetry while others recede to the background. As Albert Gelpi has noted, even though these terms "change their protean shape and color in different hands and perspectives," they are nonetheless "necessary"; moreover, "the very imprecision of such epithets—the fact that they enfold inconsistencies and rest on contradictions and paradoxes—allows us to identify and trace the volatile play and counterplay of issues and values as a given period defines itself in relation to its antecedents and sets the terms for what will develop from it" ("The Genealogy of Postmodernism" 517). While Gelpi's comments here refer to "periods of cultural history," the same principles hold when considering the various moments in an author's career.[6]

Critics agree that Warren throughout his career was particularly concerned with what he perceived as the fragmentation and alienation of the individual in the modern world. However, while this may form a consistent subject in Warren's canon, his general diagnosis and response to this problem changed quite drastically over the course of his career. In order to distinguish between these changing intellectual moments, I have described his aesthetic responses variously as modern, Romantic, and postmodern.[7] To elaborate briefly, we might consider the altering ways in which Warren conceptualized the complex relationships between the poet, the world, and the poet's medium of language. Early in his career, Warren blamed this perceived fragmentation of the individual on the state of the world—on modernity itself. Faced with the disorientation of the modern world, Warren opted for Eliot's program of tradition, authority, order, and control—an aesthetic agenda that complemented and was complemented by Warren's early Agrarian politics. From this particular modernist perspective, the poem generally stands either as a singular image of order against the world's disorder or as a "diagnostic" reflection of that disorder.[8] By the 1950s, Warren's outlook on politics and poetry had transformed itself. In conjunction with his new integrationist political views, Warren pursued a more affirmative, "therapeutic" agenda by attempting—in Romantic fashion—to reconcile the self with the contemporary world through the redeeming language and unifying imaginative vision of the poem.[9] Integration, in other words, became both a political solution and an aesthetic pattern for Warren in this period. However, as he progressed into the late 1960s and the 1970s, Warren increasingly questioned this Romantic alternative, and the momentary balance he had achieved between poet, world, and language began to shift again. In direct contrast to his earlier modernist views which held that the individual was fragmented by the complexities of modernity, Warren increasingly accepted uncertainty, flux, and fragmentation as the self's natural state. Moreover, as his career came to a close, he tended to locate the source of this fragmentation within the medium of language itself, a tendency that places Warren, philosophically at least, at the threshold of the postmodern.[10]

Although this study considers the entire range of Warren's career as a poet and attempts to define some of the complex relationships between his poetry and politics, it is in no way exhaustive or definitive; the very range and breadth of Warren's poetic canon makes any such claim implausible. Similarly, Warren's deep engagement with the issue of race extends far beyond the primary texts I discuss in detail—and far beyond the scope of a single critical monograph. I have simply attempted to offer a new conceptual framework for our understanding of Warren's poetic career, one that takes into consideration the important relationship between his poetics and politics. I agree with Harold Bloom's assessment that Warren's poetry "will be permanent in our literature" (Foreword xxvi), and I hope that this study prompts further critical inquiry and debate.

The Racialized Order of Warren's "Pondy Woods" Sequence (1929)

> In the past the southern Negro has always been a creature of the small town and farm. That is where he still chiefly belongs, by temperament and capacity; there he has less the character of a "problem" and more the status of a human being who is likely to find in agricultural and domestic pursuits the happiness that his good nature and easy ways incline him to as an ordinary function of his being. . . . Let the Negro sit beneath his own vine and fig tree.
>
> Robert Penn Warren, "The Briar Patch"

> In "The Briar Patch" Mr. Warren, with all the metaphysics of his breed, and using all the connotations of the title,—tells the world about the Negro's place in that world. . . . The white man's burden. Oh the pity of it, Iago. A separate community the ideal,—"Under his own vine and fig tree." (Which is a 'cultured' euphemism for ghetto.)—It seems to the chronicler that he's heard all of this, somewhere, before. . . .
>
> Sterling Brown, review of *I'll Take My Stand*

It is apparent from his response that the African-American poet and critic Sterling Brown had little patience with Robert Penn Warren's defense of segregation in "The Briar Patch," but, perhaps as important, his comments on this essay also reveal that he had just as little patience with Warren's racial representations in his poetry. When Brown declares that Warren's pro-segregation argument displays "all the metaphysics of his breed," he is echoing language from Warren's 1928 poem "Pondy Woods," in which a talking buzzard pithily informs a black fugitive, "Nigger, your breed ain't metaphysical." Through this repetition, Brown pointedly links Warren's politics with his poetics in order to repudiate both. Sterling Brown was keenly aware of the fact that racial representations are never without political consequences—even in poetry; indeed, as early as the 1930s Brown as a critic wrote pioneering studies of racial stereotypes in

American literature, describing the ways in which these representations reflected political trends in the country.[1] As Joanne V. Gabbin affirms, "One of Brown's earliest and most stunning contributions to critical thought is his assertion that politics and polemics have everything to do with the way an oppressed group is portrayed" (5). Gabbin goes on to assert that Brown's pioneering studies of race and literature "began the necessary work of tearing down the icons of misconception, stereotypes, and ignorance that stood fast in American society . . . [and] laid the foundations for the study of Black images in American fiction, poetry, and drama" (185). In the first three chapters of this study, I will expand upon the connection so succinctly drawn by Brown between the young Warren's poetry and politics, first by focusing closely on Warren's poetic and political texts from the late 1920s and early 1930s, and then by discussing more generally his poetry of the 1930s and early 1940s. I will show that Warren's poetry of this early period was indeed a highly politicized mode of discourse. His early regional politics—particularly his views on race— and his emerging high modernist aesthetic were complementary endeavors which drew from the same source: a general fear and mistrust of the social and cultural changes facing America in the early part of the century—particularly in the South—and a consequent desire for the stability, order, and authority of tradition in the face of this modern flux and uncertainty.

Sterling Brown obviously bristled at Warren's easy use of racist rhetoric in "Pondy Woods": even as late as a 1973 interview, he answered Warren's line "Nigger, your breed ain't metaphysical" with "Cracker, your breed ain't exegetical."[2] From a contemporary perspective, it is easy to understand Brown's irritation, for the poem certainly is a jumble of racist rhetoric and stereotypes; the "Nigger" in the poem, Big Jim Todd, is described as a "slick black buck" who is running from a lynch mob after committing an unnamed crime on his "Saturday spree." As Jim hides out in the swampy terrain of Pondy Woods, he is confronted by a talking buzzard who lectures him—on one occasion in Latin—on the inevitability of his imminent demise. Tellingly, Jim Todd has no voice and can offer no response to the buzzard's admonition. Indeed, a response would almost seem outside the realm of possibility, for Warren's Jim is merely a one-dimensional stereotype constructed from a white fantasy of blackness rather than from any real knowledge of the complex, lived experiences of African-Americans in the early part of the twentieth century. Interestingly, Sterling Brown's own poem of 1927 titled "Old Man Buzzard" presents a remarkably similar encounter between a black man and a talking buzzard, but in a revealing contrast, Brown's character Fred has voice and agency. After listening to the Buzzard lecture him for four stanzas on the pointlessness of all of his work, hope, and dreams in the face of the inevitability of death, Fred offers a witty response which shows that the buzzard hasn't told him anything he didn't already know.[3] And far from despairing, Fred still has an affirmative view of life. Simply put, Brown's character displays a complex, realistic sense of character and personality—something that is missing from Warren's cardboard representation of Jim Todd. Unlike the young Warren who wrote "Pondy Woods," Sterling Brown was acutely aware of the full implications of the rhetoric employed in Warren's poem, seeing the entire system of racist signification that is articulated within. It is perhaps this failure on the part of white America to recognize the full implications of racial stereotypes and signifiers that Brown had in mind when he offered his biting retort to Warren in the interview of 1973. Brown charged Warren with being incapable of exegesis, of being blind to the possibilities of interpretation. Unfortunately, the text Warren was incapable of interpreting in this instance was one of his own making.

Brown's early groundbreaking criticism on racial representations in literature—along with his response to Warren's rhetoric—addresses the central fact that blacks and whites comprise separate *and unequal* discourse communities in America, and this disjuncture has increasingly served as a focal point for inquiry among contemporary literary critics and theorists.[4] As Aldon Lynn Nielsen strongly asserts in *Reading Race*,

> Our language has come to act as the metaphorical veil of which W.E.B. Dubois speaks so often, separating two national groups and occluding our vision of one another. This veil is maintained between the two terms of a racial dialectic, one of which is privileged. Such privilege is evident even in the naming of the two terms. To the one side of the veil is the white thesis, which is given primacy, which is considered originary, and which names itself. To the other side of the veil, cloaked in darkness, stands the black antithesis, which is always seen as secondary, and which receives its name from the white term. That name is "nigger." (1–2)

Nielsen goes on to argue that this single epithet forms a "linguistic nexus of white thought" where a complex system of racist stereotypes and images—"frozen metaphors"—intersect (5). Anytime the word "nigger" is spoken, or anytime one of these frozen metaphors is repeated, the entire system is in fact conjured up. As an African-American, Sterling Brown has the Du Boisian double vision that allows him to view both sides of this racial dialectic. But many contemporary critics and theorists charge that white Americans, occupying the position of privilege and power, more often than not are unconscious of the other side of the veil; they have named the veil a definitive, essential, and unchangeable reality and sense no need to look beyond at the myriad individuals concealed from their sight. According to such views, Warren's use of racist rhetoric, like any invocation of racist rhetoric and imagery, both participates in and sustains the entire system of racial hierarchy—a system grounded upon a false assumption of natural, absolute, and essential differences between the races.[5]

Warren's representations of African-Americans have not gone unnoticed among critics who have devoted themselves to the study of his poetry. However, critics have not yet suggested the true complexity of Warren's various and often contradictory representations of race; nor have they considered the deeper connection between Warren's changing politics and poetics. For instance, Hugh Ruppersburg, in surveying Warren's representations of blacks, concludes, "From the beginning of his career Warren portrayed blacks in a fairly consistent manner. For the most part he avoided racist stereotypes. Yet he also did not portray blacks so as to arouse sympathy or concern for their condition" (150). Aldon Nielsen, on the other hand, argues more convincingly that the racial representations in the poetry reflect Warren's transition from an uncritical acceptance of the limiting racial assumptions of "The Briar Patch" to "an uncomfortable moral questioning of the white poet's part in the racial discourse" (115). However, Nielsen contends that even in an early poem like "Pondy Woods," Warren is already questioning racial discourse, even though it was published two years before Warren's defense of segregation in "The Briar Patch." In the pages that follow, I will provide a more contextualized reading of "Pondy Woods" which shows quite the opposite: Warren at this early stage of his career is invoking racial stereotypes in an uncritical manner. Overall, the racial representations in Warren's poetry are more complex than these critics suggest, serving a wide variety of functions at different points in his career. By reading these changing representations within their more immediate contexts, we can discern that while Warren moves in his poetry from an unquestioning acceptance of racial assumptions to a self-conscious, often discomfiting, inquiry into these same assumptions, the political context of this transition also informs in remarkable ways the changing contours of his poetry's evolving aesthetic. Indeed, the exchange between Warren's poetry and politics moved in both directions, with Warren's thinking about race sometimes acting as a cause of aesthetic changes and other times being an effect of aesthetic changes. Either way, it becomes clear that Warren's poetry was not written in a political vacuum; rather, it was in an ongoing dialogue with its changing social and historical contexts and with his own changing political and aesthetic perspectives.[6]

At the time Warren was beginning his career as a writer, the South was undergoing what critics have described as a period of general social upheaval. As Richard Gray explains, the South in the 1920s "became an inextricable part of the urban-industrial complex, and on the level of consciousness, its traditional systems of thought and belief were eroded by the new philosophies of modernism" (*Writing the South* 123).[7] The cultural battle between the old and the new manifested itself in a variety of ways, from the rejuvenation of the Ku Klux Klan and the resurgence of religious fundamentalism to the Scopes evolution trial and the ongoing national debates over race and racial violence, which would come to a head in 1931 with the Scottsboro case. In response to the historical changes facing the South in the 1920s and the social and cultural pressures that resulted, Warren, like the other Agrarians, adopted a conservative and defensive agenda which privileged tradition as a way of maintaining a coherent cultural order in the face of such change. Fellow Agrarian Allen Tate succinctly described the agenda as "authoritarian, agrarian, classical, and aristocratic" (Sarcone and Young 34). Within such a project, the continuation of racial segregation as a living remnant of the cultural past became absolutely essential, and Warren's assignment in the Agrarian symposium *I'll Take My Stand* was to argue just that.

For Warren, however, this conservative stance of the Agrarians would go beyond regional politics and would also provide the political foundation for and rationale behind his poetry's emerging aesthetic: the regionalist interests of his earliest poetry would be absorbed by a growing allegiance to the authoritarian, tradition-oriented aesthetic agenda of high modernism, outlined most convincingly by T. S. Eliot. As an undergraduate student at Vanderbilt in the early 1920s, the young Warren was taken in by the Fugitive group of poets, and his close relationships with three of these poets—John Crowe Ransom, Allen Tate, and Donald Davidson—would eventually lead to his involvement with the Agrarian writers who published *I'll Take My Stand* in 1930. As M. Thomas Inge has pointed out, there has been a great deal of confusion and interchange between the Fugitive and Agrarian labels, despite the fact that the terms refer to two distinct literary events and two largely different groups of participants. While Inge is correct in emphasizing the distinct historical realities of these two groups, some of the confusion regarding the terms has resulted from the fact that for those individuals who actively participated in both projects—namely Warren, Tate, Davidson, and Ransom—the seam between the two endeavors came to be virtually nonexistent.[8] Though the Fugitives initially placed themselves in opposition to myths of the Old South, over time they began to self-consciously view themselves as distinctively Southern.[9] The national reaction to the Scopes trial in Dayton, Tennessee, in 1925 is often viewed as the watershed moment in the transition between the Fugitive and Agrarian programs. In response to the national ridicule heaped upon the South for the so-called Monkey Trial, these four writers adopted a conservative and defensive attitude, one that privileged what they saw as the unique, humanistic, and humane attributes of a Southern, agrarian way of life over the supposedly dehumanizing effects of Northern industry, mass production, and consumer culture. As early as 1927, Tate, Davidson, and Ransom were corresponding about a "Southern Symposium" which would eventually be published in 1930 under the title *I'll Take My Stand: The South and the Agrarian Tradition*.[10]

Although Warren was not involved in the earliest of these discussions—he had left Vanderbilt and was pursuing an M.A. at the University of California—by 1928 he was definitely showing his regional leanings and interests. With Tate's assistance, he had secured a contract to write the biography *John Brown: The Making of a Martyr*, a text that illustrates the young Warren's deep-seated regional biases. Warren essentially eviscerates the legend of John Brown as abolitionist martyr, recasting him as a figure whose actions amount to nothing more than "horse rustling and murder as well as nigger stealing" (*JB* 308). He also takes advantage of every opportunity to attack Northern liberalism in all its forms; his targets range from abolitionists such as William Lloyd Garrison, Lydia Maria Child, and Wendell Phillips to authors such as Emerson, Thoreau, and Stowe.[11] Writing of his *John Brown* biography much later in his life, Warren reflected: "It is far from the book I would write now, for that book was shot through with Southern defensiveness, and in my ignorance the psychological picture of the hero was presented far too schematically" (*WSN* 320). Warren's biography of Brown also shows that at this early point in his career he refrained from approaching slavery—and, perhaps by extension, segregation—as a moral issue; instead, he tended to elide the moral question of slavery by approaching it through the framework of historical circumstance and economic necessity: "John Brown, along with the greater number of Abolitionists, thought of slavery in terms of abstract morality, and never in the more human terms of its practical workings. They saw a situation which violated justice, and they firmly believed that every victim of the situation was ready to avenge himself by cutting a throat. The slave himself was at the same time more realistic and more humane; he never bothered his kinky head about the moral issue, and for him the matter simply remained one of convenience or inconvenience" (*JB* 331–32). This tendency to avoid direct confrontation with the moral dilemmas behind Southern race relations is also apparent in "The Briar Patch." In stark contrast, Warren in the 1950s confronts these moral dimensions of race in a direct and even confessional manner.

Warren's early regional biases extended well beyond his revisionist biography of John Brown and into the contemporary political scene as well. In the fall of 1929 and just a short time before *John Brown* was published, Warren wrote Tate to tell him of his recent visit to Nashville before his return to Oxford, where he was then studying as a Rhodes scholar. In the letter Warren expresses his support for the "S. of the O.S. [Sons of the Old South] agitation" and explains with boyish enthusiasm that the "Nashville brothers . . . are on fire with crusading zeal and the determination to lynch carpet-baggers" (*Selected Letters* 167). A few months later, in January of 1930, John Crowe Ransom wrote to officially request Warren's contribution to the Agrarian symposium. Regarding the strong Southern slant to Warren's scathing biography of John Brown, Ransom writes, "As to the sentimental background, you know that I shared that from the start. My hat is off to you" (Ransom, *Selected Letters* 191). From here, he segues into the issue at hand: "What is immediately on my mind is to say: Now is the time for all good men to come to the aid of the party. Don, Andrew Lytle, Tate, and I have got things cooked up to the point where they can't be stopped. I refer to the Old South movement, about which we had a few flying words last summer" (191). After describing the plans for publication, as well as the possibility of purchasing a county newspaper as an open-ended forum for airing their Agrarian beliefs, Ransom suggests that Warren may be the candidate to address the issue of race:

Of course we have been counting on you as one of the faithful. I don't mean to mortgage your career, but only for the time being to get your article and your signature. Haven't you a burning message on the subject of ruralism as the salvation of the negro? or this, that, or the other? Don and I think that you are such a force that we don't need even to indicate to you your subject. (192)

By early March, Warren had signed on to the project, specifically requesting the subject of segregation. And by March 17, Davidson wrote to inform Warren of the deadlines for the manuscript, rallying him with words that may have provided the title of Warren's essay defending segregation: "It's up to you, Red, to prove that negroes are country folks—'bawn and bred in a briar-patch.'"[12]

While both the Agrarian symposium and his continuing studies at Oxford certainly demanded much of his time, Warren still found the energy to pursue with success his main interest, poetry. In the 1929 letter to Allen Tate in which Warren swore allegiance to the Sons of the Old South, he also informed Tate that he had just had a manuscript of poems accepted for publication by Joseph Brewer of Payson and Clarke, the same press that published his *John Brown: The Making of a Martyr*. Unfortunately for the young Warren, the firm of Payson and Clarke went bankrupt in the stock market crash, and his manuscript, titled "Pondy Woods and Other Poems," never went to press. The typescript of this unpublished manuscript still exists among the Robert Penn Warren Papers at Yale's Beinecke Library. Completed just some six months before he began working on his defense of segregation, it provides an interesting glimpse into the important connection between Warren's early regional politics and his early poetry.

The most notable formal feature in the manuscript is the fact that it is comprised of three separate sequences or clusters of poems—"Pondy Woods," consisting of nine poems, "Genealogy," consisting of seven poems, and "Images on the Tomb," which also has seven poems. The "Pondy Woods" sequence runs as follows:

"Pondy Woods"
"Tryst on Vinegar Hill"
"Kentucky Mountain Farm"[13]
"Croesus in Autumn"
"Garden Waters"
"Easter Morning: Crosby Junction"
"August Revival: Crosby Junction"
"Alf Burt: Tenant Farmer"
"The Last Metaphor"

Critics have often commented on the importance of Warren's conscious and careful sequencing of his poems, and the same care and effort obviously went into the arrangement of this early sequence, which presents the young poet's perspectives on Southern culture in the modern era. Importantly, the poem "Pondy Woods" takes on a more overtly racialized agenda in the context of the sequence; indeed, race is an important factor in this sequence, helping Warren define the unique attributes of a coherent, hierarchical Southern culture—the same "essential structure" he subscribes to in "The Briar Patch." While thematically all of the poems contrast human mortality with nature's permanence, Warren's arrangement of poems counterpoints black response to this theme with white response, and thereby demonstrates an uncritical belief in hierarchical, natural, and absolute racial difference.

Relying heavily on the style of the folk ballad, "Pondy Woods" tells the story of Big Jim Todd, "a slick black buck" who is on the run after committing some unspecified crime. In an effort to avoid the lynch mob, he has made his way to the swamps of Pondy Woods, where he has found a hiding place below a roost of buzzards. After the first three stanzas set this scene, the poem takes an unlikely turn as one of the buzzards sardonically addresses Jim on the ultimate futility of his efforts to preserve his life:

"Nigger, you went this afternoon
For your Saturday spree at the Blue Goose saloon,
So you've got on your Sunday clothes,
On your big splay feet got patent-leather shoes.
But a buzzard can smell the thing you've done;
The posse will get you—run, nigger, run—
There's a fellow behind you with a big shot-gun.
Nigger, nigger, you'll sweat cold sweat
In your patent-leather shoes and Sunday clothes
When down your track the steeljacket goes
Mean and whimpering over the wheat.

"Nigger, your breed ain't metaphysical."
The buzzard coughed. His words fell
In the darkness, mystic and ambrosial.
"But we maintain our ancient rite,
Eat the gods by day and prophesy by night.
We swing against the sky and wait;
You seize the hour, more passionate

Than strong, and strive with time to die—
With Time, the beakèd tribe's astute ally. (*CP* 39–40)[14]

The buzzard's monologue clearly defines Jim through stock racial images drawn from the assumed inferior characteristics of the black race: not as intellectually developed as whites, blacks are "more passionate," more impulsive, and consequently more criminal. Jim has apparently lost control of himself while on his Saturday spree. Though Jim is treated in a somewhat comic-ironic manner (wearing his Sunday best for his Saturday spree), the poem also conjures up bestial images with phrases like "slick black buck" and "your breed ain't metaphysical."[15]

Certainly these negative stereotypes are easily identified in the poem, but the fact that the majority of them are invoked by the buzzard and not the narrator has created some varied responses among critics. Are these representations to be taken literally? To what extent does the statement "Nigger, your breed ain't metaphysical" reflect Warren's own views? What are the consequences of such representations—both for the poet and for the reader? At one end of the spectrum, Hugh Ruppersburg argues that "Jim's blackness is not an issue, except as it defines the social helplessness of his position, but it does allow Warren to portray him as an extreme example of the hopelessly fated man" (151). Other critics have read the passage more ironically. Porter G. Raper, for example, sees the buzzard's monologue as an attack on "the Old White South and its elitist world-view" (23).[16] Most interestingly, Aldon Nielsen suggests that Warren here forecasts Derrida's labeling of metaphysics as "white mythology." Nielsen describes the buzzard as "the carrier of the ostracizing power of white discourse," concluding that "the use of the buzzard sets up a disturbance within the discourse, for it is a spokesman with whom few readers will readily identify" (117). But reading such a level of irony into these passages would suggest that Warren was already questioning and deconstructing white racist discourse even before he wrote "The Briar Patch." This seems highly unlikely, particularly since he invokes some of the same stereotypes in his essay, assigning "crime, genial irresponsibility, ignorance, and oppression" to the black community (264).[17] If we consider the particular moment of composition, and if we read this poem as the lead poem in the "Pondy Woods" sequence, it becomes apparent that Warren cannot be so readily distanced from the values disclosed in his rhetoric.

This may perhaps best be clarified by turning to the next poem in the sequence, "Tryst on Vinegar Hill." This poem was apparently composed as a companion piece to "Pondy Woods," as both poems contain reference to Squiggtown. As Jim spends the night in Pondy Woods fearing for his life, two lovers, "a nigger boy and girl," spend the night on Vinegar Hill, an African-American burying ground that overlooks Squiggtown. Together, the poems conjure up two broad categories of racial stereotypes commonly associated with African-Americans, particularly at this point in American and Southern history. On the one hand, Jim is an image of black bestiality and criminality, while on the other, the young lovers convey a naive, happy-go-lucky innocence associated with an assumed racial primitivism.[18] In the case of "Tryst on Vinegar Hill," it is important to emphasize that Warren does not attribute the characters' simplicity to their youthfulness; rather, he associates it specifically with their race. Even though this stereotype may seem more benign than that presented in "Pondy Woods," it is just as limiting. Moreover, the racism articulated in this poem is not spoken by an interloping buzzard; it is spoken by the poet-narrator who is witnessing the scene.[19]

The poem's first two stanzas describe the burying ground of Vinegar Hill where the lovers will come for their meeting. The narrator claims that the sky here seems to lie "More intimately" and "more blue" over the burying ground, as though "it drew / A primeval clarity / Up from the heart and desperate sinew / Of niggers who once were buried there" (CP 23). Here the boy and girl come "To watch the lazy sun go down." While Warren's dubious association of "primeval clarity" with the African-American body is in itself revealing, it is in the third stanza that the narrator begins to comment more directly on what he sees as the unique characteristics of the black race. Considering the irony in the fact that the boy and girl come to a place of death to celebrate their love, the narrator—echoing the buzzards of "Pondy Woods"—exasperatedly proclaims:

Niggers are the damnedest breed:
They see such things and do not need
To know they see, or even guess
Within the earth that restlessness
Of thought which arches those obscene
Fat tropic ocean tides, arches the green
Slow channels of the secret leaf; which drops
The nerves' grey filaments to stay the bone,
And whose dishonest artifice unlocks
The oak's tough bole to bud, and subtly props
The crystalline interiors of the stone.

They do not guess that thought which mocks
Itself back to its hungry elements.
They only see, and their ripe innocence
Of laughter from dark lips in twilight now
Spills; no wind, but the low dogwood's intense
White bloom spills on the dew-black bough. (*CP* 23)

Here the narrator quite literally confirms the point of view expressed by the buzzard in "Pondy Woods" when it declared, "Nigger, your breed ain't metaphysical." The narrator expresses bewilderment at what he sees as the black race's inability to look beyond mere surface realities. They neither "need / To know" nor can "even guess" the complex questions about the nature of reality that he apparently cannot escape. In other words, they cannot see beyond the physical world into the realm of the *meta-physical*. In contrast, the narrator is obviously plagued by his own metaphysical wonderings, as phrases like "restlessness / Of thought" and "thought which mocks / Itself back to its hungry elements" would seem to suggest. The poem, then, juxtaposes black consciousness—portrayed here as limited, superficial, and uncritical—with the higher mode of consciousness represented by the white poet-narrator—expansive, profound, and discriminating.[20] In the last lines of the stanza, Warren further underscores this supposedly natural racial contrast with the images of the "intense" white bloom against the black bough, an image that simultaneously seems to allude both to the moment of ejaculation and to Pound's "In a Station of the Metro." Even the poem's rhyme scheme suggests a contrast between simplicity and complexity, as the first three stanzas each begin with rhyming couplets before developing into more complex, intricate patterns of rhyme.

The narrator of "Tryst on Vinegar Hill" appears to be expressing a longing for the "easy ways" of the black race, much in the same way that poets have traditionally looked to nature itself as an emblem of a simpler, easier existence, an existence free from the burden of human consciousness. The black figures in these poems have been reduced to a part of the natural landscape; the narrator views them as more primitive and more animalistic, as being closer to nature. In short, the couple in "Tryst" epitomize the period's white stereotypes, particularly white views of black sexuality. Some thirty-five years later, Warren offered an insightful analysis of the reasons why "whites cling to the 'myth' of Negro sexuality." As is often the case in his later writings on race, he implicitly offers a sharp critique of his own early views: "there may be a complex of answers, but one is certainly that sexuality is taken to equal animality, and therefore inferiority and a justification for segregation. Segregation protects the white woman from the debasing animality of the Negro man, and at the same time, by defining an inferior and dependent status for the Negro, puts the Negro woman in a position where she, with the attraction of her special sexuality, is presumed to be sexually available—even if only to the imagination" (*WSN* 294). With this in mind, it should also be noted that the couple in "Tryst on Vinegar Hill" are described as a "Yaller gal and big black boy" (*CP* 23). The description of the girl implies that she herself may be the result of an interracial sexual union, thereby subtly encoding into the poem's text this belief in the "sexually available" black woman.

In the poem's closing stanza, the narrator tellingly describes the song of the whip-poor-will as an "uneasy questioning refrain," but the couple's only response is "to lay / The lip to lip and heart to heart again" (*CP* 23). The couple simply do not share in the narrator's anxieties, and again it should be remembered that this is attributed to their race, not their youthfulness. In the closing lines, their lovemaking becomes so potent that it provides a "spark / Of warmth" to the decaying bodies buried beneath them. Of the dead, the narrator says:

> They know their place—not anxious, not too bold—
> Poor ghosts, who once loved laughter and the sun,
> And now, when the lazy day is gone,
> Still find the ivied earth so cold. (*CP* 24)

Like the couple in "Tryst," Jim Todd in "Pondy Woods" is apparently unaware of complex ontological issues until the buzzard instructs him in the laws of human mortality. Following this lecture, Jim experiences a moment of understanding, yet he seems incapable of articulating this new knowledge:

> Pedantic, the bird clacked its grey beak,
> With a Tennessee accent to the classic phrase;
> Jim understood, and was about to speak,
> But the buzzard drooped one wing and filmed the eyes. (*CP* 40)

It is perhaps this new awareness regarding the inevitability of death that prompts Jim to leave his hiding place at dawn, and as the poem closes, the hounds can be heard tracking Jim toward his violent death. On one level, Jim's awakening to his own mortality does represent his "oneness with all human beings," as Hugh Ruppersburg suggests; however, I do not agree with Ruppersburg's contention that this effectively "cuts through the racist stereotype of the fugitive black criminal" (160). The same may be said of "Tryst on Vinegar Hill": Warren's assumption of natural and essential racial differences both contradicts and overrides any sense of universal themes. In short, these poems are explicitly racialized texts which differentiate the white race from the black race at a time when, as Grace Elizabeth Hale has shown, this assumed racial difference formed the very basis of Southern culture itself. In *Making Whiteness: The Culture of Segregation in the South, 1890–1940,* Hale analyzes the complex process through which the South constructed a segregationist culture in the late nineteenth and early twentieth centuries. "Hierarchical structures founded in the personalized social relations of specific localities lost their authority in an increasingly mobile and rapidly changing society," she argues, and as they did, the South "produced new grounds of difference to mediate the ruptures of modernity. In effect, they translated the specific and individualized linkages between identity, place, and power that had reigned in an earlier, smaller world into connections between categories of people and imagined spaces that moved far beyond local boundaries" (6). In other words, as local practices and customs lost their power in the more modern South, broad-based cultural myths of essential racial difference became more important and more commanding. "Pondy Woods" and "Tryst on Vinegar Hill" construct "imagined spaces" for such mythologizing, and Warren's commitment to these notions of natural racial difference becomes more readily apparent when we consider these poems alongside "The Briar Patch" and in relation to the rest of the sequence.

If the first two poems of the "Pondy Woods" sequence exhibit Warren's racial assumptions regarding blacks, it is in the sequence as a whole that we can discern the manner in which these assumptions formed the foundation for his representation of the hierarchical structure of the segregated South. In contrast to the stereotyped representations of African-Americans in the first two poems, in the poems that follow Warren clearly portrays whites in a more dignified, sympathetic manner. In "Kentucky Mountain Farm"—here comprised of five sections—the modern-day narrator takes a historical view of his region, considering the plight of the early settlers, the "little stubborn people of the hill" who had carved a difficult existence out of the rugged landscape. In "Rebuke of the Rocks," the opening section, the narrator describes how they struggled in human affliction and hardship against the continuity of nature's cyclical processes. In contrast to the "more passionate" lives of blacks in the first two poems, the "lean men" who reside among these hills present a picture of cold, hard discipline. To survive, they must renounce passion; their affinities must lie with the rocks that surround them:

> Instruct the heart, lean men, of a rocky place
> That even the little flesh and fevered bone
> May keep the sweet sterility of stone. (CP 35)

This appraisal of the settlers' austere character is echoed in the second section of "Kentucky Mountain Farm," titled "At the Hour of the Breaking of the Rocks." Here we are told that the lean men whose time is now past lived with a stern conviction that is out of place in the modern world:

> Beyond the wrack and eucharist of snow
> The tortured and reluctant rock again
> Receives the sunlight and the tarnished rain.
> Such is the hour of sundering we know,
> Who on the hills have seen to stand and pass
> Stubbornly the taciturn
> Lean men that of all things alone
> Were, not as water or the febrile grass,
> Figured in kinship to the savage stone. (CP 36)

The narrator's interest in these images of the historical past suggests that he longs for the discipline and conviction of the lean men. He is a victim of modernity ("the sundering we know"), cut off from the past and living a fragmented, rootless existence. This is also suggested in the poem's repetition of words like "breaking," "wrack," "tortured," "sundering," and "fractured."

In the closing section of "Kentucky Mountain Farm," titled "The Return," this attempt to recall the order of the historical past seems doomed to failure. Once again Warren contrasts nature's permanence with human discontinuity. The first stanza describes a "timeless gold / Broad leaf" falling from its bough into the stream below. As it approaches the water's surface, its reflection—a "richer leaf"—rises to meet it; it seems restored to wholeness even in death:

> A richer leaf rose to the other there.
> They touched; with the gentle clarity of dream,
> Bosom to bosom, burned on the quiet stream. (CP 38)

In contrast, the second stanza describes the "backward heart" of the narrator, which has "no voice to call" its "vagrant image [back] again." The narrator's meditations on history have revealed a seemingly irreconcilable split between the past and present. His acute awareness of time and death, along with his obsession with the historical past, stands in counterpoint to the ways in which the black characters of the first two poems reacted to human mutability.

Warren continues this contrast with "Croesus in Autumn" and "Garden Waters." In the former, the narrator describes an old man sitting on a village bench contemplating the decline of summer and the change of the seasons. He compares the old man to Croesus, the ancient ruler of immense wealth who supposedly was instructed, "Account no man happy before his death." Even though the narrator treats the old man in a comic and somewhat cruel manner, he ascribes to the old man the very intellectual qualities he denied the black characters in "Pondy Woods" and "Tryst on Vinegar Hill": the changing seasons "stir the bald and metaphysic skull" of the elder (CP 53). "Garden Waters" similarly centers on human consciousness contemplating the passage of time—"the season's wreck, / The dead leaf and the summer's chrysalid" (CP 60), but as the "Pondy Woods" sequence progresses, it becomes clear that the poems are lamenting not so much human mortality and transience as the loss of a way of life and of a coherent cultural order. Significantly, the image of the "summer's chrysalid" suggests the possibility of rebirth and renewal, a possibility the narrator repeatedly returns to as the sequence moves toward its conclusion. The modern-day narrator is alienated from the security of the old order and desires a rapprochement with its traditions. However, in "Easter Morning: Crosby Junction" Warren suggests that the promise of renewal that traditional religion offers is inaccessible to the narrator, even though he seems to desire its security:

> How may we sing who have no golden song,
> How may we speak who have no word to say,
> Or pray, or pray—who would so gently pray? (CP 17)

The narrator's modern sensibility will not allow him to partake of the promise offered by Christianity. He is too rational and too preoccupied by death, as is illustrated in "August Revival: Crosby Junction" and "Alf Burt: Tenant Farmer." In "August Revival" the preacher's promise of resurrection seems to the narrator a "chronicle too weary to be told," and he resigns himself to a more modern, more naturalistic outlook (*CP* 21). Despite this outlook, however, he can still describe with sympathy the death of a tenant farmer. While all of his life Alf Burt had struggled against pestilence, flood, and drought—struggles that call to mind the "lean men" of "Kentucky Mountain Farm"—he finally is afforded peace in death, even if it is a naturalistic peace: "And in that sleep where all things are the same / No dream can fall to stir him to remember / Thistle and drouth and the crops that never came" (*CP* 15).

The final poem of the sequence, "The Last Metaphor," confirms the poet-narrator's overall relationship to the scenes thus far described. The narrator, carrying his "mortal miseries," ventures out to once again confront the sunset and the stark countryside stripped of its foliage—natural images that foretell both his own death and perhaps that of his culture. Taking counsel "of the heart alone," he concludes "I am as the tree and with it have like season" (*CP* 54). Just as the tree has been stripped of its leaves, the narrator feels he has been stripped of his connection with a coherent culture, as his persistent sense of alienation in the sequence suggests. But as he reflects upon this metaphor, he realizes that like the tree, which is renewed with each spring, perhaps he too may somehow experience a restoration. The thought comforts him enough so that he may offer up one final metaphor:

And hence he made one invocation more,
Hoping for winds beyond some last horizon
To shake the tree and so fulfill its season:
Before he went a final metaphor,

Not passionate this, he gave to the chill air,
Thinking that when the leaves no more abide
The stiff trees rear not up in strength and pride
But lift unto the gradual dark in prayer. (*CP* 54–55)

The sequence itself stands as the poet-narrator's prayerful offering; he pays homage to his cultural past and, in doing so, hopes to maintain a sense of connection with his forebears.

Throughout the "Pondy Woods" sequence, Warren provides images that point to the inevitability of change and death, both individual and, through the attitude of the detached narrator, cultural. Like the narrators of Ransom's "Old Mansion" or "Antique Harvesters" or Tate's "Ode to the Confederate Dead," the poet-narrator finds himself in a position alienated from the society and culture he nostalgically celebrates. In spite of this, the closing lines again illustrate his desire to maintain continuity in the face of change. Like the narrator in *The Waste Land*, he has shored these fragments of the past against the ruin of the modern world, hoping for some sort of renewal. The sequence itself is comprised of fragments of his cultural heritage as a Southerner, and, importantly, these fragments have been arranged in a way that reinforces the South's racial order of both the past and the present. In other words, though the narrator feels that much of his culture has been eroded away, his belief in hierarchical racial difference provides a living link to the past. The desire to maintain the tradition and order of the past provides the thematic center of Warren's "Pondy Woods" sequence, but it also informs his defense of segregation in *I'll Take My Stand* and extends to form the foundation for his emerging high modernist aesthetic. Indeed, the fact that Warren dispersed most of the poems of this sequence among the contents of his 1935 volume *Thirty-Six Poems* suggests the ways in which his conservative regional political biases were absorbed within a growing allegiance to the authoritarian, traditionalist aesthetic agenda outlined by T. S. Eliot and the high moderns. In "The Briar Patch" Warren speaks of the desire to maintain the "integrity" of the South's traditional cultural order. Facing the threat of rising industry and social change in the South, the continuance of racial segregation—a cultural remnant of the past—becomes paramount. Similarly, the young Warren followed Eliot's belief that the modern poet must cultivate a historical consciousness and must strive to define his or her stance in relation to the poetic tradition, which likewise offers stability and continuity in the face of modern change and uncertainty. Echoing Eliot's "Tradition and the Individual Talent," Warren in 1934 will proclaim that the modern poet "must tap the old, constant, undefiled, absolute stream, . . . he must discover his own relation to poetic tradition."[21]

Rereading "The Briar Patch"

I uncomfortably suspected . . . that no segregation was, in the end, humane. But it never crossed my mind that anybody could do anything about it. When I wrote ["The Briar Patch"] . . . the image of the South I carried in my head was one of massive immobility in all ways, in both its virtues and vices—it was an image of the unchangeable human condition, beautiful, sad, tragic.

Robert Penn Warren, *Who Speaks for the Negro?*

In his introduction to the 1962 reissue of *I'll Take My Stand*, Louis D. Rubin Jr. describes Agrarianism as an "extended metaphor" which offers "a critique of the modern world" (xxviii, xxxi). For Rubin, the relationship between this "metaphor" and the actual social and political realities of the South is oddly immaterial; instead, "What matters is the vision of a more harmonious, aesthetically and spiritually rewarding kind of human existence that the book holds up. . . . *I'll Take My Stand* is not a treatise on economics; it is not a guide to political action; it is not a sociological blueprint. It is a vision of what the good life can be" (xxxii). In his introduction's concluding paragraph, Rubin again elides the book's political agenda by making a New Critical turn toward the supposedly universal values articulated in *I'll Take My Stand*: "One should read this prophetic book, then, not as a treatise on economics and politics, not as a guide to regional social structuring, but as a commentary on the nature of man—man as Southerner, as American, as human being" (xxxv).[1] To this list of qualifiers Rubin might have added "white," for the Agrarian vision of "the good life" was not so good for African-Americans living in the Jim Crow South.

The political dimensions of Agrarianism cannot be so easily erased, and Sterling Brown's scathing review of *I'll Take My Stand*, published in 1931 in *Opportunity*, attests to this fact. In the review, Brown dismisses the volume as a "romantic defense of the agrarian tradition"; he briefly lists a

number of the contributors' oversimplifications, logical gaps, and histori-
cal inaccuracies and characterizes the endeavor as nothing more than "an-
cestor worship" ("A Romantic Defense" 281). After rejecting the volume
as a whole, Brown in the second half of his brief review turns his attention
to what he believes is the real engine driving the Agrarian agenda: "The
chronicler suspected all along that there would be hidden somewhere the
unreconstructed Southerner's attitude to the Negro—the proverbial Afri-
can woodcarving in the lumber yard." From here Brown launches into his
caustic attack on Warren's defense of segregation: "In 'The Briar Patch'
Mr. Warren, with all the metaphysics of his breed, and using all the con-
notations of the title,—tells the world about the Negro's place in that
world" (282). Tellingly, however, Brown does not even bother to offer any
detailed analysis and rebuttal of Warren's argument; he simply quotes
numerous excerpts from the essay before dismissing it out of hand.
Brown was obviously confident that the readers of *Opportunity* would
share his reaction to Warren's political agenda. As Mark A. Sanders has
noted, "Brown's unequivocal dismissal [of *I'll Take My Stand*] serves as
an essential political gesture, a vehicle through which a major New Negro
publication denounces the Fugitives, as they were called, and the reigning
manifesto of southern intellectual racism" (xx).[2]

Despite what was seen so clearly by Sterling Brown, the full political
and ideological implications of Warren's early racist assumptions have not
yet been fully considered by critics who have devoted themselves to the
study of his canon. My use of the phrase "racist assumptions" requires
some clarification. Among the varying degrees of racism—ranging from
the paternalistic and condescending to the vicious and violent—Warren's
early views certainly belonged to the more genteel, paternalistic tradition
of white Southern racial superiority. The fact that Warren was an advocate
for continued racial segregation in the South does not necessarily make
him a proponent of race hatred or racial violence. At the same time, how-
ever, his support of segregation does mean that he accepted the assump-
tion that forms the backbone of segregation: an essentialist belief in abso-
lute racial difference and natural racial hierarchy.[3] If we accept Henry
Louis Gates Jr.'s definition of racism as "the penchant to *generalize* based
upon essences perceived as *biological*" ("*Race*," *Writing, and Difference*
404), Warren's early canon provides plenty of evidence of this tendency.
Nonetheless, some critics continue to insist that Warren never held racist
beliefs, despite his pro-segregation essay and his often casual, uncritical
use of racist rhetoric in his early career.[4] But in attempting to defend War-

ren's early positions, critics at times have had to play the contortionist. Consider, for example, this passage from Robert Koppelman's *Robert Penn Warren's Modernist Spirituality*, a passage that suggests "The Briar Patch" was not really arguing for segregation:

> Significantly, it was from England and with his characteristically independent perspective that Warren would compose "The Briar Patch," his controversial (though frequently misinterpreted) apparent defense of southern segregation (albeit intended to promote the specific welfare of the southern Negro) which would be his contribution to *I'll Take My Stand*. (2)

Koppelman never goes on to explain or justify this viewpoint and only comments on the essay at one other point in his book. There he claims that Warren's essay shows that he "parted company with his fellow Southern Agrarians by arguing what he believed was in the best interests of the southern Negro" (32). In short, Koppelman evades the question of racism in Warren's text by simply refusing to discuss the issue. The problem with such attempts to evade—or, in this case, erase—the issue of racism in Warren's canon is that they can result in an overly simplified, homogeneous portrayal of Warren's career as a writer. In contrast, by foregrounding the issue of race in Warren's canon—and, in this study's case, particularly in his poetry—we allow Warren to emerge as a much more complex individual than critics have heretofore suggested. The degree to which he consistently struggled with his past becomes much clearer, and his canon reveals surprising points of conflict, contradiction, and reversal.

The failure of critics to consider this level of complexity can be traced to a few recurring strategies they have employed in their readings of Warren, and nowhere is this clearer than in their analyses and appraisals of "The Briar Patch." While Warren's positions on race—particularly as expressed in "The Briar Patch," *Segregation*, and *Who Speaks for the Negro?*—have received a substantial amount of critical attention, the fact that there are two very different Warrens to consider—the conservative segregationist and the liberal integrationist—has often created problems for critics. Inevitably, it seems, critics have chosen to emphasize what they consider to be the similarities between these two points in Warren's career rather than the differences. This tendency may be traced to the fact that when literary critics approach the career of an author, they usually rely on frameworks of development, which necessarily emphasize notions of continuity, growth, and unity.[5] But such an interpretive strategy can at times be too quick to erase points of conflict and tension in favor of harmony and homogeneity. Such may be seen in a summary statement on "The Briar Patch" offered by John L. Stewart in *The Burden of Time: The Fugitives and Agrarians*:

> But, for all the limitation of his perspective, Warren wrote with that eye for naturalistic detail which already distinguished his poetry and gave his brief excursion into sociology and economics authority and concreteness not found in most of the other essays [of *I'll Take My Stand*]. Moreover, he had his vision, here so rudimentary when compared to what it would become in his long poems and the novels, of a man's compelling need to fulfill himself. *Otherwise, the essay had little connection with or significance for his development as a writer.* It was not in the least philosophical, and it was the philosophical bases of Agrarianism which counted most with him. (166, italics added)

In this appraisal, Stewart first salvages any points that he sees as similar to Warren's later writings (the origins of his development) and then deletes the rest of the essay (the racial politics) from Warren's canon. However, though Stewart may conclude that the essay is not philosophical, we cannot escape the fact that it is ideological, and the ideological underpinnings of Warren's pro-segregation argument—with their racist implications—have been given short shrift by critics.

Instead, critics have tended to read "The Briar Patch" by superimposing over the text Warren's later, more liberal ideas. In other words, they read forward in anticipation of his conversion to an integrationist position. Again, this critical tendency is one of the potential pitfalls of adopting a framework of development. In doing so, they essentially attempt to unify two vastly different positions Warren held over a span of twenty-five years. They have relied on a variety of recurring arguments to accomplish this end. Daniel Joseph Singal, for instance, in *The War Within: From Victorian to Modernist Thought in the South*, spends a significant amount of time explaining that Warren was the most progressive of the Agrarians. Pointing to fellow Agrarian Donald Davidson's dissatisfaction with Warren's essay, Singal, like Koppelman, concludes that "The Briar Patch" reveals that Warren "was already moving beyond" the Agrarians (349). A slightly different tack is taken by Marshall Walker. In *Robert Penn Warren: A Vision Earned*, Walker attempts to excuse the racist logic of "The Briar Patch" by blaming Warren's Southern background and environment. Walker claims that the defense of segregation put forth in the essay "was, in 1930, for Warren, the most humane possible expression of practical sympathy for the Negro within the structure in which both he and the Negro had been raised" (34–35). Certainly Warren was to a large degree a product of his environment, and certainly his early views on segregation were in line with much of the white Southern population at that time. However, if we were to pursue Walker's argument to its logical conclusion, we would have to wonder why segregation doesn't still exist today, for he suggests that it is impossible for an individual to see beyond the circumstances of environment. Warren himself dismisses such a deterministic viewpoint in *Segregation: The Inner Conflict in the South*, where he concludes that we cannot view ourselves simply as "prisoners of our history" (62).

Other critics, like Hugh Ruppersburg and William Bedford Clark, historicize Warren's career and canon to a greater extent than has been done before; however, when it comes time to address "The Briar Patch," they come close to compromising their claims of historicity by reading forward a full quarter of a century in anticipation of Warren's conversion to an integrationist position, which was announced first in *Segregation*. As Ruppersburg and Clark attempt to link these two texts within a developmental narrative, the details and pressures of the specific historical moments in which Warren was writing, as well as the manner in which they informed his views, tend to get lost against the backdrops of the narratives the critics have constructed. These narratives suggest that Warren's later views were natural outgrowths and extensions of his early views, so much so that an early text contains the same ideas as a later text, only in nascent form. In the case of Warren's views on race—and in the case of his views on poetry—this is not necessarily true. As I suggested in the introduction, one does not develop naturally and inevitably from a segregationist to an integrationist philosophy; nor does a poet develop naturally and inevitably from a modernist aesthetic to a neo-Romantic one. These transformations instead came about through difficult self-criticism and self-revision. While his 1930 defense of segregation does contain major contradictions, these contradictions did not make his later adoption of an integrationist position inevitable. Warren in 1930 still could have "developed" in an entirely different direction, such as that taken by Donald Davidson from a segregationist position to a more intense segregationist position.[6] This is certainly not to say that the approaches of Clark, Ruppersburg, and the other critics I've cited here are invalid; indeed, these critics have laid the foundation for our current understanding of Warren's long and diverse career. I only hope that my efforts to place Warren's texts in their more immediate contexts can fill in some of the subtle details of this complex career and its remarkable series of transformations.

In *Robert Penn Warren and the American Imagination*, Ruppersburg provides one of the more complete discussions of Warren's racial politics, but like Singal and Stewart he looks for the origins of Warren's later progressive viewpoints in the essay: "Though the essay often reflects a patronizing, paternalistic view of Southern blacks, [and] an occasional willingness to invoke expected stereotypes . . . , it also expressed surprisingly broad-minded attitudes for the time and place of its publication" (30). Again like Singal, Ruppersburg goes on to cite Donald Davidson's criticism of Warren's essay, which works to cast Warren as the least Agrarian of the Agrarians. Following this strategy, Ruppersburg is able to proclaim, "Still, for all one might say against it, 'The Briar Patch' was not thoroughly racist." Indeed, near the end of his analysis, Ruppersburg seems to be bordering on the conclusions drawn by Koppelman that Warren did not hold racist opinions at all and that he was really arguing against segregation all along. He claims to sense Warren's moral conscience coming through in the essay, pointing to certain passages on fair wages and crop prices. According to Ruppersburg, these statements "begin to suggest that racism and segregation are contrary to the very essence of what it means to be human, and American, [and] anticipate both *Segregation* and *Who Speaks for the Negro?*, which made Warren's rejection of racism and segregation unambiguously clear" (34). In essence, he implies that Warren was already against segregation at the time he wrote "The Briar Patch."

William Bedford Clark similarly invokes this type of forward-reading strategy in *The American Vision of Robert Penn Warren*. In the preface Clark announces his intention to "historicize" Warren's writing "to a degree that has not been attempted thus far" and goes on to explain that in doing so, he has tried "to avoid . . . the sometimes pernicious reductivism one finds in the work of many self-proclaimed 'new historicists'" (xii). But instead of the "pernicious reductivism" of the new historicists, Clark offers a narrative of development that carries its own potential for a reductive argument. Clark, like many others, contends that "Warren's values and assumptions proved to be remarkably consistent over the course of his career" (18). While he admits that Warren's approach to race underwent a "profound reevaluation," he still chooses to emphasize continuity

rather than to fully consider the contradictions and conflicts (18). Conse-
quently, when he enters into his discussion of the "The Briar Patch,"
Clark, like the other critics discussed above, is already reading ahead a
quarter of a century. He refers to "The Briar Patch" as a "process piece"
(28) and proceeds to group it with *Segregation* and *Who Speaks for the
Negro?*, claiming:

> What should be stressed here is the common thread that runs
> throughout Warren's thinking about race and "freedom" in the full-
> est sense of the word. No set of social circumstances, however propi-
> tious, can be depended upon to assure self-actualization. The most
> debilitating tyranny is that of the insular and misdirected self, a tyr-
> anny that enslaves men and women without respect to the color of
> their skins. (30)

Like Louis Rubin in his above-cited reading of the Agrarians, Clark here
turns to universal themes, in effect deleting the concrete cultural context
and political agenda of the essay. According to Clark's comments, the
young Warren who authored "The Briar Patch" was trying to help Afri-
can-Americans by freeing them from some type of psychological tyranny
which was worse than the Jim Crow tyranny they faced in their daily
lives. While both Clark and Ruppersburg provide valuable and insightful
readings of Warren's canon within the American cultural context, they
rely too heavily upon the developmental narratives they have constructed
when they discuss Warren's racial politics. They allow their knowledge of
Warren's later, more liberal views to infiltrate their readings of "The Briar
Patch" and sway their interpretations.[7] This tendency in Warren criticism
ultimately limits our understanding of his complexity, giving us a dimin-
ished view of his segregationist and his integrationist positions alike; in
fact, they become one and the same. In contrast, by placing Warren's early
writings on race in their immediate social and cultural contexts, it be-
comes clear that he was more committed both to segregation and to the
conservative principles of Agrarianism than critics have yet suggested.
Warren's "Pondy Woods" sequence of 1929, his "Briar Patch" essay of
1930, and even his reactions to the racially charged politics of the
Scottsboro case in the early 1930s all reveal a firm commitment to the
culture of segregation. Moreover, as I will demonstrate in the next chap-
ter, the conservative principles behind his Agrarian politics formed the
foundation of the emerging high modernist aesthetic of his early poetry.
    Although Donald Davidson's dissatisfaction with Warren's essay is of-

ten cited as evidence that Warren was somehow a liberal in conservative's clothing, the overall thrust of "The Briar Patch" is very much in line with the most conservative principles of segregation and Agrarianism. Most of Warren's argument is simply a rehashing of Booker T. Washington's "Atlanta Compromise" speech of 1895. But a third of a century had passed since then, and Washington's strategy of compliance and submission had been supplanted by the more assertive tactics of W.E.B. Du Bois and the NAACP. Moreover, it must be emphasized that Warren shows little indication that he may, as the critics mentioned above suggest, have been wavering in his commitment to segregation; on the contrary, throughout the essay he affirms the principles of segregation and displays an unyielding belief in essential and hierarchical racial differences between blacks and whites, a belief that is, of course, necessary for a commitment to segregation. While Ruppersburg contends that Warren's statements on equal justice, equal compensation for work, and fair crop prices show that he was somehow already rejecting racism and segregation, these statements are not necessarily based on some higher moral imperative that has integration as its end goal. On the contrary, they are carefully constructed concessions in an economically based argument designed to secure the continuation of racial segregation in the agrarian South in the face of encroaching industrialism from the North. Even in his brief comments on the practice of lynching, Warren approaches the issue from an economic perspective rather than a moral one.[8] Indeed, Warren's commitment to "equal right before the law" for Southern blacks may not have been as firm as Ruppersburg suggests, for as I'll discuss later, evidence shows that Warren's views on the Scottsboro case of the early 1930s and to the Supreme Court's 1932 decision that challenged the Southern justice system were anything but sympathetic to the plight of the falsely accused Scottsboro men.

Warren wrote "The Briar Patch" with two main goals in mind: first, to show that industrialism would not provide a better life for Southern blacks and, second, to defend the Southern system of segregation as a culture. Significantly, at the time he was writing this pro-segregation essay for *I'll Take My Stand*, Warren was keenly aware of both the project's intended national audience and the growing moral controversy surrounding the issue of segregation in this national arena. In a letter to Allen Tate dated May 19, 1930, Warren tells Tate that the thesis of his essay is "pressing him hard" and expresses knowledge that his topic is explosive: "The negro is a delicate subject and one which could be most easily attacked;

consequently, for my own good and the good of others, I can't afford to pull a boner in dealing with it" (*Selected Letters* 185). Fearing such attacks from unsympathetic readers, Warren's defense of segregation is one that makes what may be termed humane concessions to African-Americans in the South; nonetheless, he is still firmly committed to the continuation of segregation as culture. His logic, stated very simply, runs something like this: If we want to maintain segregation in the South—which we do—we must ensure, through legal protection and adequate opportunity, that blacks are able to make a viable living as tradespeople, sharecroppers, and subsistence farmers. Otherwise they will provide a cheap source of labor that will continue to lure even more industry to the South. This, in turn, will undermine the place of the white laborer in the marketplace, fan the flames of race hatred, and further erode the integrity of the Southern agrarian cultural order.

The greatest contradiction in Warren's essay is that he proposes just means (legal protection and adequate opportunity) to achieve unjust ends (the continuation of racial segregation). In light of this contradiction, we may conclude that segregation and inequality were, in theory at least, separate things in the young Warren's mind. At the same time, however, "The Briar Patch" shows that Warren was well aware of what Thurgood Marshall would argue some twenty-four years later: separate is inherently unequal. This is particularly apparent in his discussion of the plight of the "educated Southern Negro," where Warren makes it unambiguously clear that he wants nothing to do with blacks in the social sphere. These passages show a real awareness of the social barriers facing Southern blacks:

> He has money in his pocket, but he is turned away from the white man's restaurant. At the hotel he is denied the bed which he is ready to pay for. He likes music, but must be content with a poor seat at a concert—if he is fortunate enough to get one at all. The restrictions confront him at every turn of his ordinary life. But his answer to another question might do something to clear both his and the white man's mind. Does he simply want to spend the night in a hotel as comfortable as the one from which he is turned away, or does he want to spend the night in the same hotel? A good deal depends on how this hypothetical Negro would answer the question. (253–54)

As Warren continues, it becomes obvious that he believes the correct answer is the former option. And if this is what the hypothetical black professional wants—a hotel as comfortable as the white man's—then he'll simply have to wait patiently until the Southern black population has made itself "economically free" to an extent that comfortable hotels are owned, operated, and patronized by blacks. The other option—that he wants to stay in the same hotel as the white man—is ludicrous to Warren, as his subsequent comments illustrate:

> But the Negro radical, or the white radical in considering the race problem, would say that he wants the second thing—he wants to go to the same hotel, or he wants the right to go to the same hotel. The millennium which he contemplates would come to pass when the white man and the black man regularly sat down to the same table and when the white woman filed her divorce action through a Negro attorney with no thought in the mind of any party to these various transactions that the business was, to say the least, a little eccentric. (254)

For the young Warren who wrote this essay, the South without segregation was a preposterous supposition. Warren would undoubtedly have included the likes of W.E.B. Du Bois among such radicals. Not many years after Booker T. Washington had risen to prominence following his Atlanta Compromise speech, Du Bois in *The Souls of Black Folk* had mounted a full frontal assault on Washington's "attitude of adjustment and submission," pointing out that, along with the resulting disfranchisement and dwindling educational opportunities, Washington's counsel of "silent submission to civic inferiority" would certainly "sap the manhood of any race in the long run" (36, 37). Warren at this point in his career shows little sympathy for such an argument. Instead, in formulating his response to the demands of the hypothetical Negro-turned-radical, Warren presumptuously assumes the persona of Booker T. Washington himself:

> "My Friend," Washington might well reply to such a critic, "you may respect yourself as a man, but you do not properly respect yourself as a Negro." To him the critic would be suffering from a failure to rationalize his position, from the lack of a sense of reality, and from a defect in self-respect, for the last implies the first two deficiencies. . . . Many negroes undoubtedly possess a self-respect; in others, something else, such as fatalism or humor, may partially serve its purpose in making the situation comfortable. But the more dynamic attitude is to be expected when, and only when, the Negro is able to think of

himself as the member of a group which can afford an outlet for any talent or energy he may possess. (254–55).

In other words, Warren expects blacks in the South to accept their present position of economic, social, and civic inferiority, to simply grin and bear it. If they have any desire to pursue what Du Bois termed "the higher aims of life," they'll have to wait until the black population can support such endeavors. While Warren later would contend that when he wrote "The Briar Patch" he ultimately wanted equality for blacks within a system of social segregation, it's quite clear in the text of the essay that he was willing to put up with a good amount of inequality in order to maintain the separation of the races.[9] What is quite remarkable in these passages is that Warren implicitly shows a degree of awareness of the debilitating psychological effects suffered by many black Americans living under segregation, yet he still professes little sympathy for their plight; instead, he has the audacity to claim that a black who wants a better life has no self-respect. In a 1969 interview with Marshall Walker, Warren would describe himself as having been "too young" or "too stupid" at the time he wrote the essay to understand "the brutality of the [segregation] system in its psychological way" (Watkins et al. 159).

Warren's comments on the demands made by the "Negro radical" may be seen as a direct response to the more assertive tactics employed by the NAACP during the 1920s. Following World War I, and especially following the terrible racial violence of 1919, the NAACP redoubled its efforts to dismantle Jim Crow, with leaders committing themselves to nothing less than "first-class citizenship" for African-Americans. Most notable among the group's legal efforts was the high-profile campaign to make lynching a federal crime. As Grace Elizabeth Hale has shown, even though the number of lynchings decreased in the early decades of the twentieth century, the symbolic value of lynching became more profound in the South as twentieth-century consumer culture, technology, and mass media transformed lynching "into a modern spectacle of enduring power" (201).[10] In contrast to the more remote and private forms of vigilantism of the past, there was "something new about lynchings in public, attended by thousands, captured in papers by reporters who witnessed the tortures, and photographed for spectators who wanted a souvenir and yet failed to get a coveted finger, toe, or fragment of bone" (202). These "spectacle lynchings" or "lynch carnivals," Hale asserts, were not about a lingering frontier past but about strengthening the culture of segregation, creating a new southern future in which an expanding consumer culture created and maintained rather than blurred and transformed racial difference. Lynchings ensured that a black man or woman was not just, as Du Bois had stated, "a person who must ride Jim Crow in Georgia," but also someone who could be publicly tortured and killed, prevented even from being a person. (229)

Hale argues that the emergence of a national consumer culture both threatened segregation—by providing the possibility of raceless economic exchange in increasingly national markets—and at the same time provided opportunities to reinforce essential racial difference through the commodification of race and the proliferation of stereotyping in, for example, name brand advertising such as Aunt Jemima or the Gold Dust Twins. The commodification of spectacle lynchings through the distribution of photographs, postcards, and even sound recordings likewise used consumer culture to maintain the color line. The 1916 torture and burning of Jesse Washington in Waco, Texas, was promoted in the press and took place in the town's public square in broad daylight, witnessed by a crowd of fifteen thousand. Photographs of the lynching were distributed as postcard souvenirs, selling for ten cents apiece.

With this "peculiarly modern" transformation of lynching, more seemed at stake than ever before as the NAACP pursued their public, national campaign against this barbaric practice. While the NAACP was successful in getting the Dyer Anti-Lynching Law through the House of Representatives in 1922, it was filibustered by Southern senators and never voted on. Along with the more strident efforts of the NAACP to assert black equality, it must be remembered that the Harlem—or New Negro—Renaissance of the 1920s was providing more positive, realistic, and complex representations of black America. Conversely, and seemingly in direct proportion, the same years after World War I saw a resurgence of the Ku Klux Klan, whose membership swelled from 100,000 in 1919 to over 4 million in 1924. In 1926—the year after the Scopes trial, which scholars often cite as the spark that ignited the Agrarian group— the Klan staged a 40,000–member parade down Pennsylvania Avenue in the nation's capital.[11] Certainly the battle lines on race and segregation had been clearly drawn by the time Warren sat down to write his prosegregation essay.

When we consider Warren's essay in this context—particularly his comments on black radicalism—whatever positive points critics like to cite regarding the essay begin to pale as we realize that these points are little more than minor concessions which the young Warren feels will be necessary to make for segregation's ultimate survival. In contrast to his later writings in the 1950s and 1960s which approach integration as a moral issue, Warren's 1930 defense of segregation revolves primarily around economic factors. Most notably, even when he points out that "the fate of the 'poor white' and the Negro are linked in a single tether" and that the white workman must "concede the Negro equal protection," his ultimate goal is the same: the maintenance of a segregated society. And the assumption underlying a system of social segregation is an essentialist belief in natural racial difference and natural racial hierarchy.

The primary emphasis of "The Briar Patch" may be seen in the essay's closing paragraphs. Warren turns abruptly from his brief discussion of equal protection and equal pay, pointing out that it is "hardly even the major issue" (260). Not surprisingly, as he begins his final affirmation of segregation, he adopts the paternalistic tones of the Old South and falls back upon an idealized, romantic—and racist—portrait of the happy-go-lucky existence of blacks in the rural South:

> In the past the Southern Negro has always been a creature of the small town and farm. That is where he still chiefly belongs, by temperament and capacity; there he has less the character of a "problem" and more the status of a human being who is likely to find in agricultural and domestic pursuits the happiness that his good nature and easy ways incline him to as an ordinary function of his being. (260–61)

Warren goes on to state that the goal of the South should be to maintain the "integrity" and "dignity" of its agrarian lifestyle, "to preserve its essential structure intact" (263, 264). In order to maintain that structure, segregation must continue, and in order for segregation to continue, Warren concedes, blacks must have some opportunity for economic growth and development. This, according to Warren, will carry the added benefit of seeing "crime, genial irresponsibility, ignorance, and oppression replaced by an informed and productive Negro community." But even though Warren can envisage the development of the black community in the South, he still is no closer to conceiving of a day without segregation in the South—as he definitively proclaims in his concluding paragraph: "Let the Negro sit beneath his own vine and fig tree" (264).

The Conservative Modernist Aesthetic of Warren's Early Poetry, 1923–1943

> We shall essay
> The rugged ritual, but not of anger.
> Let us go down before
> Our thews are latched in the myth's languor,
> Our hearts with fable grey.
>
> Robert Penn Warren, "History"

In a letter of November 1932, written to Allen Tate and Caroline Gordon, Robert Penn Warren launches into an uncharacteristic and curiously virulent attack on the literary critic C. Hartley Grattan for an essay titled "New Voices: The Promise of Our Youngest Writers," which had recently been published in *Forum and Century*. His response to Grattan's essay provides an intriguing glimpse into the degree and depth of Warren's early conservative—and at times reactionary—beliefs. Grattan's leftist essay traces the development of several different groups and movements among young writers in America; one of the groups he discusses at length is "that variously designated the Agrarians, the Fugitives, and the Neo-Confederates" (285). Grattan offers warm praise for the writers, particularly Caroline Gordon for her first novel *Penhally*. In his letter to Tate and Gordon, Warren describes Grattan's appraisal of the Fugitive-Agrarian group as follows:

> By the way, there is an article in the *Forum* for November by Grattan (whom John R. [Ransom] terms a plumber out of a job), who deals handsomely with the Nashville people. He says you are the finest poet of your generation and that John is distinguished. Then he says that *Penhally* is by far the best piece of work produced down here. Unfortunately he gives the wrong reasons for his opinions, even when one is inclined to agree with the opinion. Carolyn is riper for Communism than you; therefore she is a better writer. "Better" is not

the word. "Important" is probably the word. There's some good ad-
vice in the article: love niggers more and better and wait for the
"revolution," and the band-wagon will stop and pick you up. (*Se-
lected Letters* 217)

From there, having set off on this particular tangent on race, Warren
launches into a related attack on Thomas Mabry, a former colleague at
Vanderbilt, who had recently taken a position at Fisk, the historically
black university in Nashville: "Tom Mabry has definitely decided to com-
mercialize his talent for nigger-loving. He took the job at Fisk, although
he tried to hold the Vanderbilt one at the same time" (217). These particu-
larly venomous comments provide interesting insights into the degree of
Warren's early conservatism on race and suggest the close relationship
between his early political and literary ideologies.

Significantly, nowhere in his essay does Grattan even mention the is-
sue of race, but for Warren the decidedly Marxist slant of Grattan's com-
mentary becomes closely associated with racial politics. As William
Bedford Clark has recently pointed out, Warren's racist comments in this
letter should be considered in the context of the increasingly politicized
and internationally publicized Scottsboro trial which was by then well
under way. By the time Warren was writing this letter, the defense of the
Scottsboro men had been wrested away from the NAACP by the Interna-
tional Labor Defense, a Communist Party agency, and was made into an
international cause célèbre.[1] While the Communist involvement in the
case—and Grattan's own political slant—certainly must be considered as
a source of Warren's ire, it is perhaps equally important to note that the
letter to Tate and Gordon was written only a week after the Supreme
Court ordered a new trial for the Scottsboro men in their *Powell v. Ala-
bama* decision, declaring that the Scottsboro men had been denied both
the right to a fair trial and the right to counsel.[2] Moreover, their decision
challenged the systematic exclusion of blacks from Southern juries. Al-
though Warren's attack on Grattan suggests his hostility toward Commu-
nism, his repeated comments on "nigger-loving" also reveal a general re-
sentment against outside interference with the Southern way of life, even
if this interference is coming from the Supreme Court of the United
States. Considering the timing of these remarks, then, Warren's vitriolic
rhetoric seems like little more than the knee-jerk response of a defensive,
reactionary Southern Agrarian.

Warren's sentiments regarding the Scottsboro case may also be
gleaned from a 1933 letter to Seward Collins. There Warren expresses his

support for fellow Agrarian Frank Lawrence Owsley's reactionary, defensive article titled "Scottsboro, the Third Crusade: The Sequel to Abolition and Reconstruction," which would be published in the *American Review*. Warren writes, "I hear that you took Owsley's article on the Scottsboro situation. I am delighted, for I think he has got to the root of the matter" (*Selected Letters* 221). In his article Owsley essentially blames all of the South's past and present racial problems on Northern interference and clearly longs for the paternalistic myth of the Old South. Of reconstruction, for instance, Owsley writes, "The white race disciplined him [the Negro] severely for his conduct during reconstruction. At length, however, with outside interference largely removed, old friendships were renewed between the races; new ones were formed until something of the old affection which had existed between the black man and white man returned. His condition gradually improved; though he has never yet been given back the ballot nor allowed to sit on juries. The experience of reconstruction was too bitter to be soon forgotten" (271). In response to the current Communist support for the Scottsboro men, Owsley sternly warns Southern blacks not to seek outside help, saying that "the Negro in the South" would be "in a worse plight than he was after reconstruction. He would find himself face to face with an embittered white race, outnumbering his race three to one, with whom he would have to make his peace; and the terms would probably be more severe than before" (284).[3]

But Warren's reaction to C. Hartley Grattan's essay encompasses not only race and politics but also aesthetics. In fact, the most instructive thing about Warren's comments is the manner in which race, politics, and aesthetics fuse as the borders between these realms momentarily disintegrate. This becomes particularly clear if we consider the text of Grattan's essay. In his wide-ranging assessment of America's young writers, Grattan makes his political persuasion abundantly clear. He states that he finds the work of the younger generation of American writers both "discouraging" and "heartening": discouraging in that they all portray "disintegration, disorder, hopelessness, and confusion," heartening in that they all demand "construction, order, hopefulness, and clarity of thought" (284). From this assessment, Grattan goes on to imply that the new generation of writers contains the seeds of a decidedly leftist social revolution:

> The young are not patriots if by that word you understand a blind loyalty to the existing order. They are of a bigger mold than mere saluters of the flag. With their profound conviction that the conventional American ideology is decaying, they look forward to a new

outlook which will have as its animating principle the participation of all in the boons and usufructs of society. This is not to imply that the young are revolutionists and have given their minds to a particular cause. Some few have taken that step, of course, and unless the conditions of life in America are bettered in the next few years, more and more will follow the same path. The new writers know too much about the under side of American life to be fobbed off by glittering generalities and stupid appeals to moribund traditions. (283)

Interestingly enough, Warren would probably agree with Grattan's assessment of the decay in American culture, but their chosen responses to this diagnosis places them at opposite ends of the political—and literary—spectrum. Indeed, the caustic nature of Warren's attack on Grattan is understandable when we consider that they represent polar opposites on race, politics, and aesthetics. Grattan's essay promotes a radical, revolutionary ideology and ultimately seeks a total social revolution; in contrast, Warren adheres to a conservative, reactionary ideology—he is suspicious of change and committed to maintaining traditional forms of social order. This is the stance Warren assumes in "The Briar Patch" and at the end of the "Pondy Woods" sequence, which expresses a hope or prayer for a renewal through the past.

For Grattan, however, looking to the past is unrealistic and irresponsible, as his comments on the Agrarians and Fugitives make abundantly clear. While Grattan warmly praises Tate, Ransom, and Warren for their individual talents as writers, he also claims that their "ideology tends to be cryptic and esoteric and to the crudest apprehension, merely an escape into a Southern past which never existed." As Warren notes in his letter to Tate and Gordon, Grattan reserves his highest marks for Caroline Gordon's novel *Penhally*, which, according to Grattan, "presents a tangible image of the sort of life the Agrarians worship," but which is also "honest enough to show how it has been disintegrated and defeated by forces impossible to control." Grattan concludes that the murder of Nicholas Llewellyn at the end of the novel symbolizes the fact that "the Agrarian movement is, in the final analysis, a similarly despairing but highly dramatic protest of representatives of an old way of life before they go down to final defeat" (286). Such an analysis of the Agrarian group must have infuriated Warren, particularly because at the end of his essay Grattan manages to appropriate the Agrarian movement within his grand narrative of Marxist revolution: "We have advanced from dilettantism to agrarianism, to uncanalized protest, and finally to Communism. There can be no doubt that there is plenty of evidence to show that the young writers insist that the old American world and its values has decayed, is decaying, and that a new world and new values must be required" (288).[4]

But it is perhaps Grattan's recognition of escapism and nostalgia in Agrarianism that proved most irksome to Warren, for in his own literary reviews of the period, these are the very characteristics for which Warren reserved some of his harshest criticism. Indeed, in light of Warren's solidifying aesthetic principles, to be labeled a nostalgic sentimentalist would be a great insult. But if Warren's backward-glancing poetry of the period isn't "merely an escape" into the past, then what is it? The answer may be gleaned from some of Warren's own criticism from the same period. In a November 1927 review, for instance, Warren writes that Edith Sitwell's *Rustic Elegies* is "vitiated by the undisciplined intrusion of Miss Sitwell's nostalgia." Labeling her poetry "sentimental" and "nothing more than romantic escape," Warren concludes by offering this interesting qualification: "And escapist poetry, to be more than this, must exhibit, I think, a sort of understanding of the world from which it flees" ("The Romantic Strain" 23, 24). Warren clarifies this statement in another essay-review published six months later. Reviewing new scholarly texts on Hawthorne, Frost, and Sherwood Anderson, he attacks Anderson, claiming that "Anderson lacks the intellectuality which would give meaning to the theme of individual escape and the duty to oneself. Only in 'Winesburg' was there a hint of this" ("Hawthorne, Anderson and Frost" 402). Warren develops his position by positing that there are in fact two forms of "escapist literature," the higher order exemplified by Joyce, the lower by Anderson. I will quote the entire concluding paragraph, because I believe his comments on Joyce's strengths—particularly when contrasted with Anderson's perceived weaknesses—may help elucidate the aesthetic principles Warren himself aspired to as a young poet:

> There seem to be two impulses which may give rise to an escapist literature. One is the rejection by judgement, which presupposes an imaginative comprehension of the special world renounced. The other is motivated by fear, by incomprehension. The first variety often produces by the terms of its very revolt the most full and subtle expression of its age. The work of James Joyce is of this type; he at least understands the wrecked and fragmentary tradition from which he turns away. He has the vigor to make his own beginnings and his atavism possesses an intellectual validity which gives "Ulysses" its magnitude. One manifestation of this is a superior objectivity. In

Anderson there is only the inchoate impulse, the symbol of "dark laughter." Anderson's work falls into the second classification, the projection of whose premise ends in sentimentality. Mr. Chase senses this discrepancy; Mr. Fagin, on the other hand, glorifies the blind, uninformed escape and romanticizes the failure in adaptability and lack of mental toughness. Anderson is not an "expression of America," as Mr. Fagin would put it; he does not succeed in making his subjective portrait significant. But there remains "Winesburg, Ohio," with its fine objectivity. (401)[5]

The fact that Warren's criticisms of Anderson are quite similar to Grattan's characterization of the Fugitive-Agrarian writers may help to explain the severity of Warren's reaction to Grattan. More important, however, the contrasts Warren draws here begin to suggest the values and characteristics he privileges in his own emerging aesthetic, an aesthetic that is clearly aligned with the modernist program then being outlined by Eliot. He juxtaposes Anderson's weak subjectivity with Joyce's superior objectivity, Anderson's vague sentimentality with Joyce's mental toughness and intellectual vigor, Anderson's fear and incomprehension with Joyce's judgment and comprehension. In addition, he sees in Joyce an atavism that can make its own beginnings in relation to the past—an assessment that echoes Eliot's own appreciation of *Ulysses* and the "mythical method."[6] In short, Warren sees in Joyce greater discipline and self-control and, perhaps most important, an intellectual connection to the past. Once again, Warren in turning away from the ruined present seeks a renovation of the past rather than Grattan's proposed future revolution. But in order to avoid mere nostalgia and romantic sentiment, such an attempt must be marked by a rigorous discipline, and Warren clearly found this desired discipline in Eliot's aesthetic project, which espoused an almost scientific objectivity and a firm commitment to order, hierarchy, and tradition.

As many critics have noted, however, such an aesthetic program is grounded in an identifiable political unconscious, and the political unconscious behind this particular brand of modernism has often been portrayed as, at the very least, antidemocratic and authoritarian, and in the most extreme cases, fascistic and totalitarian.[7] Wyndham Lewis and Ezra Pound would obviously represent the most extreme cases, and while the young Warren certainly does not fit into the category of Pound or Lewis, we can still draw a connection between his conservative segregationist beliefs and his conservative and authoritarian aesthetic. For my present discussion, the most useful overview of the modernist aesthetic Warren adopted is provided by Michael Levenson's *A Genealogy of Modernism*. Levenson's more moderate analysis traces the evolution of modernism from the early avant-garde efforts up to 1922 and the publication of *Ulysses* and *The Waste Land* and, perhaps most important, the founding of Eliot's *Criterion*, which "exemplifies the institutionalization of the movement, the accession to cultural legitimacy" (213). In reviewing the transition from the early avant-garde modernism to the "high" modernism advocated by Eliot—the branch of modernism Warren aligned himself with—Levenson offers this summary of contrasts:

> A fundamentally individualist perspective has become aggressively anti-individualist. The cult of inner experience has passed to outer control; personal expression has given way to critical discipline. In the place of freedom and spontaneity, art is now characterized in terms of order, restraint and authority. A revolutionary justification is exchanged for a traditionalist. Self-expression yields to self-suppression. The primacy of emotion yields to the primacy of reason. (211)

The characteristics of Eliot's modernism outlined here—tradition, order, discipline, objectivity, and reason—are the same characteristics Warren lauds in Joyce, and they are also the characteristics and principles found in his own early poetry. Faced with the disorder of the modern world, Warren opts for Eliot's program of tradition, authority, order, and control.

Many critics have commented on Warren's early affinities with Eliot, but they have limited their comments primarily to matters of style and theme. However, Eliot's aesthetic agenda informs Warren's early poetry more completely than has been heretofore suggested. When Warren was introduced to Eliot's poetry through his association with the Fugitive poets at Vanderbilt, the impact was profound. Warren was, in his own words, "completely overwhelmed" by *The Waste Land*; he memorized it and was capable of reciting it in its entirety (quoted in Blotner 35). And Allen Tate—who along with John Crowe Ransom would comprise Warren's primary influences among the Fugitive poets—remembers that Warren covered his dormitory room walls with murals depicting scenes from Eliot's poem.[8] Critics have often portrayed Ransom and Tate as distinct, even competing, influences upon the young Warren. According to this interpretation, Warren acquired from Ransom his admiration of the metaphysical poets and his early penchant for an objective formalism, and from Tate his attraction to Eliot and the archetypal modernist thematics of alienation and determinism.[9] But according to Eliot's modernist tenets, Ransom and Tate were not necessarily competing influences, for Warren's interest in the metaphysical poets, while perhaps fanned by Ransom, certainly complemented Eliot's larger modernist project and his proposed return to tradition. Significantly, Warren himself identifies the affinities between Ransom and Eliot in his 1935 essay "John Crowe Ransom: A Study in Irony," and in doing so, he also indicates his own aesthetic dispositions.

Over the course of this particularly revealing piece, Warren draws a running parallel between the two poets, asserting that they are both responding to the modern "dissociation of sensibility" that Eliot identified in his essay "The Metaphysical Poets." According to Eliot's diagnosis, the metaphysical poets were the last generation of truly intellectual poets who possessed "a mechanism of sensibility which could devour any kind of experience"; in contrast, the poets who followed, including the poets of the modern era, "thought and felt by fits, unbalanced" (quoted in Warren, "John Crowe Ransom" 94). The metaphysical poets, then, become a particularly important model for Eliot in his call for a harder-edged, more intellectual poetry: the modern poet, Eliot claims, must look beyond simply the heart and "into the cerebral cortex, the nervous system, and the digestive tracts" ("The Metaphysical Poets" 250). Interestingly, Warren sees Ransom and Eliot occupied by the same theme (dissociation of sensibility) and the same goal (unification of sensibility), and he also sees them employing the same tool, irony. But while Ransom's irony is "psychological," Eliot's irony "may be called historical: the ignoble present is suddenly thrust into contrast with the noble past" ("John Crowe Ransom" 110). In concluding, Warren again emphasizes the thematic similarities between Ransom and Eliot, and indirectly illustrates the fact that both the Agrarian project and Eliot's modernist project had their impetus in the same conservative desire for order and control in the face of modern flux and change:

> But the theme in the poetry of both men is similar: "Where there is no vision the people perish." Both have experienced a necessity for order, and, in consequence, have concerned themselves with disorder as the overt subject matter of their poetry. Both have diagnosed the disorder in terms of dissociation of sensibility, although Ransom, on this point, has been more general. (111)

It was perhaps Eliot's rapprochement with tradition that most attracted Warren, particularly if we consider his argument in "The Briar Patch" on the need to maintain the integrity of the Southern cultural order in the face of modern change. While it is obviously impossible to pinpoint the exact point at which Warren became disaffected with Agrarianism, we may view this 1935 essay as a sign of the manner in which his Agrarian desires for order and a continuous relationship with the past were eventually subsumed within his emerging and solidifying modernist aesthetic. This trend may also be seen in a revealing criticism Warren makes regarding Ransom's first volume, *Poems About God*. Warren describes these early poems as too provincial and "perhaps nostalgic, turning to an order of life which the poet since that time has analyzed and defended with more formidable social and economic doctrine" ("John Crowe Ransom" 104). This particular point of criticism may help to explain Warren's dispersal of the poems from his "Pondy Woods" sequence among the text of *Thirty-Six Poems*, which was published in 1935, the same year as this essay. Warren perhaps was afraid that the specifically regional thrust of the "Pondy Woods" sequence would be misinterpreted as sentimental nostalgia, especially by a critic like Grattan. Even though Warren was still active in the Agrarian cause, participating in a second Agrarian symposium titled *Who Owns America?*, Eliot's aesthetic philosophy allowed him to view his own poetry as part of a broader cultural movement that went beyond regional politics, yet had a similarly conservative agenda.[10]

Maintaining the past in poetry—what Warren refers to as the "old, constant, undefiled, absolute stream" of poetic tradition—requires discipline, objectivity, and the cultivation of a historical consciousness. According to the aesthetic program Warren adhered to—and as his own early poetry illustrates—all three of these principles go together. First and most obviously, the early poetry is marked by a disciplined reliance on closed, traditional forms and a hard objectivity which guards against emotion and nostalgia. In *Thirty-Six Poems*, for instance, the overwhelming majority of poems in the volume are written in closed forms with regular, often intricate rhyme schemes; a handful of the others—"Aubade for Hope," "Letter to a Friend," "Aged Man Surveys the Past Time," "Eidolon"—are written primarily in blank verse. Even the most technically complex poems of the volume rely on rhyme as a means of control, and these, quite significantly, tend to echo Eliot both formally and technically. Such is the case in "The Return: An Elegy," "Letter from a Coward to a Hero," and "So Frost Astounds," whose rhymes, coming at irregular intervals, often suggest the rhythmic qualities of Eliot, especially his "Pru-frock."

Warren's echoing or imitating of other poets—be they Eliot and Pound or Donne and Marvell—has been noted by numerous critics, but none have suggested the important role imitation played in Warren's emerging aesthetics. Imitation, according to Warren's early views, is not merely apprentice work; instead, it provides an important tool whereby the poet establishes a relationship with the tradition. Warren suggests the value of imitation in a 1936 review of an anthology titled *Trial Balances,* in which poems of thirty-two young poets are accompanied by critical commentary by established poets and critics. Warren's review declares the best of these thirty-two poets to be the ones "who have most definite affiliations with other poets, past and contemporary" ("Straws in the Wind" 174). For Warren, the only way you can make yourself new and original is in relation to the poetic tradition, both past and present. Again commenting on these young imitators, Warren writes: "These young poets, as I have said, are the most 'imitative,' and they are, not too paradoxically, the most 'original'" (174). Warren cautions, however, that a poet must have the disciplined sensibility and taste to know what constitutes the tradition that should be imitated. As a warning, he closes by criticizing the poetry of Robert Liddell Lowe, which, according to Warren, "is decidedly not Mr. Lowe's own. It is merely an imitation of something he read, perhaps in the *Atlantic Monthly* or *Harper's.* It is simply that Mr. Lowe, a young man of talent, has been 'imitating' the wrong stuff" (175). Warren's authoritarian judgments here call to mind Raymond Williams's explanation of the ideological tendencies of modernism. In *The Politics of Modernism,* Williams, like Levenson, distinguishes the traditionalist modernism of Eliot from the earlier avant-garde modernism, pointing out that while modernism's representatives remain consistently "anti-bourgeois," they "either choose the formerly aristocratic valuation of art as the sacred realm above money and commerce, or the revolutionary doctrines . . . of art as the liberating vanguard of popular consciousness" (34). Warren's critical comments, along with his own poetry of the period, place him in the aristocratic wing, which privileges tradition and control over greater freedom and self-expression.

Warren similarly suggests the paradoxical relationship between imitation and originality in his 1934 lecture titled "Modern Poetry, or Modernism in Poetry." Here he defines the appropriate relationship between the modern poet and the poetic tradition, explaining that the modern poet must strive to be new, but that this may be done only by cultivating a relationship with the past:

> We may say, then, that the poet cannot take over bodily the old poets. He must be new, he is alive and they, alas but happily, are dead. He cannot transpose their forms, though in all conscience he must strive for their ultimate effect. He realizes that tradition does not mean imitation. He cannot transpose their forms, for their forms depend on what they had to say; but he must study, however, the ways in which they got their effect. He realizes that if he is to be a poet at all he must be new. And he realizes that if he is to be a poet at all he must tap the old, constant, undefiled, absolute stream, that he must discover his own relation to poetic tradition. (RPW Papers)

How similar Warren's assessment of the role of tradition seems to be to Eliot's. In "Tradition and the Individual Talent," Eliot likewise portrays the paradoxical relationship between the poetic past and the poetic present:

> Tradition is a matter of much wider significance. It cannot be inherited, and if you want it you must obtain it by great labour. It involves, in the first place, the historical sense, which we may call nearly indispensable to anyone who would continue to be a poet beyond his twenty-fifth year; and the historical sense involves a perception, not only of the pastness of the past, but of its presence; the historical sense compels a man to write not merely with his own generation in his bones, but with a feeling that the whole of literature of Europe from Homer and within it the whole of literature of his own country has a simultaneous existence and composes a simultaneous order. The historical sense, which is a sense of the timeless as well as of the temporal and of the timeless and of the temporal together, is what makes a writer traditional. And it is at the same time what makes a writer most acutely conscious of his place in time, of his contemporaneity. (4)

The result of this "great labour" that Eliot describes is that the balance in poetry shifts decidedly away from the principle of self-expression—"the spontaneous overflow of powerful feelings," say, of the Romantics—to the principle of self-suppression and self-control. In opposition to the subjectivity and freedom of Romanticism, Eliot opts for the objective order and control of classicism. As Eliot insists, "the poet must develop or procure the consciousness of the past and . . . he should continue to develop this consciousness throughout his career. . . . The progress of an artist is a continual self-sacrifice, a continual extinction of personality" (6–7). Warren again concurred with Eliot. In his 1936 essay "Literature as a Symptom," Warren contrasts objectivity with subjectivity, claiming that by striving for objectivity, the poet creates a work that "is not forever tied to his own personality, and the act of parturition is, indeed, complete. The work may be, therefore, a genuine creation" (267). In contrast, Warren derides the writer who pursues the doctrine of self-expression. According to Warren, such a writer sees his work as nothing more than "a scaffolding or stage on which he may parade, a device to permit the expression, ultimately, of his own personality. His speculative questions . . . are but a means to an end, an end which, we have been assured in recent years, is of great importance and magnificence. That end is self-expression; just that" (267–68). Warren's 1933 essay on the nineteenth-century Southern poet Sidney Lanier also illustrates the depth of his early aversion to Romantic subjectivity. Warren blasts Lanier's undisciplined "emotionalism" as the worst element of Romanticism: "Lanier merely recapitulated in a vulgar and naïve version what today may appear as their [the Romantics'] fallacies and confusions, the unsatisfying quality of their work. He was the final product of all that was dangerous in Romanticism: his theory of personality, his delusion of prophecy, his aesthetic premise, his uninformed admiration of science, his nationalism, his passion for synthesis, his theory of progress" ("The Blind Poet" 44–45).

In contrast to what he felt were the slovenly, subjective excesses of Romanticism, Warren based his early poetry upon principles of discipline and objectivity, which he viewed as necessary tools for the cultivation of a historical consciousness. He forswore self-expression in favor of a controlled, objective dialogue with the past and its traditions. A good example of this may be seen in Warren's poem "The Garden," first published in Poetry in 1935 and, shortly after, in Thirty-Six Poems. The poem is a response to Andrew Marvell's poem of the same name and closely follows Marvell's metrical rhythms and stanzaic structures. Victor Strandberg categorizes Warren's "The Garden" as a "poem of passage" which chronicles the "experience of a forced, one-way passage into a ruined world" (Poetic Vision 21). Strandberg sees most of Warren's early poems dividing fairly evenly between two possible responses to such a passage, one being filled with "nostalgia and regret," the other being guided by "guilt, dread, and despair" (47). But it should be noted that the objective and impersonal voice Warren adopts in these poems—and particularly in this one—guards against the sentimentality often associated with nostalgia; instead, Warren's objective voice and formal restraint produce a less emotional and more cerebral response to the sense of loss. Warren in this poem contrasts Marvell's world, in which the poet still possessed a unified sensibility, with the modern world and its sense of dislocation and separateness.[11] The poem, then, is a broad comment on the coherent past and the disordered present, but the imitation that forms the basis of the poem conveys an important meaning in itself. The poet has consciously and laboriously drawn the form of the past forward into the present, thus providing a moment of control and order in the face of modern decay and chaos: the "ruined state" of the poem's third stanza. While Marvell's garden is lush and timeless, Warren's poem, being set in early autumn, admits signs of death and decay. But even though the garden has already been won by the early autumnal frosts, the sun, a constant, has the power to provide the garden a momentary reprieve against time and death:

> How kind, how secret, now the sun
> Will bless this garden frost has won,
> And touch once more, as once it used,
> The furlèd boughs by cold bemused.
> Though summered brilliance had but room
> In blossom, now the leaves will bloom
> Their time, and take from milder sun
> An unreviving benison. (*CP* 59)

As is the case in much of his early poetry, Warren proves himself an astute technician when operating in the formal vein. Along with a subtle use of alliteration and assonance which helps to create a languid tone, he counterpoints caesuras with enjambed lines to create a sense of momentary pause and release. At the same time, just as the sun can provide the garden with a momentary respite from the ravages of time, the power and constancy of the poetic tradition, present in the form of the poem, can provide a momentary respite for the poet lost in the flux of modernity. Warren's strategy here calls to mind Frost's belief that poetry provides a "momentary stay against confusion"; here the stay against chaos is provided by the traditional form of the past, which is retrieved from the past and which acts as a sort of scaffolding for the modern poet. It is only after this reprieve has been won—erected from the past—that the poet may envision the "sacrament that can translate / All things that fed luxurious sense

/ From appetite to innocence" (*CP* 59). Warren's poem, then, is a medita-
tion on the relationship between the past and present, but more specifi-
cally on the relationship between the "constant, undefiled" poetic tradi-
tion and the poet lost in modernity and suffering from a dissociation of
sensibility.

Warren continues this contrast in the series of poems he wrote in the
metaphysical manner in the few years after "The Garden" was pub-
lished—and, not inconsequentially, in the years following his John Crowe
Ransom essay, which discusses so extensively the metaphysicals and
Eliot's perceived dissociation of sensibility. These poems—"Bearded
Oaks," "Monologue at Midnight," "Picnic Remembered," and "Love's
Parable"—would be gathered together in his 1942 volume *Eleven Poems
on the Same Theme*, and they have been viewed by turns as meditations
on lost love or lost innocence or, more recently, as intensely personal
statements on Warren's strained first marriage.[12] But like "The Garden,"
these poems can be read as a broader commentary on the modern poet
seeking a relationship with tradition and struggling with the modern dis-
sociation of sensibility. The modeling of these poems again goes beyond
mere imitation, forming a part of the poem's essential meaning as it car-
ries an implicit contrast between the present and the past. All of these
poems masterfully recreate the metaphysical mood, as Warren attempts
to reconstruct the unified sensibility of the past which could, Eliot
claimed, "devour any kind of experience" and make poetry out of it. War-
ren's efforts produce elaborate extended metaphors and conceits worthy
of the seventeenth-century poets, metaphors that can variously compare
the lovers in the poems to twin atolls ("Bearded Oaks"), flies trapped in
amber ("Picnic Remembered"), a diseased body ("Love's Parable"), and
the dying flame of a match framed within a watching eye ("Monologue at
Midnight"). But Warren's recurring emphasis in these poems ultimately
inverts the metaphysicals. For while Donne was capable of envisioning
and celebrating a perfect, timeless love in "The Canonization," "The An-
niversary," and "A Valediction: Forbidding Mourning," all of Warren's
metaphysical poems focus on themes of diminution, loss, and separate-
ness. In fact, Warren at times seems to be making a direct comment on
Donne. In "Love's Parable," for instance, the second stanza calls to mind
Donne's true lovers in "A Valediction: Forbidding Mourning," but in War-
ren's poem this state of perfection has passed, unappreciated, and all that
is left is "ironic residue." Significantly, in the sixth stanza Warren relates
the condition of the lovers to the condition of the world: before their love

began to fail, "all the world proportionate / And joyful seemed" (*CP* 76). Even though this comparison seems fairly conventional at this point in the poem, Warren repeats it in the penultimate stanza, and in doing so, he makes a broader cultural statement. After lamenting the decaying relationship between himself and his lover, which is now described with images of "fungus," "rot," and "inward sore," he exclaims: "Are we but mirror to the world? / Or does the world our ruin reflect . . . ?" (*CP* 76). With this question, the diminished relationship of the lovers becomes a symptom of the modern condition.

While such a diagnosis on the state of the modern world may appear oblique and indirect in these poems—implicit, say, in the contrast between their orderly forms and their disorderly themes—the other poems in *Eleven Poems on the Same Theme* provide a much more direct statement on modernity. Of these, "Terror" and "Pursuit" are particularly revealing for the way in which Warren uses his numerous allusions to the Bible, myth, and literature to help paint a bleak portrait of the modern condition. As he shows in "Terror," the modern world has been loosed from the moorings of traditional belief and myth. Consequently, the individual, with "no adequate definition of terror," seeks meaning through either the courting of violence and death or the struggle for mere survival. Warren illustrates these responses with contemporary references to U.S. volunteers fighting in the Spanish Civil War, the rise of fascism and Nazism in Europe, and the experimental efforts of surgeon Alexis Carrel. For instance, Warren points out the peculiar irony in the fact that some U.S. volunteers went from Spain to Finland, where they ended up fighting the Russians, their recent allies in Spain: "They fight old friends, for their obsession knows / Only the immaculate itch, not human friends or foes" (*CP* 78). According to Warren, the volunteers are not fighting for any moral or even political principle; they are simply driven by a vacant desire to confront death.

But Warren jarringly places such contemporary references alongside allusions to the Bible (Jacob and "the crime of Onan") and Shakespeare (Clarence, from *Richard III*, and the "criminal king," Macbeth), thereby illustrating through contrast the modern world's unique poverty of spirit and lack of meaning. The following passage provides a good example of his method:

You know, by radio, how hotly the world repeats,
When the brute crowd roars or the blunt boot-heels resound

In the Piazza or the Wilhelmplatz,
The crime of Onan, spilled upon the ground;
You know, whose dear hope Alexis Carrel kept
Alive in a test tube, where it monstrously grew, and slept.[13]

But it is dead, and you now, guiltless, sink
To rest in lobbies, or pace gardens where
The slow god crumbles and the fountains prink,
Nor heed the criminal king, who paints the air
With discoursed madness and protruding eye,
Nor give the alarm, nor ask tonight where sleeps
That head which hooped the jewel Fidelity,
But like an old melon now, in the dank ditch, seeps;
But you crack nuts, while the conscience-stricken stare
Kisses the terror; for you see an empty chair. (CP 78)

Through the allusion to Onan, Warren portrays the fascist rallies in Italy and Germany as acts of collective masturbation. At the same time, the allusion offers a sharp contrast to the image of Alexis Carrel's scientific experiments. In the Book of Genesis, Onan is put to death by the Lord for practicing coitus interruptus, but in the poem, the strict Biblical codes that sanctify procreation are undermined by the new god, science, which now professes to hold the keys to life and survival. Warren suggests that without some form of traditional codes to govern and guide behavior and to create value and meaning, we are reduced to a naturalistic existence, a struggle for mere survival; unlike Macbeth, "the criminal king" who is hounded by guilt in the form of the murdered Banquo's ghost, the modern "you" of the poem is "guiltless." Warren himself explains the significance of this allusion: "The *criminal king* at the end of the poem is, of course, Macbeth, who can see Banquo's ghost because he still has the *adequate definition of terror* despite his attempts to 'reason' himself out of it. . . . Macbeth still sees meaning, and in a sense *kisses the terror*. But the *you* of the poem sees only an empty chair" ("Author's Note" 543).

The bleak portrait of modernity presented in this poem is fairly typical of the group as a whole, and it suggests another important distinguishing characteristic of Warren's early poetry. Late in his career, Warren would claim that poetry can serve two functions in society: a diagnostic function and a therapeutic function. By this he means that literature can either reveal the symptomatic ills of a society or it can provide a means of coping with and potentially curing those same disorders. At the time Warren made this distinction in his 1975 book *Democracy and Poetry*, he clearly believed the therapeutic function to be of a higher order. However, if we consider the recurring thematic emphasis of his early poetry—loss, ruin, disorder, decay, and naturalism—we would have to conclude that this work is without a doubt of the more diagnostic sort. The naturalistic emphasis in "Terror" runs through much of Warren's early poetry, from "To a Face in the Crowd" up to "The Ballad of Billie Potts." In these poems in particular, Warren portrays the modern individual cut off from the past and living a naturalistic existence as a "nomad" or "wanderer." Indeed, in his 1939 essay "The Present State of Poetry: In the United States," Warren contends that the central question facing the modern poet is "Can man live on a purely naturalistic level?" (391). But beyond Warren's proposed rapprochement with tradition which I have described, he rarely suggests a solution to this problem. Instead, as in his characterization of Ransom and Eliot, he sees a "necessity for order" in the modern world, and so "disorder" becomes his primary subject matter ("John Crowe Ransom" 111). Significantly, Warren's political orientation is based upon the same basic assumptions: disorder is the diagnosis and the maintenance of tradition is the proposed solution.

Warren, however, eventually lost faith in both his Agrarianism and his early poetry's aesthetic and thematic emphasis, as I will illustrate in the chapters that follow. A sense of dissatisfaction with this aesthetic program is already apparent in 1939 in "The Present State of Poetry." Warren describes what he views as the dismal state of affairs in American poetry. He first discusses the limitations of the proletarian writers, the regional writers, and the formalists, and then goes on to say that "the general effects of free verse on American poetry have already been achieved" (394). While at this point in his career Warren can still point to Eliot as "the most important single influence on American poetry," by the end of the essay he reaches an impasse:

> But these considerations are, in one sense, considerations of style. There are other, more general, considerations. Why is our poetry so fragmentary, and so dispersed from any abiding central impulse? Why do some of our very best poets produce such a small body of work? Why is poetry so cut off from the public? Why have the efforts to write in the larger modes failed or been so partial in their success? (398)

As a response to these questions, Warren quotes from a review by the critic F. Cudworth Flint, published a few years before in the *Southern Review*. Interestingly enough, Warren's *Thirty-Six Poems* is one of the five volumes Flint considers in the review.[14] Warren concludes his essay by offering these ruminations on the questions he has just posed:

> The answer may be the answer given by F. Cudworth Flint: "what our culture chiefly needs at present is an artistic focal point, a center of unity, more formally evident than can be supplied by a collection of short poems. We need a structure of life and art capable of appealing both to the simple and to the learned. In other words, we do not need beliefs, of which we have almost too many (scepticism is a product of intellectual overcrowding); we also need a mythology, and a mythology credible, and capable of being embodied in poetry of *epic* magnitude. The day of leviathans is not over; or if it is, the worse for us. . . . We are still, in spite of everything, human beings. Who will show us our myths?" (398)

Flint is clearly calling for what may be termed a more therapeutic vision of art and poetry, and while Warren's quoting of Flint may seem to suggest a certain degree of sympathy for Flint's viewpoint, his closing comments express doubt that such an aesthetic program is possible in the modern era. In fact, Warren seems uncertain about the worth of poetry altogether:

> But perhaps we do not need to have our myth pointed out to us. Perhaps we may know it, and know it too well, knowing that, as Stevenson said, "it provides no habitable city for the soul of man." And in the midst of our competing beliefs, one belief may be lacking: the belief that poetry is worth writing. (398)

Racial Themes and Formal Transitions in Warren's Early Fiction

But the pain, strangely enough, seemed to be attached to the compulsion, as though in some way I did not want to go into that remembered world.

Robert Penn Warren, "'Blackberry Winter': A Recollection"

Following the publication of *Selected Poems: 1923–1943*, Robert Penn Warren entered a period lasting approximately ten years in which he published no poetry. Warren would end this break with the 1953 publication of *Brother to Dragons*, a text in which he squarely confronts the issue of race in a personal, perhaps even confessional manner; the Romantic subjectivity and themes of *Brother to Dragons* also indicate a radical departure from his early poetry's more objective, formalist aesthetic. Conventional wisdom has held that Warren's break from poetry was the result of his turning his attention to fiction, and indeed he was very productive as a writer of fiction over these years, producing *At Heaven's Gate* (1943), the Pulitzer Prize–winning *All the King's Men* (1946), *The Circus in the Attic and Other Stories* (1947), and *World Enough and Time* (1950). However, critics have grown increasingly speculative regarding the nature of Warren's decade-long poetic silence. Mark Miller, for instance, has argued that even though Warren was not writing lyric poetry over this decade, the texts he did write—particularly his fiction—allowed him to experiment and search for a poetic form more appropriate to his increasingly complex and more redemptive artistic vision. In contrast, James Perkins contends that Warren's reimmersion in the issue of racial politics led him to a reconciliation with the South which in turn allowed access to his own personal past as a subject for poetry.[1] Both of these scenarios are correct; in fact they are interrelated. Perkins suggests it was primarily Warren's work on *Segregation* in the mid-1950s that led to his poetic breakthrough, but Warren's fiction shows that he was confronting the subject of race much earlier. At the same time, he was experimenting with forms and moving inevitably closer to the subjective and autobiographical impulse that would lead him back to poetry.

Significantly, the subject of race infiltrates, either obliquely or explicitly, all of Warren's early works of fiction, beginning with his first novel *Night Rider* (1939) and extending through *Band of Angels* (1955). In *Night Rider*, *At Heaven's Gate*, and *World Enough and Time*, racial issues enter only as a way of advancing the plots of the novels, but in *All the King's Men* and *Band of Angels*, race pervades the texts more completely, informing the entire meanings of the novels.[2] The legacy of slavery interrupts *All the King's Men* in the form of the Cass Mastern story, and *Band of Angels* is narrated by Amantha Starr, a mulatto who is raised as though she were white only to be sold into slavery upon her father's death. The issue of race was increasingly on Warren's mind and in his work, and between the mid-1930s and the early 1950s he experienced a profound transformation of opinion, moving from the segregationist stance of "The Briar Patch" to the integrationist position announced in *Segregation: The Inner Conflict in the South* (1956). At the same time, and particularly over the course of his ten-year break from poetry, Warren also began to explore the possibilities of a more subjective and autobiographical foundation for his work—and for his return to poetry. Showing signs of dissatisfaction with the more objective narrative forms of his first two novels, Warren began to experiment with the liberties offered by the romance form, while simultaneously moving toward autobiography. The implications of these sometimes intersecting political and aesthetic shifts—which culminate in Warren's personal confrontation with race in *Brother to Dragons* and his adoption of a Romantic aesthetic—can be traced in three early works of Warren's fiction: the 1935 story "Her Own People," the 1946 masterpiece *All the King's Men*, and the story "Blackberry Winter," published the same year. The latter two works in particular show Warren intensifying his personal investigations into the charged issue of race and confronting his own past experiences in the segregated South.[3] In a parallel manner, they also reveal his growing desire to merge the private and public, the personal and the political—a tendency that anticipates the direction his poetry takes with *Brother to Dragons* and his adoption of a subjective yet politically engaged Romantic aesthetic.

Warren at times claimed that he began to reconsider his position on segregation not long after his essay "The Briar Patch" was published in 1930. The often overlooked 1935 story "Her Own People" shows him re-examining the assumptions evident in his earlier defense of segregation. In "The Briar Patch" Warren had expressed little understanding of or concern over the psychological effects of segregation on Southern blacks, going so far as to suggest that blacks who wanted equality lacked "self-respect" since they were apparently incapable of rationalizing their position. "Her Own People" shows Warren investigating the real power race and economics can hold over individual identity. In the story he explores some of the complex, intertwined economic and psychological forces at work in the segregated South—and the nation at large, for that matter. The story considers the ways in which blacks negotiate with white economic power, the effects of a consumer culture oriented toward whiteness, and the evasiveness of whites who benefit from this system. The main character, Viola, is a young black domestic who by the end of the story assumes an attitude of noncompliance reminiscent of Melville's Bartleby. In this sense, the story may be seen as a curious example of what Harold Bloom calls *apophrades:* "the return of the precursors . . . in colors not their own" (*A Map of Misreading* 90).

Before the story opens, Viola has been a servant of the Allens, a wealthy white couple who brought her with them when they moved from Alabama to Tennessee. She has recently quit, and the Allens find out that Viola has apparently lied to them about her rent situation in order to get more money from them. Mrs. Allen angrily confronts Viola, who admits the facts but calmly denies Mrs. Allen's charge that her actions amount to lying and stealing. Exasperated by Viola's unyielding responses, Mrs. Allen tells her to go back "to Alabama to your own people," and, "I don't ever want to see you again." To this, Viola calmly replies, "I wouldn't never say that about you, Miz Allen, . . . I wants to see you" (*CA* 186). In the story's conclusion, the Allens are informed that Viola has not left her bed for the three days since Mrs. Allen sent her away. The Allens visit her briefly, provide money to cover Viola's bus fare, and wash their hands of any further responsibility.

As William Bedford Clark points out, Viola is in many ways an adaptation of the stereotypical tragic mulatto figure. Her bizarre and seemingly inexplicable behavior in this story underscores the power that a white economy and white perceptions of blacks can have over black identity itself. As Langston Hughes explained in his 1926 essay "The Negro Artist and the Racial Mountain," blacks must cope with the "urge within the race toward whiteness, the desire to pour racial individuality into the mold of American standardization, and to be as little Negro and as much

American as possible" (1630). We can gather from the story that Viola is a character who follows this urge to whiteness—not for whiteness itself, but for all that is associated with it: economic opportunity, political power, and privilege. Early in the story, Mr. Allen refers to Viola as a "white-folks' nigger," to which Mrs. Allen adds, "She's ashamed of her nigger blood, all right," and points out that Viola often complained that "niggers are dirty" (CA 178). The latter comment resounds with irony, considering the detailed description of the Allens' filthy house that opens the story. Either Viola has simply been telling the Allens what she thinks they want to hear, or she has been conditioned to literally believe this. If the former were the case, we might be inclined to view her denial of stealing and lying as a sign of justification based upon the belief that she was only taking what was rightfully hers. However, the latter possibility—that Viola has been thoroughly conditioned to accept and strive for white standards—seems more likely in this particular instance, and as Mr. Allen points out rather sardonically, Viola has simply been following their own example of crass materialism. The additional money Viola "stole" went to the purchase of a new coat, much to the consternation of Mrs. Allen, who gave Viola plenty of hand-me-down clothes. When his wife calls Viola a fool for blowing her money on a coat she didn't need, Mr. Allen responds, "Niggers . . . know how to live. Just like the good book says, 'Man does not live by bread alone.' Now Viola works all winter and you teach her to save money and when she gets it saved, she knows what to do with it. . . . She got herself a new coat. Now that nigger's got a sense of values" (CA 182).

Viola's spurning of her own racial identity is also evident in her chosen isolation from other blacks in the community, and by her superficial desire to emulate the Allens' lifestyle through her clothing. Her landlord Jake reports to the Allens: "She doan never go nowhere I knows of no way. She just comes in er-nights and gits herself all dressed up in them clothes you give her and combs her hair. She doan go nowhere, she just sets there in that room a time, then she gits in the bed. . . . She doan ack like she wants no friends . . ." (CA 181).

On hearing this, Mr. Allen reflects, "The trouble . . . is that we ought never brought her from Alabama away from her own people" (CA 181). What he fails to realize is that he and his wife *are* her own people, for they are what Viola aspires to be a part of; as Mr. Allen put it earlier, Viola is a "white-folks' nigger." This is perhaps the reason behind Viola's odd response when Mrs. Allen says she never wants to see Viola again. Viola desires to both see and be seen by Mrs. Allen because she has entirely accepted the identity the Allens project onto her as her own self. To be dismissed from their presence is to lose her identity. Viola's Bartleby-like retreat from the world and her refusal to leave her bed at the end of the story signal her new awareness of the futility of her aspirations toward acceptance. She will never be more than a "white-folks' nigger" in the eyes of the Allens, who at the end of the story show no signs of enlightenment, and no signs of assuming responsibility for the disturbed Viola.

Though it is fair to identify Viola as a variant of the stereotypical tragic mulatto, Warren's representation marks a significant investigation on his part into the real power race holds over individual identity. At the same time, it is an objective work of fiction within which it can be hard to locate the author himself. Indeed, though much of Warren's fiction touches upon racial issues, fiction provided enough distance to allow him to deal with the subject in a detached and even abstract way; as a result, it can at times be difficult to determine exactly where he stands among his fictive characters. This sense of detachment would become increasingly unsatisfactory for Warren, and would lead him to invest himself more heavily in the subjective and personal forms of his later poetry. As he explained in a 1956 interview, "The poem is a way of knowing what kind of a person you can be, getting your reality shaped a little bit better. . . . it's a way of living" (Watkins et al. 16). Late in his career, Warren often stated that his poems represented him more fully than his novels: "I think poems are more *you*" (Watkins et al. 242). In contrast, consider Warren's comments on Faulkner's racial views as they related to his fiction: "The drama in which Faulkner sought his knowledge emerges in forms that constitute an enormously complicated intellectual as well as imaginative structure, an objective structure. We think of Benjy and Jason and Caddie, and Christmas, and Sutpen, but we do not think of Faulkner; Faulkner remains taciturn, enigmatic, sealed, his reality absorbed into the objective thing created. And this is why, when he did give an opinion or express a personal view, we may feel let down and defrauded; what the 'Squire' says is sometimes thin, or contradictory" (*WSN* 297). In "Her Own People" Warren similarly deals with race through the objective structure of the narrative, but in *All the King's Men* and "Blackberry Winter" he shows signs of dissatisfaction with objective forms, and reveals a growing desire to bridge the gap between the personal and the political, the private and public worlds.

All the King's Men is almost universally considered Warren's best novel, and many critics have also viewed it as an important transitional work in Warren's canon and career, particularly in regard to Warren's changing views of form, subjectivity, history, and race. In *Robert Penn Warren and American Idealism,* John Burt argues that the novel shows Warren moving from the realism and naturalism of his earlier work to an intensive engagement with romance which climaxes in *Brother to Dragons.* Burt sees Warren's negotiations between romance and realism as a struggle to find "neutral territory" between idealism and pragmatism, between the authenticity of the private imagination and the obligations to the public, social world (126). More recently, Jonathan Cullick argues that *All the King's Men* is an important milestone in Warren's development away from objectivity and toward autobiography: "As [Jack] Burden envisions himself connected to history, he places less distance between himself and the story he narrates. His development reflects Warren's development from *John Brown* to *Jefferson Davis* and *Portrait of a Father*" (101). Finally, in regard to race, Carl Freedman demonstrates that *All the King's Men* is a "transitional work, in which one can locate both the pressure of the old order . . . and a nascent awareness that the construction of a healthy southern culture requires the white South squarely to confront its evil racial history" (139). All of these transitional aspects of the work forecast and inform the direction Warren's poetry would take with *Brother to Dragons* and his adoption of a subjective yet politically engaged aesthetic that attempts to bridge the gap between the private and public spheres.

As critics have often noted, *All the King's Men* is both a political novel, whose subject is Willie Stark, and a personal story of conversion, whose subject is Jack Burden, the novel's narrator. The deeper significance of these two stories, however, comes out only through the novel's third story, whose subject is Cass Mastern. The Cass Mastern episode, which takes up almost the entirety of the fourth chapter, reconciles the personal and the political elements of the novel even though it goes against the flow of the main plot. While the novel as a whole increasingly moves from the political arena to the private sphere, the Mastern narrative progresses the other way; more specifically, it shifts from Cass's private sin of adultery to an awareness of the cultural sin of slavery. As Carl Freedman argues, "political power, though the overriding manifest theme of *All the King's Men,* ultimately functions as a code for a more basic concern with sexual relations; and that sexuality, in turn, encodes a still more fundamental preoccupation, one that the novel shares with most serious southern literature—namely, race, slavery, and the historic guilt of the South" (128).

As Warren was writing *All the King's Men,* he occupied the Chair of Poetry at the Library of Congress for the year 1944–45; there, along with fulfilling his duties, he immersed himself in the narratives of former slaves that had been collected by the WPA. It was also at the Library of Congress that Warren ran across an account of the Lewis murders, which would eventually serve as the subject of *Brother to Dragons.* These pursuits, combined with his inclusion of the Cass Mastern narrative in *All the King's Men,* show that Warren in the 1940s was intensifying his personal investigations into the charged issue of race and confronting his own past experiences in the segregated South. In *All the King's Men* Jack Burden, and by extension the reader, confronts the racial legacy of the South through the story of Cass Mastern. Even though Jack has literally tried to leave the Cass Mastern story behind him through his successive moves, the package containing Cass's journal, letters, photograph, and ring keeps following him. The legacy of the past—particularly, in this case, the historical legacy of slavery—cannot be left behind.

Through his encounter with the Cass Mastern story, Jack formulates a new metaphor through which to view his own place in the world, a metaphor that emphasizes complicity and responsibility. However, it takes a long time for Jack to accept this metaphor:

> Cass Mastern lived for a few years and in that time he learned that the world is all of one piece. He learned that the world is like an enormous spider web and if you touch it, however lightly, at any point, the vibration ripples to the remotest perimeter and the drowsy spider feels the tingle and is drowsy no more but springs out to fling the gossamer coils about you who have touched the web and then inject the black, numbing poison under your hide. It does not matter whether or not you meant to brush the web of things. Your happy foot or your gay wing may have brushed it ever so lightly, but what happens always happens and there is the spider, bearded black and with his great faceted eyes glittering like mirrors in the sun, or like God's eye, and the fangs dripping. (*AKM* 188–89)

Significantly, this view of the world as "one piece" will be transformed into an important foundational principle in Warren's later poetry—his theory of an "osmosis of being." Both the web of being in *All the King's Men* and the later theory of an osmosis of being can certainly be linked to Coleridge's theory of the One Life, and as many critics have noted, Warren's work on the novel coincided with his intensive study of Coleridge's

Rime of the Ancient Mariner. There are many parallels between the works, and *All the King's Men* anticipates Warren's later poetic themes in many ways. Still, as John Burt points out, Cass's imagery is a bit more horrific than Warren's redemptive theory of an osmosis of being.

Cass comes to his horrific knowledge of complicity only at a terrible cost. His affair with Annabelle Trice leads to the suicide of his friend Duncan Trice, the destructive and obsessive guilt of Annabelle, and the selling of Annabelle's slave Phebe down the river and probably into forced concubinage. Thus the private sin of Cass's affair with Annabelle becomes inextricably intertwined with the public, societal evil of slavery. After Duncan's suicide, Annabelle's slave Phebe finds his wedding ring under his pillow. Annabelle becomes convinced that Phebe knows of the adulterous affair that drove Duncan to take his own life, and she reads Phebe's gaze as a reproach for her secret sin. Later, Cass himself expresses his inability to face the accusation implicit in the black gaze, an image that powerfully reappears in *Brother to Dragons*. Overwhelmed by the fact of his lifelong participation in the system of slavery, Cass eventually sets his slaves free and courts his own death:

> They had kissed my hands and wept for joy, but I could take no part in their rejoicing. I had not flattered myself that I had done anything for them. What I had done I had done for myself, to relieve my spirit of a burden, the burden of their misery and their eyes upon me. The wife of my dead friend had found the eyes of the girl Phebe upon her and had gone wild and had ceased to be herself and had sold the girl into misery. I had found their eyes upon me and had freed them into misery, lest I should do worse. For many cannot bear their eyes upon them, and enter into evil and cruel ways in their desperation. (*AKM* 183)

This sense of hopelessness amid the communal guilt of the South burdens Cass more heavily than his adulterous behavior. He admits that he was aware of slavery's evils before his affair and its consequences, but the selling off of Phebe links him to this evil in a more intimate manner. Cass even states that he "could have managed somehow to live with" the fact that he betrayed his friend. "But I suddenly felt that the world outside of me was shifting . . . and that the process had only begun of a general disintegration of which I was the center. . . . it was as though the vibration set up in the whole fabric of the world by my act had spread infinitely and with ever increasing power and no man could know the end" (*AKM* 177).

For Cass, the distinction between the private and public dimensions of responsibility and guilt has dissolved.

Like Cass's, Annabelle's change of character comes not so much from her act of infidelity itself as from her relationship with Phebe, which raises her private guilt and shame to a more public level. For both Cass and Annabelle, the boundaries between personal, private sin and public, communal sin have vanished, and this is a burden neither can successfully live with. They cannot even look back nostalgically to a time of innocence before their adulterous affair, because they were already partners in the larger crime of slavery before that personal transgression. With the Cass Mastern episode, Warren creates a narrative that probes the psychological effects of slavery on those who perpetuated and benefited from the system. Cass comes to the realization that the private and public selves cannot be so easily separated. The realm of personal responsibility extends far beyond the interior self to one's place in society and history, and the web of being does not allow us to flee from responsibility in the same manner as Jack's deterministic theory of the Great Twitch does. Instead, it forces us to accept the burden of our time and place in history, and to assume our parts in the broader political realities of our moment. In this way the novel reflects Warren's conversion on the race issue and his decision in the 1950s to confront the subject in a more personal, autobiographical manner. While Jack Burden's conversion experience certainly remains problematic, as critics have often noted, at the end of the novel he can finally accept Cass Mastern's theory of the web of being; he prepares to go "into the convulsion of the world, out of history into history and the awful responsibility of Time" (*AKM* 438).

While the Cass Mastern story points thematically to Warren's desire to blur the distinctions between the personal and the political realms, the use of Jack Burden as the narrator in *All the King's Men* also shows him taking important formal steps toward the more personal, subjective aesthetic of his later poetry. *Night Rider* and *At Heaven's Gate* were both narrated from a third-person point of view, but Warren apparently grew dissatisfied with this perspective and its sense of detachment and objectivity. As he worked on converting the play *Proud Flesh* into the novel *All the King's Men*, he determined that he needed a narrator who was a part of the story, and whose own personal retelling of the events would actually become more important than the novel's plot itself. The decision was a breakthrough for Warren, and in a 1946 letter to Donald Davidson he comments on his growing reliance upon a first-person point of view: "I couldn't find any other way into this particular book. The first-person narrative may be what Allen [Tate] once called it, the great alibi of the novelist. But I tend to find more and more that I write my best when I write with a very formally defined sort of mask, another person's self. My next novel, I fear, will be of the same sort, but with a very different narrator" (quoted in Blotner 527). In short, Warren was becoming more interested in the sort of "internal" dramas that would characterize his later poetry.[4]

"Blackberry Winter," published the same year as *All the King's Men*, marks another important step in Warren's progress toward a subjective aesthetic. Randy Hendricks astutely describes the story as a "'poetic,' personal effort," and argues that it marks a "watershed in Warren's career as well as a link between the early and late poetry" (49). Warren's own comments on the story's process of composition support this view of the story as an aesthetic breakthrough which was particularly relevant to his return to poetry. In "'Blackberry Winter': A Recollection," an essay included in the 1959 edition of *Understanding Fiction*, Warren made an important distinction between the story and all of the other fiction he had written up to that point:

> As a matter of fact, most of my stories and all of my novels (except two unpublished ones) have started very differently, from some objective situation or episode. . . . And I sometimes think it strange that the last story I ever wrote down and presumably the last I shall ever write (for poems are great devourers of stories) should have sprung so instinctively from the world of simple recollection—not a blackberry winter at all, but a kind of Indian summer. (643)

That Warren, writing this reminiscence in the late 1950s after his return to poetry, should refer to poems as "devourers of stories" indicates the extent to which he had successfully recast himself in the 1950s as a poet first and foremost. The composition process Warren describes in his reminiscence anticipates the autobiographical impulse that would help him to end his decade-long poetic impasse.

But Warren's use of personal experience goes beyond mere recollection, for he always attempts to raise the events of personal past to a more generalized and contemporary level of significance. In the case of "Blackberry Winter," Warren explains in his essay that the story began as a simple act of remembrance; having just completed *All the King's Men* and while enduring a harsh and unusually long Minnesota winter, he found himself entering the "remembered world" of his Southern childhood: "I was going back into a primal world of recollection. I was fleeing, if you wish. Hunting old bearings and bench-marks, if you wish. Trying to make a fresh start, if you wish. Whatever people do in their doubleness of living in a present and a past" (640). But he carefully counters this sense of "fleeing" to the past by also detailing the complex variety of contemporary circumstances that influenced the story's composition—the end of the war, his reading of Melville's poetry, his completion of *All the King's Men*, and his intensive study of Coleridge. Though the story may have had its beginnings in a recollection of the past, Warren contends that it is inextricably linked to the complexities of the contemporary moment:

> So what had started out for me as, perhaps, an act of escape, of fleeing back into the simplicities of childhood, had turned, as it always must if we accept the logic of our lives, into an attempt to bring something meaningfully out of that simple past into the complication of the present. And what had started out as a personal indulgence had tried to be, in the end, an impersonal generalization about experience, as a story must always try to be if it accepts the logic of fiction. And now, much later, I see that the story and the novel which I had then only lately finished, as well as the study of Coleridge, all bore on the same end. (642–43)

One of the ways Warren attempts to address the "complication of the present" is through the story's remarkable treatment of racial issues. The story shows that for a Southerner of Warren's age and background, the personal recollection of the past necessarily includes a confrontation with the emotionally charged issue of race.

"Blackberry Winter" is a story of lost childhood innocence, as Seth, the middle-aged narrator, recalls his initiation into the world's ironies, limitations, and potential for evil. Through the events of the story, he becomes more acutely aware of his place in the world, particularly his place in the racial and class structures of the South. The story takes place on a particularly cold June morning when he was a boy, and is framed by his encounters with a wandering vagrant who spends the morning working on Seth's parents' farm at the behest of Seth's mother. At the end of the story, Seth's father dismisses the vagrant in a potentially violent confrontation, and Seth follows the wanderer down the road, pestering him with innocent questions. The tramp—whom Warren in his reminiscence describes as "a creature altogether lost and pitiful, a dim image of what, in one perspective, our human condition is" (640)—responds by threatening to cut Seth's throat. But along with this encounter with the tramp which initiates him into a world of class distinctions and resentments, Seth has an experience that opens his eyes to his own place within the Southern racial order. As this is a coming-of-age story set in the segregated South, part of the innocence lost is the comfortable myth of racial amity and harmony.

Seth's family's farm houses a few families of black tenants, and on this particular morning Seth passes time, as he often does, by visiting the cabin of Dellie and Old Jebb, and their son Little Jebb. On this visit, Seth's views of life in Dellie and Jebb's cabin are dramatically changed. Dellie, who cooks for Seth's family, is home sick with her son Jebb when Seth stops by. Seth recalls that Dellie and Jebb "had the name all over the community for being clean and clever Negroes. Dellie and Jebb were what they used to call 'white-folks' niggers'" (CA 77). Like "Her Own People," this story examines the manner in which white characters perceive blacks, but unlike the Allens, who always refer to Viola as a "nigger," the boy Seth seems conscious of his racial rhetoric. Seth points out that Dellie and Jebb's cabin has always been cleaner than the other tenant cabins, whose occupants are "shiftless" by comparison; however, on this morning Seth notices that a recent storm has strewn trash across the yard:

> Up toward the porch, the ground was not clean any more. Old pieces of rag, two or three rusted cans, pieces of rotten rope, some hunks of old dog dung, broken glass, old paper, and all sorts of things like that had washed out from under Dellie's house to foul her clean yard. It looked just as bad as the yards of the other cabins, or worse. I had never thought of all that filth being under Dellie's house. It was not anything against Dellie that the stuff had been under the cabin. Trash will get under any house. But I did not think of that when I saw the foulness which had washed out on the ground which Dellie sometimes used to sweep with a twig broom to make nice and clean. (CA 78–79)

In his reminiscence, Warren claims this passage was in some ways influenced both by the recent war and by his reading of Melville's poem "The Conflict of Convictions." Melville in the poem says the impending Civil War would reveal "the slimed foundations" of the world. Warren's physical description of the yard, as well as the manner in which it affects Seth, foreshadows Seth's revelation regarding his relationship with Dellie and her family. As Seth narrates the action, it becomes apparent to the

reader—though probably not to the young Seth at the time of the story—
that Dellie resents Seth's intrusion, particularly since she is sick and in
bed. When she informs Seth that she is "Mighty sick," he does not take
the cue to leave her in peace but only says, "I'm sorry." Dellie's response
indicates her sense of hollow frustration:

> The eyes remained fixed on me for a moment, then they left me
> and the head rolled back on the pillow. "Sorry," the voice said, in a flat
> way which wasn't question or statement of anything. It was just the
> empty word put into the air with no meaning or expression, to float
> off like a feather or a puff of smoke, while the big eyes, with the
> whites like the peeled white of hard-boiled eggs, stared at the ceiling.
> (*CA* 79)

It is apparent that Little Jebb has been ordered to sit quietly by the
hearth so that his mother can rest, but Seth approaches him to engage him
in play: "I was asking him to get out his train and play train.... Jebb didn't
want to get the train out, but I told him I would go home if he didn't" (*CA*
80). Jebb finally gives in. Presently the boys, lost in their play, become too
loud for Dellie to bear. Following a particularly loud outburst from Jebb,
she interrupts them:

> "Come here," the voice said from the bed.
> Jebb got up slow from his hands and knees, giving me a sudden,
> naked, inimical look.
> Jebb went to the bed. Dellie propped herself weakly up on one arm,
> muttering, "Come closer."
> Jebb stood closer.
> "Last thing I do, I'm gonna do it," Dellie said. "Done tole you to be
> quiet."
> Then she slapped him. It was an awful slap, more awful for the kind
> of weakness which it came from and brought to focus. I had seen her
> slap Jebb before, but the slapping had always been the kind of easy
> slap you would expect from a good-natured, grumbling Negro
> woman like Dellie. But this was different. It was awful. It was so awful
> that Jebb didn't make a sound. The tears just popped out and ran down
> his face, and his breath came sharp, like gasps.
> Dellie fell back. "Cain't even be sick," she said to the ceiling. "Git
> sick and they won't even let you lay. They tromp all over you. Cain't
> even be sick." Then she closed her eyes. (*CA* 80–81)

Seth's reaction is to flee, and his running away can be attributed to a variety of factors. First, his comfortable, projected image of Dellie as a "good-natured, grumbling Negro woman" has suddenly been challenged. He catches a glimpse of her as an individual capable of deep anger and resentment. At the same time, he also may feel some responsibility for Dellie's striking of Jebb, for he pressured Jebb into playing; he senses this accusation in Jebb's "naked, inimical look." But perhaps the most important factor in his fleeing is a nascent awareness that the "they" Dellie refers to actually includes him. She resents Seth's intrusion, and she probably resents the fact that Seth's parents allow his intrusion. Her slapping of Jebb, then, is a transference of her desire to slap Seth for interrupting her rest in the first place. In portraying Dellie in this manner, Warren undermines one of the sentimental props of the Southern racial order: the idealization of the Mammy figure. Warren's commentary in "'Blackberry Winter': A Recollection" explains the personal origins of this scene, as well as his rationale for including it:

> Even if the boy would see no irony in that echo of J.E.B. Stuart's fame [through the character of Old Jebb], he would get a shock when Dellie slapped her beloved son, and would sense that the blow was, in some deep way, a blow at him. I knew this, for I knew the inside of that prideful cabin, and the shock of early recognition that beneath mutual kindliness and regard some dark, tragic, unresolved something lurked.... The story ... was now shifting emphasis from the lyricism of nostalgia to a concern with the jags and injustices of human relationships. What had earlier come in unconsciously . . . now got a conscious formulation. (642)

Even though Warren concludes his reminiscence by saying that the story is not autobiographical in the strict sense of the word (of its characters he says, "I never knew these particular people, only that world and people like them"), the composition process he describes begins to suggest the autobiographical impulse he will follow upon his return to poetry. According to Warren, in the 1950s he had "a complete change of attitude toward what constituted the germ of a short poem." In contrast to the more "abstract" nature of his earlier poetry, the poems he began to write in the 1950s were more concrete and tended to be drawn from his own personal experience: "when I went back to writing short poems, the poems were more directly tied to a realistic base of facts. They're more tied up with an event, an anecdote, an observation. . . . They were closer to me, closer to my observed and felt life. They had literal germs. That doesn't mean they were autobiographical in the rigid sense of the word. But they were tied more directly to the sort of thing that might become a short story. . . . tied closer to the texture of casual life, incidental observations, direct experience. They moved into that world, [the] poetry did" (Watkins et al. 130).

Confession and Complicity
in *Brother to Dragons* (1953)

> Nothing we were,
> Is lost.
> All is redeemed,
> In knowledge.
> But knowledge is the most powerful cost.
> It is the bitter bread.
> I have eaten the bitter bread.
> In joy, I would end.
>
> Robert Penn Warren, *Brother to Dragons*

Although conventional wisdom has held that Warren's ten-year hiatus from publishing poetry was mainly the result of his turning his attention to fiction, Warren on a number of occasions explained that during this decade he still attempted to write poems but could not finish them. In his own words, he "lost the capacity for finishing the short poem."[1] Considered in its context, and considering the remarkable changes that occur in his poetry upon his return, Warren's hiatus suggests that he went through an aesthetic crisis. He wrote his way out of this poetic impasse with the 1953 publication of *Brother to Dragons*, a text in which he confronts his own early views on race in a deeply personal manner and lays the foundation for his poetry's new aesthetic. The fact that Warren broke out of his impasse by directly addressing racial themes in such a personal way suggests an important relationship between his evolving racial politics and his evolving poetics; it is as though his personal confrontation with race was a necessary step in the process by which he defined his new aesthetic, an aesthetic that may best be described as Romantic.

Critics in recent years have increasingly drawn attention to Warren's poetic affinities with Romanticism, culminating in Lesa Carnes Corrigan's thorough study *Poems of Pure Imagination: Robert Penn Warren*

and the Romantic Tradition. According to Corrigan, in the 1940s as War-
ren wrote "A Poem of Pure Imagination," his famous New Critical study
of Coleridge's *Rime of the Ancient Mariner,* he underwent a "form of
'conversion' experience that shaped his spiritual outlook as well as his
aesthetic philosophy" (13).[2] Corrigan shows that following Warren's re-
turn to poetry in the 1950s, his work is essentially Romantic, distin-
guished by a "sacramental vision of the universe" which reconciles differ-
ences and celebrates what Coleridge called the One Life that links all
humankind and nature. Warren parallels Coleridge's concept of the One
Life with his own theory of an "osmosis of being," a concept he outlined
in his seminal 1955 essay "Knowledge and the Image of Man." Corrigan's
study convincingly establishes Warren's close relationship with the Ro-
mantic tradition of poetry, showing that Romanticism's underlying phi-
losophy and aesthetic principles provided him with a way out of his poetic
impasse. His breakthrough, however, involved more than an immersion
in Romanticism. Indeed, Warren's "conversion" experience had impor-
tant political contexts, antecedents, and consequences, all of which inter-
sected with the charged issue of race.

It is more than mere chance that the poetic conversion Corrigan de-
scribes coincided with Warren's reimmersion in the race issue in the
1950s and early 1960s and his public adoption of an integrationist posi-
tion. Surveying the work Warren produced over these years, one sees that
he became nothing less than obsessed by racial politics and the historical
legacy of slavery, returning to these subjects again and again in texts of
this period: in the long poem *Brother to Dragons* (1953), in the novels
Band of Angels (1955), *Wilderness* (1961), and—to a lesser extent—*Flood*
(1963), in the contemporary social criticism of *Segregation: The Inner
Conflict in the South* (1956) and *Who Speaks for the Negro?* (1965), and
in the historical criticism of *The Legacy of the Civil War* (1961). Mark
Jancovich claims in *The Cultural Politics of the New Criticism* that the
segregation debates of the 1950s "gave Warren a concrete image of the
process of defining a moral identity, and of the interrelation between the
self and others" (131). Following Jancovich's suggestion, close examina-
tion of Warren's political and poetic texts of the period reveals that his
political and aesthetic views evolved in a reciprocal and parallel fashion,
influencing one another in an ongoing dialogue. This is especially appar-
ent if we consider Warren's poetry alongside his two inquiries into con-
temporary racial politics, *Segregation* and *Who Speaks for the Negro?*
Looking at Warren's poetry within this politicized context provides a

deeper, more nuanced portrait of his poetry's themes and underlying assumptions, while at the same time shedding light on the complex nature of the transformation that occurred with his return to poetry in the 1950s. Moreover, by examining Warren's political and aesthetic conversions in conjunction with one another, we can begin to sense that these conversions were parallel consequences of a much deeper and more profound ideological shift in Warren's worldview, a shift that took place cumulatively over his ten-year poetic impasse. In light of the dramatic differences between Warren's worldviews of the early 1940s and early 1950s, it is possible to liken his story of change to that of Jack Burden in *All the King's Men:* "It is the story of a man who lived in the world and to him the world looked one way for a long time and then it looked another and very different way. The change did not happen all at once. Many things happened, and that man did not know when he had any responsibility for them and when he did not" (*AKM* 435). In the case of Warren, the fact that the change may have taken place gradually and cumulatively does not diminish its magnitude. By the early 1950s, he clearly looked at the world around him in a very different way.

The effects of Warren's changing worldview appear most strikingly in his new views on racial politics and poetry, which contradict or contrast sharply with his earlier beliefs; however, they are also apparent in his altering positions on a host of related themes involving self and identity, the complex relationships among determinism and will and individual responsibility, the social function of literature, and the process of an individual's response to the flux and uncertainty of the contemporary historical moment. In all of these areas of thematic inquiry, Warren in the 1950s articulated new positions that contrast with his earlier views. And just as there are significant connections between Warren's conservative Agrarian politics and his early, tradition-oriented modernist aesthetic, so too there are meaningful, revealing parallels in the way he approached his poetry and politics during the 1950s and early 1960s. Indeed, at times it becomes difficult to tell where his aesthetic philosophy ends and his political philosophy begins. So while he may have helped to develop the New Criticism and its apolitical literary values, Warren nonetheless came to believe in a vital, necessary relationship between his own art and the particular social and political realities of the moment. Warren's new poetry of this period is characterized by a more personal, autobiographical voice, but it is by no means a voice withdrawn or isolated from the pressures of the contemporary historical moment. Instead, Warren felt the personal landscape of his new poetry was vitally connected to the contemporary social and political world. As he explained in a 1966 interview, "Social tensions have a parallel in the personal world. The individual is an embodiment of external circumstances, so that a personal story is a social story" (Watkins et al. 70). So even though Warren shifts to a more personal, autobiographical poetry, he would still contend that the personal story revealed in the poems exhibits the pressures and realities of the social world. This is illustrated by the fact that Warren's poetry of this period and his more overtly political texts on segregation and the civil rights movement share fundamental similarities in method, manner, and voice. In the two endeavors, he employs a number of similar metaphors, tropes, and rhetorical strategies and, perhaps more important, in both he moves from the detached objectivity of his earlier works—be it the objective formalism of his early poetry or the academic detachment of "The Briar Patch"—to a more subjective voice which reflects a deeper level of personal engagement with his subject matter, and with the contemporary historical moment.

Along with this shift to a more autobiographical voice, Warren's Romantic poetry is premised upon two interrelated concepts that are new to his poetry of the 1950s: an underlying belief in a unity, or "osmosis," of being which unites and redeems all life and experience, and an understanding (and representation) of the self as a willed "development" in time. Each of these concepts manifests itself in Warren's poetry through a variety of tropes and strategies which I will discuss in greater detail later in chapter 7; for now, I would like to suggest the ways in which these concepts are equally relevant to his prose writings on race.

The central operational metaphor of Warren's Romantic aesthetic is his theory of an osmosis of being, and through it he develops and articulates a belief in poetry's therapeutic social relevance. Upon his return to poetry in the 1950s, the rejuvenated Warren increasingly saw poetry as an agent for reconciling differences and illustrating the fundamental unity of human experience: as he argued earlier in the conclusion of his 1946 essay on Coleridge, poetry is a "myth of the unity of being" which reconciles "the self-divisive internecine malices which arise at the superficial level on which we conduct most of our living" ("A Poem of Pure Imagination" 399). In his 1955 essay "Knowledge and the Image of Man," Warren assimilated these views more completely, developing his central premise that the individual exists "in the world with continual and intimate interpenetration, an inevitable osmosis of being, which in the end does not deny, but affirms, his identity" (187). For Warren, it is a given that the individual "disintegrates his primal instinctive sense of unity" through the tumult and transgression of social experience; however, he believes that through the creation of knowledge, this experience may be redeemed and the individual may be restored to a "more precious" unity, a "unity presupposing separateness" (187). Accordingly, Warren's poetry of this period consistently relies upon motifs and metaphors of synthesis, integration, and reconciliation, and this tendency has not gone unnoticed among critics. As Lesa Carnes Corrigan notes, Warren's poetry shows that "Redemption is available only through the sustained reconciliation of opposing forces" (91). Other critics have hinted at the more public dimensions of this tendency in Warren's work. As Robert S. Koppelman explains, "Warren ultimately works toward a reconciliation of the private 'self' with the public and natural worlds" (13). Similarly, Randy Hendricks broadly asserts: "It can be reasonably argued that the integration of the personality is the major theme of works whose seemingly broad scope is reflected in such titles as *Segregation, Who Speaks for the Negro?* and *The Legacy of the Civil War*" (83).

Koppelman's and Hendricks's suggestions that there is a public element in this equation become more keenly relevant when we consider the manner in which the boundaries between Warren's poetry and politics often became blurred during this period in his career. In contrast to the modernist aesthetic of his early poetry, which privileged the hierarchies of tradition, the Romantic themes and strategies of his new poetry paralleled and underscored his more egalitarian political emphasis by positing a unity of being that transcends differences and dissolves hierarchies. In fact, during this period Warren often approached the subject of race and the political issue of integration by employing the same metaphors and tropes that inform his poetry's Romantic aesthetic. In *Segregation*, for instance, he defines the conflict over segregation less as a public political issue and more as a personal "inner conflict" of "self-division"; integration—on both a public and a personal level—becomes the corrective, much in the same way that his poetry seeks to document the integration of the divided, fragmented self into a unified moral being. In *Who Speaks for the Negro?* we can similarly sense that the debates over racial integration became a real-life testing ground for Warren's Romantic assumptions, particularly his belief in a fundamental unity of being and his strategy of reconciling—or integrating—opposites, a pattern seen over and over again in his poetry. At one point in the text, for example, he suggests that "the integration of the Negro into American society would be . . . a correlative of the integration of the personality, white or black" (171). Later in the text, he emphasizes that integration is not merely a political issue, but a symbol of possibilities, both public and personal: "The word *integration*, in fact, does not refer, clearly and distinctly, to one thing. It refers to a shifting, shadowy mass of interfusing possibilities. It refers, in short, to the future" (415). Just as he defined poetry as a therapeutic myth which reconciles superficial differences by affirming the fundamental unity of all human experience, Warren in a 1958 interview described race as a living symbol of a unity that contains diversity: "Race isn't an isolated thing—I mean as it exists in the U.S.—it becomes a total symbolism for every kind of issue. They all flow into it. And out of it. . . . It gives a little variety to life. At the same time, it proclaims the unity of life" (Watkins et al. 46). Throughout his work of the 1950s and 1960s, Warren sought to construct a symbolic unity that transcended the world of poetry and influenced his meditations on contemporary racial politics as well.

Along with outlining his metaphor of the osmosis of being, "Knowledge and the Image of Man" provides a rationale for Warren's adoption of a personal voice, perhaps the single feature that most distinguishes his new poetry from his earlier works.[3] Departing from his earlier poetry's privileging of objectivity, Warren now argues that in order to play a therapeutic role in society, poetry must be "drawn from the actual world and charged with the urgencies of actuality. . . . It is not a thing detached from the world but a thing springing from a deep engagement of spirit with the world" (191–92). At the same time he was articulating and putting into practice this new Romantic aesthetic, Warren's own "deep engagement" with the public world centered most specifically and concretely on the issue of race—as it did for much of his adult life—and the subjective voice he adopted in his poetry projected itself to his nonfiction writings on race as well. As Jonathan Cullick explains, "'The Briar Patch' . . . maintains academic distance from the topic. The later narratives, *Segregation: The Inner Conflict in the South* and *Who Speaks for the Negro?* show an author who has become discontent with the voice of a detached narrator. . . . they are personal narratives, grounded in interviews and shaped by the autobiographical impulses of the narrator. They are narratives of connection" (51). This general movement from detachment and objectivity to subjective engagement actually began with Warren's fiction of the 1940s—as discussed previously—and culminates in *Brother to Dragons*, the poem that ended Warren's break from poetry; through the inclusion of R.P.W. as the narrator in *Brother to Dragons*, he laid to rest the more objective, detached voice characteristic of his early poetry. Significantly, Warren also confronted and attempted to move beyond his own early views on race in *Brother to Dragons*. The poem thus marks a watershed moment in his evolving perspectives on both poetry and race, and indicates a correlative evolution between his aesthetics and politics. The voice he adopted in the poem actually formed the foundation for his later inquiries into segregation and the civil rights movement, and Ralph Ellison sensed just such a connection not long after the publication of *Segregation*. In a 1957 interview with Warren, Ellison remarked, "In recent years your work has become more intense and has taken on an element of personal confession which is so definite that one tends to look, for example, on *Segregation* and *Brother to Dragons* as two facets of a single work" (Watkins et al. 33).

Along with the shift toward personal expression in Warren's poetry came a new method of representing the self, a method that seems to have led Warren away from the element of determinism that pervaded his early poetry. Earlier in his career, Warren had claimed that modern poetry is essentially consumed by the single question "Can man live on a purely naturalistic level?" While he was never a proponent of deterministic thinking, Warren's early poetry was often dominated by deterministic themes and a related sense of alienation. The only real solution his early poetry offered was a proposed rapprochement with the traditions of the past. Now, however, in contrast to an individual being controlled by deterministic factors, Warren portrays the self actively creating its values and destiny in spite of deterministic factors. As he explains in "Knowledge and the Image of Man," the individual, through a "progressive understanding" of the osmosis of being that unites all life, "creates new perspectives, discovers new values—that is, a new self—and so the identity is a continually emerging, an unfolding, a self-affirming and, we hope, a self-corrective creation" (186–87).

While Warren scholars have linked his theory of an osmosis of being with the Romantic tradition, they have generally failed to consider that his rhetoric of the developing self likewise has its literary roots in Romanticism. As Clifford Siskin persuasively demonstrates in his pioneering study *The Historicity of Romantic Discourse*, "development" is a central strategy and formal feature of all Romantic discourse, its characteristic way of representing the self as a mind that grows and develops: "With the Romantic redefinition of the self as a mind that grows, writing became an expressive index to that growth—the product, as we still understand it, of a developing creative imagination" (3). Through the strategy of development and the formal features it includes, the random events of an individual's life may be ordered into patterns of willful and meaningful growth. Critics have generally read Warren's newly articulated theory of the developing self as though it were transparent, accepting development as a psychological truth rather than considering the various formal features and rhetorical strategies it entails.[4] At this point in his career, Warren embraces this strategy both in theory and in practice, and this element of Romantic discourse he adopted influenced not only his poetry but also his nonfiction writings on race. This view of the self as a willful, developing moral identity allowed him to move away from the more deterministic views of the self he entertained earlier in his career.[5] At the same time, development as a strategy of self-representation allowed Warren to recoup and redeem the past, including his early views on race. In other words, Warren represents his own conversion from a segregationist to an integrationist position through the very developmental theories he outlines in "Knowledge and the Image of Man." In that essay, he explains development as a secular version of the fortunate fall, transforming transgression into a "felix culpa" which leads the self to a deeper, "more precious" sense of moral awareness and a restoration of unity. Development thus allows us to redeem the past, including Warren's own early views on race.[6] In a way, his earlier errors almost become an asset, providing a deeper, more authentic awareness of the moral complexity of human nature. Such is the resolution of *Brother to Dragons*, but this motif also appears in *Segregation* and *Who Speaks for the Negro?* As Jonathan Cullick points out, *Segregation* and *Who Speaks for the Negro?* both follow narrative patterns of return, reconciliation, and redemption, and these patterns "serve as instruments for illustrating connection within the matrix of time" (3). Through these patterns Warren recovers and redeems the past and offers an effective counterpoint to the deterministic emphasis of his earlier work.[7]

With this shift away from determinism, Warren can again be compared to Jack Burden in *All the King's Men*. Over the course of the novel, Burden moves from his deterministic Great Twitch theory to the acknowledgment of will and responsibility which comes from his acceptance of Cass Mastern's competing theory in which "the world is all of one piece. . . . like an enormous spider web" (*AKM* 188). But while Warren treats these themes objectively in *All the King's Men*, his move away from determin-

ism and toward an emphasis on will and responsibility is seen in a frankly
personal, confessional way in his poetic and political texts of the 1950s and
early 1960s. Warren now spurns strictly deterministic explanations of
human motivation and behavior, particularly in *Brother to Dragons* and
Segregation. At the same time, he offers a pointed critique of his own
early assumptions, both aesthetic and political. In both of these texts, War-
ren moves away from the backward-looking, traditionalist premise of his
earlier work and now accepts the burden of his own time and place in
history. For a white Southerner in the 1950s, the burden of the contempo-
rary moment was felt most acutely in the debates over integration leading
up to and following the Supreme Court's *Brown v. Board of Education*
decision of 1954. Between the mid-1940s and mid-1950s, then, Warren
was prompted to accept the burden of the moment and to develop a per-
sonal aesthetic of "deep engagement" with the world. By considering the
contexts of these remarkable changes, and by considering the correspon-
dences between his altering poetics and politics, we can perhaps begin to
speculate as to the political and ideological rationale behind his adoption
of a Romantic aesthetic—as well as perhaps the reasons behind his ten-
year poetic impasse.

It is impossible to pinpoint an exact moment or cause behind Warren's
repudiation of his early pro-segregationist views and his adoption of a
more liberal perspective; more than likely a wide range of social and cul-
tural disruptions caused the ideological structure supporting his early be-
liefs—and his early poetics—to give way. At a reunion of the Fugitives
held in May 1956 at Vanderbilt, Warren reflected back upon the war years
and offered some cryptic remarks on how and why he lost his interest in
Agrarianism, which for him would always be tied inextricably to his de-
fense of segregation:

> I can only speak of what it signified for me—what Agrarianism sig-
> nified for me. And of late years I have tried to give it some thought,
> and I must confess that my mind tended to shut up on the subject for
> about ten years. It seemed irrelevant at one stage to what I was think-
> ing and feeling, except in a sentimental way—I mean at the level of
> what these things signify. I ceased to think about it during the war
> years. Before we got in the last war, just before it and several years
> after, there was the period of unmasking of blank power everywhere.
> And you felt that all your work was irrelevant to this unmasking of
> this brute force in the world—that the de-humanizing forces had

won. And you had no more relevance in such discussions as we used to have. (Watkins et al. 19–20)

It is important to note here that the period during which he came to feel that Agrarianism was irrelevant corresponds with the period of his poetic impasse. Warren's early conservative poetic principles were ideologically consistent with his conservative Agrarian political views, and thus it follows that the ideological shift that caused Warren to lose faith in his political principles would also undermine his faith in his poetic principles. It may be useful to recall Warren's discouraged tone in the conclusion of his 1939 essay "The Present State of Poetry: In the United States," which shows that he was already sensing that poetry was perhaps irrelevant to the events of the modern world. Writing at the start of the World War II— at approximately the time when he says he ceased thinking of Agrarianism—Warren concludes his review of American poetry by gravely declaring that "in the midst of our competing beliefs, one belief may be lacking: the belief that poetry is worth writing" (398). What was it, then, that prompted the profound transformation in Warren's worldview over these years, leading him to articulate new aesthetic and political values? On a personal level, as Mark Miller and Lesa Carnes Corrigan have noted, the end of his first marriage and his new, happier life with Eleanor Clark surely played a large role in the changing tone of his new poetry. But looking at the changing landscape of race politics can perhaps provide insight into the underlying ideological shift Warren experienced.

During those years when Warren published no poetry, many factors influenced and altered the landscape of racial politics in America. The most obvious factor was the war itself, which forced many to reconsider their views on race, both through the debates over integrating the armed forces and through the terrifying logic of the Nazis' racist thinking.[8] In *Race: The History of an Idea in America*, Thomas F. Gossett points out that the racist ideology of the Nazis which led to the holocaust provided Americans with concrete images of the logical outcome of racist thinking:

In the 1930's and 1940's, the country was treated to the spectacle of just how far a nationalism based upon race might go in Germany and, to a lesser extent, in Italy. The racist mouthings of Hitler, Goering, Goebbels, and their racist philosopher Alfred Rosenberg were a compound of horror and absurdity. Americans realized with a shock, especially after World War II, that the Nazis had meant exactly what they said—that they were perfectly willing to carry out their beliefs by a program of genocide—by killing literally millions of Jews and other peoples they regarded as inferior. The recognition that race prejudice is not merely regrettable but also highly dangerous was no longer limited to the minorities who suffered from discrimination or to the students of racism. (445)

This new awareness described by Gossett, coupled with America's new role as world leader, led many to begin demanding justice and equality for all Americans, regardless of their race or ethnicity. In fact, the issue of racial justice increasingly took center stage in the national spotlight in the years following World War II. In 1946 President Truman created the President's Committee on Civil Rights to investigate race discrimination in the United States. In their report published in 1947, titled *To Secure These Rights*, the committee called for an end to both racial segregation and all forms of racial discrimination. That same year Jackie Robinson became the first African-American to break major league baseball's color barrier. A year later Truman ordered an end to race segregation in the nation's armed forces. Most significant, in the early 1950s a number of cases challenging segregation in public schools were making their way through the justice system, and in 1952 *Brown v. the Board of Education of Topeka, Kansas* came before the Supreme Court of the United States for argument. On May 17, 1954, a unanimous decision was handed down, ruling that "separate but equal" was unconstitutional. Over this period of years, the moral landscape underlying the issue of segregation became clear to more and more Americans, but not all were responding positively to the changes taking place. During the 1948 presidential election, the Democratic Party's aggressive civil rights stance led to the Dixiecrat rebellion against the party. Strom Thurmond, the Dixiecrat candidate, received more than a million votes and carried four Southern states. And in the years following the Supreme Court's *Brown* decision, the South would grow increasingly recalcitrant regarding the new law of the land, a development that prompted Warren in 1956 to write *Segregation: The Inner Conflict in the South*.

In this altering cultural and political landscape, Warren clearly left behind the conservative principles, both political and poetic, of his younger days. The publication of *Brother to Dragons* in 1953 ended Warren's decade-long hiatus from poetry, and in nearly every aspect—form, voice, style, and theme—the poem signals a definitive departure from the aesthetic and themes of his early poetry. The significance of *Brother to Drag-*

ons in Warren's canon may be gathered from the fact that it has generated more criticism than any other poetic text he produced—and more than any of his novels save *All the King's Men.* Furthermore, Warren would twice return to *Brother to Dragons:* in 1976 he would rework it as a two-act play, and in 1979 he would publish a "new version," dramatically revised to better reflect the looser, more open style of his poetry in the 1970s. Even though critics generally tend to favor the later version, the 1953 version, my subject for the moment, stands as a watershed moment in the transformation of Warren's poetry, and of his views on race. Considering the poem's historical subject matter—the brutal axe murder of a slave by Lilburn and Isham Lewis, nephews of Thomas Jefferson—it is not surprising that critics have often read *Brother to Dragons* as a broad statement on the American consciousness and the American past, particularly its faults and sins. As William Bedford Clark succinctly puts it, the poem is a "reminder of the disparity between American dreams and American realities as well as of certain contradictions within our national character" ("Canaan's Grander Counterfeit" 145).

In addition to these broader historical themes, *Brother to Dragons* is also a deeply personal poetic statement, but critics have generally failed to consider the implications of Warren's decision to include himself among the cast of characters as "R.P.W.: *The writer of this poem*" (*BD* 2). The work is subtitled "A Tale in Verse and Voices," and certainly the most prominent voice belongs to R.P.W., who holds a dialogue with the disembodied voices from the historical past. R.P.W. has been characterized by critics as both "a commentator on the action" and a "spokesman for modern man" (quoted in Dooley 101), but as Dennis Dooley has argued, his presence is more central to the poem's meaning than such labels would suggest. In what is the most extensive analysis of R.P.W., Dooley points out that R.P.W.'s "conversion" from cynicism and despair to a sense of hope based on "mature spiritual wisdom" acts as a framing device for the action of the poem (111). But even Dooley fails to consider the complicated issue of self-representation that goes hand in hand with the poem's subject *and* subjectivity: namely, in a poem whose central event is a symbol of racial injustice, how does Warren, placing himself within the text, represent his own racist past?

I would like to consider exactly what is at stake if we are willing to read R.P.W. less as a generic spokesman for modernity and more as Warren himself, an equation Warren certainly encouraged in the poem's introductory material. Critics have generally hedged from such an immediate association, reading R.P.W. instead as a type of modern-day Everyman. Hugh Ruppersburg, for instance, maintains that R.P.W. at certain points "clearly *is* Warren" while at other times he "strikes the modernist pose of a time-wearied cynic; skeptical and contemptuous of visions and ideals" (70–71).[9] This tendency to distance Warren "the poet" from R.P.W. "the character" may be linked, first, to the formalist tendency to separate poet from persona and, second, to the fact that R.P.W. for most of the poem is not a very likeable fellow. However, I am more willing to consider the possibility that these latter, negative characteristics that Ruppersburg describes are not necessarily a pose; instead, I believe Warren's representation of R.P.W. is intended to be indicative of his own early views and beliefs. Moreover, reading such a split between R.P.W. and the real-life Warren, as Ruppersburg does, contradicts the poem's thematic emphasis on human complicity, personal guilt, and redemption. In fact, the poem's thematic emphasis and resolution *demand* that we read R.P.W. literally as Warren's own voice. This becomes particularly clear if we consider the importance of race and racism in the poem. Foregrounding race in our approach to *Brother to Dragons* reveals the true complexity involved in Warren's confrontation with his own racist past. Dennis Dooley has argued that R.P.W.'s conversion frames the conversion of Jefferson; however, it is equally important to emphasize that R.P.W.'s own racism frames the racism of the poem's other characters, and it is this culture and history of racism represented in the poem that implicates all of the white characters in the crime of Lilburn Lewis.

It would be difficult to overestimate the importance of race in the text of *Brother to Dragons*. It is an inescapable force in the poem, providing the central, concrete, human issue from which Warren developed the poem's more abstract and general themes. Indeed, race pervades the entire text, influencing the poem's composition, determining its radical subjectivity, and underscoring its main themes and resolution. Interestingly, however, few critics have confronted the issue of race in *Brother to Dragons* with any directness; instead, they generally have subsumed race within broader discussions of the poem's more universal themes. For instance, most critics have failed to even consider the significance of R.P.W.'s repeated use of racist rhetoric, which is surprising considering the fact that the poem centers around the murder of a slave.[10]

In terms of theme, critics agree that on the broadest level *Brother to Dragons* is a poem about issues such as original sin, the banality of evil, human complicity and guilt, and redemption. This being the case, the foregrounding of R.P.W.'s obvious racism is essential to the poem, for in order to offer any thematic resolution on issues such as these, Warren must first confess his own sins: he must implicate himself within the white system of racist rhetoric and representation that gives rise to the murder of the slave George. Indeed, how could Warren hope to speak with any authority on the issue of communal guilt without first admitting his own personal sins? Consequently, while *Brother to Dragons* certainly may be viewed most broadly as a meditation on original sin and complicity, it is more specifically a meditation on American sin, even more specifically a meditation on the Southern sin of slavery, and most specifically a meditation on Warren himself and his own involvement in the particular sin of racism. While *Brother to Dragons*, then, may be viewed as a confessional poem, it must be noted that Warren attempts to project his confessional voice by placing it within a framework that endows both personal and national history with mythic significance. While Robert Lowell once lamented, "Alas, I can only tell my own story," Warren here believes he is constructing a mythic narrative that contains *everyone's* story and could speak specifically to American culture in the post–World War II era.[11] As Warren explains in his introductory notes to *Brother to Dragons*, "Historical sense and poetic sense should not, in the end, be contradictory, for if poetry is the little myth we make, history is the big myth we live, and in our living, constantly remake" (xii). By emphasizing that the issue discussed by the characters is "a human constant," Warren prompts the reader to search the contemporary moment for specific resonances in American culture (xii). In this way, *Brother to Dragons* becomes a cautionary myth for American culture of the 1950s.

Indeed, Warren's emphasis on human depravity and evil in the poem is intended as a corrective to the increasingly complacent and homogeneous culture of America during the 1950s, the period Lowell would dub "the tranquillized *Fifties.*" This was the cultural milieu that made the Reverend Norman Vincent Peale's *The Power of Positive Thinking* a runaway best-seller. The feel-good theology of Peale, with his credo of "stop worrying and start living," struck a chord with Americans suffering from Cold War paranoia. But Warren's notes for the poem reveal that he was influenced by the sharply contrasting message provided by the more orthodox theologian Reinhold Niebuhr. These notes contain numerous references to and quotes from Niebuhr's two-volume work *The Nature and Destiny of Man*, a text that attacks the "essentially easy conscience" of the modern individual and seeks to restore the doctrine of original sin (23). Niebuhr traces the various trends of idealism and naturalism that have shaped western culture, arguing that in the end, neither naturalism nor idealism can measure the individual "in a dimension sufficiently high or deep to do full justice to either his stature or his capacity for both good and evil" (124). As one early reviewer of the first volume summarized, Niebuhr "puts sin right back in the spotlight" ("Sin Rediscovered" 38). Warren clearly felt that the easy message of someone like Norman Vincent Peale was not only naive but dangerous, and like Niebuhr, Warren in *Brother to Dragons* attempts to restore a belief in humanity's capacity for evil. But while this may be the broad and abstract message of the cultural myth Warren projects, the issue of racism remains as the concrete core of the poem.[12]

Warren's notes for the poem, preserved among the Robert Penn Warren Papers, suggest the extent to which the issue of race influenced the poem's composition, acting as a catalyst for his imagination as he developed his poem's broad thematic significance.[13] These notes reveal that, along with Niebuhr, Hannah Arendt's recently published book *The Origins of Totalitarianism* was a prominent influence on Warren as he worked toward his poem's meaning. Published in 1951, Arendt's groundbreaking study traces the origins of the modern totalitarian states back to nineteenth-century imperialism and anti-Semitism. Warren's notes indicate that he was particularly interested in Arendt's discussion of the emergence in the nineteenth century of race-thinking "as a principle of the body politic" (Arendt 185). Most revealingly, Warren's notes contain a number of specific references to Arendt's depiction of the racist culture of the Boers in South Africa, with Warren in fact equating Arendt's depiction of the Boers with the brutal murder of the slave George at the hands of Isham and Lilburn. For instance, at one point Warren writes:

> <u>NB</u> If Lilburn killed George because he saw in the Negro the "black parody" (Hannah Arendt & Boers) the dark "self" to be expurgated— (ie a purified & therefore an "ideal" act perverted)—then Jefferson's repudiation of Lilburn is a parallel crime—that is, an attempt to purify the self by exclusion, suppression, <u>not</u> by "love," ie absorption. "Evil" the "food of good"—eat it assimilate it, love it (RPW Papers)

Warren echoes this thematic equation at another point in his notes, writing:

NB In repudiating Lilburn, Jefferson repeats Lilburn's Crime—Lilburn kills George to get rid of his "dark self" (Cf Arendt) & Jefferson repudiates Lilburn for same reason (RPW Papers)

In *The Origins of Totalitarianism* Arendt paints a damning portrait of the Boers, showing that their emerging identity as a distinct people was based almost entirely on their racist beliefs which formed through their encounters with the native African population. She explains that the Boers "were never able to forget their first horrible fright before a species of men whom human pride and the sense of human dignity could not allow them to accept as fellow-men. This fright of something like oneself that still under no circumstances ought to be like oneself remained at the basis of slavery and became the basis for a race society" (192). In short, the Boers provide a classic example of a society and culture that defines itself through essentialist notions of race and through the demonization of the racial other. Considering his own early representations of blacks and his prewar pro-segregation viewpoint, Warren must have drawn some troubling analogies between Arendt's portrait of the Boers and his own experience in and allegiance to the segregated South. Interestingly, in this same period when segregation in America was under attack, South Africa was instituting apartheid as the law of the land. The situation in South Africa, Arendt's discussion of the South African Boers, and his own memories of the segregated South perhaps all combined to spark Warren's imagination as he cultivated his poem's thematic significance. But Arendt's study provided yet another connection for Warren to imaginatively pursue by linking the racism of the Boers with the anti-Semitism of the Nazi regime and its horrific "final solution." In the wake of the Nuremberg war crime trials and the revelations of Nazi atrocities, this particular correlation was not lost on one reviewer of *Brother to Dragons*, who wrote, "The dead Jefferson [of *Brother to Dragons*] looks at the obscene underside of the stone and—he can do no other—he licks his lips: he knows, now. Most of us know, now, that Rousseau was wrong: that man, when you knock his chains off, sets up the death camps" (Jarrell 161).

While Warren's notes show that the issue of racism provided the matrix from which the poem's broader and more abstract themes originated, in the text of the poem he suggests the way in which his own early views on race determined the poem's unique form and subjectivity. Since the poem specifically details the potential outcomes of racism, his own past racism figuratively implicates him in Lilburn's crime. Therefore, to not

include himself in the poem—to simply strive for an objective state-
ment—would be a form of evasion. Both his theme of complicity and his
own personal history demand a confessional voice that admits personal
sin and accepts personal responsibility for that sin. R.P.W. himself sug-
gests this line of reasoning when he recounts to Jefferson an earlier at-
tempt to write the poem in ballad form. After reciting from memory the
opening lines of this earlier attempt, R.P.W. explains why the ballad form
failed to suit the poem's needs:

> Yes, it began about like that, but the form
> Was not adequate: the facile imitation
> Of a folk simplicity would never serve,
> For the beauty of such simplicity is only
> That the action is always and perfectly self-contained,
> And is an image that comes as its own perfect explanation
> In shock or sweetness to the innocent heart.
>
> But first, our hearts are scarcely innocent,
> And any pleasure we take in the folk simplicity
> Is a pleasure of snobbish superiority or neurotic yearning.
> And second, the action here is not explained
> By anything in the action. It is explained,
> If explainable at all, by our most murderous
> Complicities, and our sad virtue, too.
>
> No, the action is not self-contained, but contains
> Us too, and is contained by us, and is
> Only an image of the issue of our most distressful self-definition.
>   (BD 43)

The ballad form, according to R.P.W., would have allowed for evasion by
providing too much distance, particularly for the poet, and this would
undermine the theme of complicity. Furthermore, in order for Warren to
speak to the reader about "our" complicity with any authority, he must
first be willing to take responsibility for his own transgressions. Warren
therefore must go against his early poetry's principle of objectivity and, in
a startling reversal, must enter into the poem's action undisguisedly as
himself, R.P.W., "the writer of this poem."

   In addition to influencing the poem's composition and form, the issue
of racism provides the functional way in which the poem's white charac-
ters become implicated in Lilburn's murder of George. In a sequence of

scenes, Warren repeatedly invokes the image of the black "gaze," which is read as a sign of reproach by white characters.[14] For these characters—including R.P.W.—to confront the gaze of the black face is to confront their own complicity in racial injustice, to glimpse their own hearts of darkness. Lucy Lewis, for instance, is forced to face not only her blood relationship as mother to the cold-blooded murderer Lilburn, but also her own implication in the crime through her adherence to the racist ideology of slavery. Lucy's revelation comes when she is confronted by George's battered form, victim of a severe beating at Lilburn's hands. Lucy has sent George to the settlement to find Lilburn, then on a three-day drunken spree, but George returns alone. His bloody image standing before Lucy portends his eventual murder. Lucy touches George's face with the idea of comforting him, but the physical contact momentarily paralyzes her with some devastating, albeit unspecified, new knowledge:

> Yes, I touched it, and that instant
> Of contact had all the terribleness of knowledge.
> My mind was saying the pure and simple thing,
> The sort of thing to live by and make the day good.
> It was saying, simply: *This poor boy is hurt,*
> *Get water, bathe his blood, bind up the wound.*
> But I could not move to execute the good thing.
> And that is strange—isn't it?—when the good thing
> Lies clear and simple, but faculty is frozen.
> Ah, had I got the water, bathed the wound,
> Then everything might have been different, and the small
> Obligation fulfilled had swayed the weight of the world.
> But, no—and to this day I know no reason
> Why then I could not act for the recognized good.
> I stood and saw the black face blown with pain.
> I saw the irrevocableness of the gaze fixed on me.
> I saw my hand move out, weightless and witless and slow,
> To glimmer white through the dark and thickening air.
> And there was nothing else in the world left,
> Like a wet sponge passed over a child's slate. (*BD* 82–83)

The "irrevocableness" of George's gaze paralyzes Lucy, and her inability to act represents a moment of moral chaos and anxiety. The "good thing" appears obvious to her, yet the moment of physical contact prevents her from acting on the principle. While her moment of confusion and paralysis is partly the result of knowing that her own son perpetrated this act against George, it is also the result of her sudden and painful awareness that George is, in fact, human, not mere chattel. This is Lucy's terrible, unnamed knowledge: she senses her own complicity in Lilburn's violence through her participation in slavery. To do the good thing and bind George's wounds would be to confirm his humanity, thereby undermining the notions of racial difference she has been raised to believe in. Since her culture has provided many "moral" arguments for the subhuman status of the African race, she faces a moral dilemma. She can either go against her cultural beliefs and act on her innermost recognition of George's humanity, or she can *not* act and thereby maintain her cultural beliefs. Her decision to not act, then, is in fact an effort to preserve her system of morality. This effort to preserve her beliefs ultimately fails, however, for as the closing image suggests, her Lockean slate of experience is wiped clean by this new and terrible knowledge, reducing her world to nothingness.

Thomas Jefferson is likewise unnerved by what he interprets as a personal reproach in the faces of his slaves. After Lucy's death, R.P.W. describes how Lilburn is left alone in the house to feel the weight of black eyes watching him. This description prompts Jefferson to launch into a brief diatribe on the power of the "picklock gaze," a diatribe that indirectly reveals his own anxiety and guilt over slavery:

> Spy—yes, they spy—they spy from the shadow.
> They spy from the darkest corner of the hall,
> They serve you the dish and stand with face blandly
> Averted, but sidewise that picklock gaze has triggered
> The tender mechanism of your destructive secret.
> Oh, they've surprised you
> At meat, at stool, at concupiscence; and with sardonic detachment
> Have even inspected your face while you turned inward
> To the most soul-searching meditation. And when
> You turn inward, at the heart's darkest angle you meet
> The sly accusation and the shuttered gleam
> Of that sidelong eye. (*BD* 108–9)

These lines call to mind comments made by the real-life Thomas Jefferson in his *Notes on the State of Virginia*. There Jefferson argues for the greater beauty of the white race and expresses a certain amount of disgust and perhaps even dread over "that eternal monotony, which reigns in the countenances, that immovable veil of black which covers all the emotions of the other race" (133). To both the real-life Jefferson and the Jefferson of *Brother to Dragons,* the black face presents an unreadable text. Jefferson suggests that it is impossible to penetrate this "immovable veil of black," but in a sense it is a veil of his own construction, formed through an adherence to the racist discourse and ideology of slavery which denies black humanity and individuality and which reduces all blacks to the "eternal monotony" Jefferson describes.[15]

Following Jefferson's indirect confession, R.P.W. presses him further, pointing out the obvious inconsistencies between his ideals and the reality of his life: "Well, this is impertinent, but to build Monticello, / That domed dream of our liberties floating / High on its mountain, like a cloud, demanded / A certain amount of black sweat" (*BD* 109). However, R.P.W. does not end by simply accusing Jefferson of hypocrisy; rather, he implicates himself by admitting to his own destructive feelings of race hatred. R.P.W. in fact incriminates himself throughout the poem with his easy use of racist epithets and his casual reliance on racist assumptions. But at this point in the poem, he self-consciously confesses to his own racism in a remarkable manner. R.P.W.'s interrogation of Jefferson essentially becomes an interrogation of Warren himself and his Agrarian past, since Jefferson stands as something of an icon for the Agrarian ideal. R.P.W.'s comments echo the moral anxiety evident in Jefferson's description of the "picklock gaze" of his slaves:

> Sure, I know well—who doesn't know down home?—
> The intolerable eye of the sly one, and the foot
> Soundless, and the sibilant confabulation below
> The threshold of comprehension.
>
>> What the hell did you say?
>> Me, Boss? You mean me?
>> Who the hell you think I mean, you black bastard?
>> Me, Boss?
>> Yes, you—what the hell was that you said?
>> Boss, I did'n say nothin.
>
> It is always nothing, but always there around you:
> And in the deep vessel of self now the dark
> Lees and dregs are disturbed, uncoil now, and rise
> To murk the clear, rational ichor of innocence.
> No use to say now you've dealt justly with individuals

Or held the most advanced views on the race question.
Do you think the Dark Inquisitor can be deflected
By trivialities like that? (*BD* 110)

If we are willing to read R.P.W. undisguisedly as Warren himself, this passage becomes a remarkably honest confession, particularly since the racism R.P.W. confesses here is more malicious than what is usually attributed to Warren in "The Briar Patch." It is also significant that these comments come before Warren's more frequently cited "confessions" in *Segregation* and *Who Speaks for the Negro?*, and in one sense, the closing lines of this passage would seem to undermine these very texts before they are even written. For Warren here suggests that no matter how progressive or liberal he may become on the race issue, he can never escape the sins of the past. As Jefferson later comes to realize in the poem, "Nothing we were, / Is lost" (*BD* 195).

Some may argue that Warren is to some degree blaming his racism on his Southern background by saying that everyone "down home" knows these feelings. However, in the passages that immediately follow this confession, R.P.W. goes on to argue at length that we can blame neither history nor our environment; instead, we must assume responsibility for our beliefs and actions even in the face of determinism. Just after R.P.W.'s confession, Jefferson suggests that Lilburn's crime was perhaps inevitable, that "Lilburn is Lilburn" and was somehow destined to kill George. To this R.P.W. counters:

Yet the accomplished was once the unaccomplished
And the existing was once the non-existing,
And that transition was the agony of will
And anguish of option—or such it seems
To any man who has striven in the hot day and glare of contingency
Or who has heard the breath of darkness stop
At the moment of revelation. And such it seems
To all who would lay a strong hand strongly on life,
And as for the others, let us wish them well
In the ineluctable sterility of their various sanatoria
Where all the light is like a light from snow,
And hope that there's always somebody to change the bedpans.
No, that is wicked. We know we all need grace,
And pity too, and charity is the index
Of strength, and the worship of strength is but the index

Of weakness, but, by God, that's still no reason
To regard all history as a private alibi-factory
And all God's gleaming world as a ward for occupational therapy.

For if responsibility is not
The thing given but the thing to be achieved,
There is still no way out of the responsibility
Of trying to achieve responsibility. (*BD* 111–12)

Although R.P.W. acknowledges the deterministic forces of history at work in our lives, he nonetheless affirms his belief in human will, and this belief carries with it an assumption of individual responsibility. Through R.P.W.'s many racist comments and through his confession of racial enmity cited above, Warren acknowledges and admits the depth of his past opinions with a bluntness that never really infuses his prose works on race. But the theme of personal responsibility as delineated in the poem goes beyond merely admitting past errors; it also involves the aggressive struggle to change ourselves. According to Warren, this is the true way that we "achieve responsibility." Importantly, R.P.W.'s inconsistent racial rhetoric provides an index to Warren's own struggle to overcome the racism of his past. Aldon Nielsen finds puzzling R.P.W.'s inconsistent rhetoric on matters of race, describing his "apparently unmotivated switching back and forth between the use of the epithet 'nigger' and the noun, 'Negro'" and concluding that "the two names are synonymous for R.P.W. in a way that they had not been . . . in the preceding century" (122). But this inconsistency is in fact necessary to the poem's theme of personal responsibility and change, for in order to suggest personal growth, Warren must represent what he has changed from. Warren's contradictory racial rhetoric accentuates the tension between his past and present selves and also suggests the incomplete and ongoing nature of the personal struggle toward self-revision. R.P.W.'s racist comments exist as a reminder of a past self that can never be completely left behind; the ghost of the past continues to haunt the present, creating tension as it conflicts with R.P.W.'s other comments on black characters which attempt to go beyond the constructed veil of racist rhetoric and stereotyping. As Jefferson realizes near the end of the poem, the past with all of its failings is essential to any dreams of the future we may harbor: "the dream of the future is not / Better than the fact of the past, no matter how terrible. / For without the fact of the past we cannot dream the future" (*BD* 193).

 Perhaps the most striking example of R.P.W.'s vacillating rhetoric occurs near the end of the poem. The year is 1951, and he has returned to

Rocky Hill, the scene of the murders, a second time. While standing on a bluff overlooking the Ohio River, he loses himself in contemplation of the past and our knowledge of it:

> I then thought
> Of all who had come down the great river and are
> Nameless, or if we know their names, then what
> Is the truth we know? What if
> We know the names of the niggers by the wall,
> Who hunkered there and moaned? Yes, we know each name,
> The age, and sex, and price, from the executor
> Who listed all to satisfy the court:
> Towit Ceolio one hundred and fifty dollars
> William one hundred and Ten dollars Frank
> *four hundred and thirty-five dollars*, et cetera.
> But that is all—no face, no form, no wish of the heart.
>
> Yes that is all, and thus we know the names
> Of those who went with Meriwether west. . . .
> We know that much, but what is any knowledge
> Without the intrinsic mediation of the heart? (*BD* 211–12)

This is a moment of supreme irony in which Warren both foregrounds his racist rhetoric and simultaneously undermines it in a fascinating way. He once again invokes the racist epithet "nigger," a word that dehumanizes and denies individuality. Yet at the same time, he points out that simply substituting a proper name for a racist epithet does nothing in and of itself to purge one of racist beliefs and attitudes, for the name contains "no wish of the heart," no essential humanity. Therefore, as R.P.W. continues his speculation, he concludes that knowledge must be accompanied by "the intrinsic mediation of the human heart."

This statement resonates backward throughout the poem, for the text of *Brother to Dragons* itself may be considered the product of such mediation of the heart, with R.P.W. investigating the "facts" of the historical record in a very personal, even painful, way. Perhaps Warren's most powerful elaborations on this reconciling theme derive from his more complex representations of the slaves, and most particularly Aunt Cat, who nursed Lilburn when he was an infant. At one point in the poem, when R.P.W. is describing the relationship between Lucy and her slaves, he self-consciously avoids the sentimental and stereotypical racial representations of the Old South apologists. After stating that Lucy's slaves had "loved" her, R.P.W. quickly qualifies his use of the word:

> They'd loved Miss Lucy—or if the word *love*
> Sounds too much like old Thomas Nelson Page
> To sit easy on our stomachs salivated with modernity,
> Then we can say that in the scale of subordination,
> The black, that victim of an obsolescent
> Labor system (we can't, you see, just say
> "Immoral labor system," as I'd near done,
> For that wouldn't be modern, except for people
> Who want things both ways)—well, to start again:
> The victims of the obsolescent labor system
> Had been conditioned, by appeals to the ego,
> To identify themselves with the representative
> Of the superordinate group, i.e., the mistress—
> In other words, they liked her "tol-bul well."
> Might say: "Miss Lucy, she ain't done so bad."
> Might say: "Ole Miss, she know a nigger feel."
> In other words, the humanity of the poor slave
> Could rise above the system's corrupting arrangement,
> Ignorance, resentment, slyness, sloth, despair,
> The limen of anguish and the bar of rage,
> To recognize the human hope of another person;
> And if that is not love, then it's something better. (*BD* 105–6)

Aunt Cat becomes the supreme example of love that can rise above all circumstances. Through her, Warren's abstract theme accrues a more definite, concrete reality as he attempts to peer through the "immovable veil of black" and locate the real humanity and complex motivation hidden within. Aunt Cat exemplifies just such human complexity—and, significantly, her love for Lilburn is perhaps what Warren most celebrates in the poem. Aunt Cat's love is anything but pure, being motivated in part by competition with Lucy, and at times it is even difficult to distinguish from hate. Yet Warren still affirms it as a love that exists in spite of human degradation and limitation. Aunt Cat continues to love Lilburn even after he cruelly repudiates her love following his mother's death. And to R.P.W., "that love is valid, / And to be prized" (*BD* 92). It is to be prized because it is a love that exists as a sheer act of human will despite degrading circumstances. Significantly, Warren gives Aunt Cat the last word in the poem among the speakers from the historical past, and her closing words reveal that she is able to love Lilburn even after his monstrous actions. This is not some Old South myth of a slave's fidelity; rather, Cat's love for Lilburn is based on the "intrinsic mediation of the heart." After Lilburn's death, she still holds in her mind the image of him as the weak and helpless baby she nursed and cared for. She describes her feelings upon visiting Lilburn's grave:

> Fer then I knowed whar my Lil come to stay,
> Lak comin home and git inside the door.
> My Lil, he come inside my heart to stay
> And hang his hat and taken ease, and all
> My heart git singin and the fire dance bright. (BD 202–3)

Aunt Cat's love for Lilburn is possible only through what R.P.W. defines as the intrinsic mediation of the human heart, the ability to recognize the hopes, wishes, and fears of another person. She is able to love Lilburn because she can recall an image of his weakness and vulnerability, his humanity. Likewise, the portrait of Aunt Cat in the poem is a product of the heart's mediation—this time by Robert Penn Warren himself. The representation of Aunt Cat is a clear sign of Warren's changing views on race, for it contains passages that, as Aldon Nielsen explains, "illuminate the human reality hidden by the discourse spoken by the white characters, passages in which he attempts to show how black slaves may have acted within the confines of their states" (120). Warren's empathetic representation of Aunt Cat results from a struggle to break free from the racist thinking of his Agrarian past, and its complexity contrasts sharply with his one-dimensional, racist portrayals of blacks in such early poems as "Tryst on Vinegar Hill" and "Pondy Woods."

But Warren's meditation on Aunt Cat goes beyond mere self-reflection and in fact dovetails with the Romantic visionary moment with which the poem concludes, for both moments in the poem are built upon the human capacity for empathy. We can see in the poem's conclusion the move toward synthesis that will become so central to his Romantic aesthetic. According to Warren, it is the intrinsic mediation of the human heart that leads in the end to self-transcendence through a recognition of our common humanity; here, the personal and confessional aspects of the poem are extended to assume a broader, more universal significance:

> In so far as man has the simplest vanity of self,
> There is no escape from the movement toward fulfillment.

And since all kind but fulfills its own kind,
Fulfillment is only in the degree of recognition
Of the common lot of our kind. And that is the death of vanity,
And that is the beginning of virtue.

The recognition of complicity is the beginning of innocence.
The recognition of necessity is the beginning of freedom.
The recognition of the direction of fulfillment is the death of the
    self,
And the death of the self is the beginning of selfhood.
All else is surrogate of hope and destitution of spirit. (*BD* 214–15)

Following this moment of mysticism and self-transcendence, R.P.W. is able to reenter the world and accept his newfound responsibility; he is "prepared / To go into the world of action and liability," a world he now considers "Sweeter than hope" (*BD* 215). This acceptance of the present, an acceptance filled with hope, is unlike anything in Warren's early poetry and marks a clear departure from his early worldview. It is important to note, however, that this is in no way a self-congratulatory resolution to the poem. Warren still emphasizes human complicity—especially his own—and R.P.W.'s many racist comments stand as a reminder of past sins, which, according to Warren, can never be left behind. Nonetheless, *Brother to Dragons* is more hopeful than anything in Warren's early canon. He offers a positive alternative to strictly deterministic outlooks, and he frees himself from his early thematic emphasis on alienation and solipsism by stressing our common humanity. This will be transformed in Warren's 1955 essay "Knowledge and the Image of Man" into the central operational metaphor for his emerging Romantic aesthetic: the osmosis of being. While *Brother to Dragons* has been read as an investigation into the sins of the past, the history under investigation is not merely American history but also Warren's own personal history. The poem makes it clear that we can neither repudiate nor deny the sins of the past and our own complicity in evil; we must instead confront "the terror of our condition" (*BD* 192). For Warren, as his inclusion of R.P.W. shows, such a confrontation must begin with oneself. Warren continues this confrontation with his past views on race in *Segregation: The Inner Conflict in the South,* and the confessional nature of both of these texts becomes a central feature of his emerging Romantic aesthetic, whereby the self becomes the primary subject of inquiry for the poetic act.

Segregation

The Inner Conflict in Robert Penn Warren

We are the prisoners of our history.
Or are we?

Robert Penn Warren, *Segregation: The Inner Conflict in the South*

Following the publication of *Brother to Dragons* in 1953, Warren would continue his sustained literary investigation into race with the publication of *Band of Angels* in 1955 and *Segregation: The Inner Conflict in the South* in 1956. From the winter of 1950–51 through August of 1956, Warren was *always* working on projects that focused specifically and directly on race. He first began contemplating *Brother to Dragons* in the mid-1940s, but it was not until the winter of 1950–51 that he had settled on the subjective form and managed to complete half of the poem.[1] By the time *Brother to Dragons* was published in August of 1953, he was already at work on his next novel, *Band of Angels,* and even before *Band of Angels* appeared in print, he was working on *Segregation.*

Band of Angels chronicles through first-person narrative the plight of Amantha Starr, an illegitimate mulatto who is raised by her white father as a privileged white daughter on his plantation, only to be sold into slavery following his death. Despite being what critics regard as one of Warren's weaker efforts as a novelist, the book still presents an interesting episode in his ongoing inquiry into the central role race plays in American history, culture, and literature.[2] Leslie Fiedler described the book as a complex literary hybrid in which Mark Twain meets Margaret Mitchell, a "novel of miscegenation" transformed into a "feminine bosom book" and "erotic historical romance" (413). As the book's opening question—"Oh, who am I?"—indicates, the central issue of the book is the construction of identity (*BA* 3). The novel illustrates, on the one hand, the arbitrary nature of the color line and, on the other hand, the power of race to determine the self. Through the figure of Amantha Starr, Warren presents a complex and diminished portrait of the self as a socially determined construct. Amantha Starr consistently allows her sense of identity and self to be controlled by the way others perceive her, particularly by the way others alternately designate her white and black, daughter and slave, wife and concubine. Amantha comes to this realization soon after she discovers her status as chattel: "Who had I, Amantha Starr, been before that moment? I had been defined by the world around me. . . . in and of myself, or so it seemed, I had been nothing. I had been nothing except their continuing creation" (*BA* 52). She continues to hold this view of herself up until the novel's concluding pages. Numerous other characters in the novel similarly shift identities through name changes but, unlike Amantha's, these changes usually occur as a matter of free will. Amantha's sense of identity is so contingent upon others that she at one point accepts an entirely deterministic view of the self as a product of history: "what you are is an expression of History, and you do not live your own life, but somehow, your life lives you, and you are, therefore, only what History does to you" (*BA* 112). Citing this passage as an example, Forrest Robinson argues that Warren's "pronounced tendency toward determinism" is part of a pattern of "bad faith" strategies Warren relies upon for evading the guilt of slavery and its legacy (528). But to suggest that Warren is advocating Amantha's outlook is mistaken. Determinism is indeed a continuing concern in Warren's oeuvre, and it is particularly relevant to the way he attempts to explain and justify his own evolving views on race, yet Warren obviously rejects the facile logic of Amantha Starr, as is evidenced by *Brother to Dragons* and *Segregation*, texts in which he asserts the need to accept individual responsibility in spite of deterministic factors. Even the resolution of *Band of Angels* finally rejects deterministic explanations of the self. Amantha Starr, after years of fleeing her past and journeying further and further west, comes to accept her purposeful role in the construction of her fate: "I had been involved in the very cause of the world, and whatever had happened corresponded in some crazy way with what was in me, and even if I didn't cause it, it somehow conformed to my will, and then somehow it could be said that I did cause it, and if it had not been for me then nothing would ever have happened as it happened" (*BA* 303). Even though she is a weak and often annoying character, and even though her conversion experience seems abbreviated by comparison, Amantha's pattern of change follows that of Jack Burden and R.P.W.; her moral outlook shifts from a deterministic view of the self which denies responsibility to an acceptance of will, responsibility, and complicity. The resolutions of all three of these narratives reflect Warren's own shifting assumptions on this complex knot of issues, and his new positions on these issues are made especially explicit in *Segregation: The Inner Conflict in The South*.

As Warren was completing *Band of Angels*, the nation's attention turned to consider the effects of the Supreme Court's 1954 *Brown v. Board of Education* decision, which ruled "separate but equal" unconstitutional. When Jack Jessup, Warren's brother-in-law and an editor at *Life*, suggested that Warren write a piece for the magazine on the resultant desegregation efforts in the South, he jumped at the opportunity.[3] To prepare for the task, Warren returned to the South in the fall of 1955 and journeyed through five Southern states, along the way engaging in conversations with a broad spectrum of individuals—black, white, segregationist, and integrationist. His article, "Divided South Searches Its Soul," was published in *Life* in July of 1956; an expanded version of that article titled *Segregation: The Inner Conflict in the South* was published by Random House two months later. Perhaps prompted by the national audience available to him through *Life*'s readership, or perhaps haunted by the specter of his former segregationist beliefs, Warren chose to approach his controversial subject in a direct and very personal manner, echoing and extending the confessional voice of R.P.W. in *Brother to Dragons*. In its frank subjectivity, its racial subject matter, and its thematic approach to the individual's place in history, *Segregation* stands as a fitting prose counterpart to *Brother to Dragons* and can help to illustrate the complementary relationship that exists between the political and poetical transformations Warren experienced.[4]

As discussed earlier, even when critics consider Warren's career-long engagement with racial politics, they have tended to search for continuity and consistency in his canon. But such a tactic often overlooks the blatant contradictions and conflicts in his varying positions on racial politics. *Segregation* is a text that readily reveals these conflicts, as Warren pointedly contradicts and even condemns both his early stand on segregation and his early representations of race. Less obviously, but perhaps more significantly, *Segregation* also reveals his new view of the individual's place in history, and this new perspective offers a way out of the trap of determinism and rebuts his former conservative, traditionalist ideology. Finally,

Segregation suggests the political implications and consequences of Warren's new poetic theories, particularly his advocacy of a subjective and personal voice, and his recurring strategies of reconciliation and synthesis.

Despite the fact that much of *Segregation* is devoted to the words of others, the book's opening passage reveals the text to be very much a reflection of Warren himself. In the opening paragraph, Warren makes it unambiguously clear that he is not a detached observer; instead, he asserts that the conflicts which are taking place in the South are in fact taking place within him as well:

> I was going back to look at the landscapes and streets I had known—Kentucky, Tennessee, Arkansas, Mississippi, Louisiana—to look at the faces, to hear the voices, to hear, in fact, the voices in my own blood. A girl from Mississippi had said to me: "I feel it's all happening inside of me, every bit of it. It's all there."
>
> I know what she meant. (3)

Since Warren concludes with a self-interview, his confessional reflections both pervade and frame the entire text, echoing through form his assertion that all he is reporting in the text is actually taking place within.[5]

These opening remarks are followed by a personal recollection of an earlier trip Warren made through Mississippi on Highway 61. He contrasts his recollections of this trip of some twenty-five years before with the images he was faced with during his return journey through the South. Through these images and reflections, Warren comes face to face with the grim reality hidden behind the Agrarian myth of the South he had earlier fabricated for the "Southern Negro":

> It seems like a thousand years since I first drove that road, more than twenty-five years ago, a new concrete slab then, dizzily glittering in the August sun-blaze, driving past the rows of tenant shacks, Negro shacks set in the infinite cotton fields, and it seems like a hundred years since I last drove it, last week, in the rain, then toward sunset the sky clearing a little, but clouds solid and low on the west like a black range of mountains frilled upward with an edge of bloody gold light, quickly extinguished. Last week, I noticed that more of the shacks were ruinous, apparently abandoned. More, but not many, had an electric wire running back from the road. But when I caught a glimpse, in the dusk, of the interior of a lighted shack, I usually saw

the coal-oil lamp. Most shacks were not lighted. I wondered if it was too early in the evening. Then it was early no longer. Were that many of the shacks abandoned? (4)

Warren here contrasts his current perceptions of the region with his perceptions of some twenty-five years before—around the time he published "The Briar Patch." In doing so, he attempts to convey his emerging awareness of the devastating poverty endured by Southern blacks living under the tenant farming system, a reality he sidestepped in "The Briar Patch." Indeed, the scene described presents a disturbing contrast to Warren's idyllic portrayal in "The Briar Patch" of the life and opportunities available for African-Americans living in the rural South. There, he had determined that the "Southern Negro" is "a creature of the small town and farm . . . [who] by temperament and capacity . . . is likely to find in agricultural and domestic pursuits the happiness that his good nature and easy ways incline him to as an ordinary function of his being" ("Briar Patch" 260–61). Now, however, the stark details of the scene impinge upon his consciousness. Noticing the dilapidated state of so many of the tenant shacks, he at first concludes that they surely must be vacant or abandoned. He also notes a sign of "progress": that some now seem to have electricity. But as darkness descends upon the landscape, Warren is gradually enlightened to the possibility that the run-down shacks are in fact not abandoned, and his reflections on this possibility suggest both his growing awareness and perhaps a growing sense of guilt.

This sense of guilt also pervades the passage that immediately follows. Warren describes passing a family of black tenant farmers who are walking alongside the darkened road, and his metaphorical description strikingly contrasts white privilege and progress with the stasis of black poverty:

The light of the car snatches past, and I think of them behind us in the darkness, moving up the track beside the concrete, seeing another car light far yonder toward Memphis, staring at it perhaps, watching it grow, plunge at them, strike them, flick past. They will move on, at their pace. Yes, they are still here. (*Seg* 5)

James Justus has asserted that Warren's later texts on race "represent an awakened consciousness more than they do a ravaged conscience" (*Achievement* 141). While this certainly may be the case, Warren in passages like these nonetheless displays a considerable sense of personal guilt over his early views on race and segregation. In the "Briar Patch," he had argued that if blacks hoped to pursue the higher goals in life, they would have to wait until the black population was capable economically of supporting such endeavors. But this metaphorical scene from *Segregation* shows that in the quarter-century that has elapsed, little if anything has changed for these rural blacks living under the tenant system.

As Aldon Nielsen has shown, there are passages in *Segregation* and, later, *Who Speaks for the Negro?* "in which the author observes as a stereotype literally dissolves before his eyes" (115). As an example, Nielsen cites a passage in which an "Uncle Tom" preacher suddenly steps out of character, much to the consternation of the reporter who has come to interview him. Significantly, it is Warren himself who prompts this chain of events. Warren has accompanied a media crew to sit in on an interview with the preacher, who has been identified by the journalists as an example of a black segregationist. But before the interview has begun, Warren abruptly asks the preacher about the humiliation suffered by blacks under segregation:

> I break in—I don't think the machinery is going yet—and ask about humiliation as a bar to Negro fulfillment.
>
> "Segregation did one thing," he says. "No other race but the Negroes could build up as much will to go on and do things. To get their goals."
>
> What goals? I ask.
>
> "Just what anybody wants, just everything people can want to be a citizen," he says.
>
> This isn't what the journalist has come for.
>
> Things aren't promising too well. Uncle Tom is doing a disappearing act, Old Black Joe is evaporating, the handkerchief-head, most inconveniently, isn't there. The genie has got out of the bottle clearly labeled: *Negro* segregationist. (*Seg* 39)

Warren's question, asking so directly about the humiliation that goes hand in hand with segregation, is one that he perhaps could not even have framed twenty-five years earlier, for in "The Briar Patch" he expressed little sympathy for blacks who would pursue equal social standing. In fact, Warren argued there—audaciously assuming the persona of Booker T. Washington to make his case—that blacks who did pursue such a goal lacked "self-respect" because they had failed to "rationalize" the reality of their position. Happily, Warren in *Segregation* refrains from such presumptuous representations. In contrast, the questions he is now capable of asking in *Segregation* show what Justus describes as an "awakened consciousness," and Warren goes on to devote several passages to other comments by blacks on the need for dignity and self-respect—and the manner in which segregation assaults these basic human needs. Furthermore, Warren's questions begin to admit that these very real and debilitating challenges are unique to the black experience: he asks his black interviewees, "Is there any difference between what the Negro feels at the exclusions of segregation, and what a white man feels at the exclusions which he, any man, must always face at some point?" One respondent succinctly puts it, "Yes, it's different . . . when your fate is on your face" (*Seg* 43). In contrast to the primarily economic emphasis of his 1930 defense of segregation, these passages illustrate that the issue of segregation has been restructured in Warren's mind and conscience as a question of morality and justice.

While Warren's newly expressed willingness to consider the acute psychological effects of segregation and racism on blacks is perhaps quite obvious, his changing attitudes toward history are more subtle. But like his changed views on race, Warren's perspectives on history and the individual's relation to it stand in marked contrast to the views of tradition and history expressed in his early career. In fact, he dismisses and even belittles his early attempt to use the past and tradition as a fixed anchor against the tide of modern flux and change. Importantly, he also challenges those who would view history either as an excuse for or as a vindication of continuing racial injustice. The former attitude emerges from a limited, deterministic view of history; the latter derives from a glorified and sanctified view of the past. Warren develops these ideas within a historical context in *The Legacy of the Civil War*, where he labels the war's psychological legacy to the South and the North as the Great Alibi and the Treasury of Virtue, respectively.[6] Early in the text of *Segregation*, Warren introduces the view of history as excuse. While on the airplane heading south, he enters into a conversation on segregation with a transplanted Northerner who concludes, "It is hard to claw out from under the past and the past way" (8). Later, he echoes this statement just before the self-interview that concludes the text. Here he quotes a taxi driver who claims that "race prejudice . . . ain't our hate, it's the hate hung on us by the old folks dead and gone" (62). These deterministic views of history, which roughly correspond to Amantha Starr's views cited above, are not unlike the way the young Warren felt about the South's resistance to change. In a 1969 interview, he stated that his early stance on segregation "was part of that fatalism that was deeply engrained in the Southern mind" (Watkins et al. 158).[7]

As Warren continues in *Segregation*, he shows that others view history with an uncritical reverence that, rather than excusing racial injustice, vindicates and sanctifies it. In another early scene, Warren relates a brief encounter with a white teenager from Atlanta whom he met at Fort Nashborough, the original settlement of Nashville. The teen expresses an interest in and respect for history but, prompted by questions from Warren about rising racial tensions in Atlanta, he is just as quick to express a deep-seated hatred for blacks. When Warren fails to echo these sentiments, the boy walks away in disgust, leading Warren to reflect:

> This, too, is a cliché. The boy, standing on the ground of history and heroism, his intellect and imagination stirred by the fact, shudders with that other, automatic emotion which my question had evoked. The cliché had come true: the cliché of hate. And somehow the hallowedness of the ground he stood on had vindicated, as it were, that hate. (11)

Ironically, the ground the boy stands on is hardly hallowed, for as Warren has earlier pointed out, the fort "is a replica, smaller than the original and not on the right spot, exactly" (10). The boy's one-dimensional view of history, like the fort he stands in, is a distortion of the past. Such a view of history does not allow for a full conception of the past with all of its faults, failings, errors, and sins, and consequently neither does it allow for a full conception of its greatness. It is just such a glorified, uncritical view of the past that Warren debunks in *Brother to Dragons*. But we may say that the young Warren himself at times held such glorified views of the past, as evidenced in both his early politics and his early poetry.[8] As a young man, Warren sought to preserve the traditionalist culture and values of the agrarian South—including segregation and its enforced racial hierarchy—in the face of modern change and uncertainty. Similarly, in his poetry he sought to impose order over modern chaos and discontinuity through the disciplined use of the past. Warren near the end of *Segregation* strongly attacks these very views, exposing such backward-looking, tradition-oriented strategies as ineffectual and even irresponsible. In opposition to such views, he counters that we must accept the challenges of our own particular historical moment; we must face the reality we have been born to.

In the context of the desegregation debate then consuming the South, Warren defines the reality Southerners must face as "the fact of self-division"—a deep intellectual and moral conflict which results when an individual is forced to negotiate between competing values and beliefs (52). Warren's new poetry will similarly address the problem of self-division, countering with Romantic strategies of synthesis and reconciliation. But in *Segregation*, he places these issues in a concrete political context. While in "Knowledge and the Image of Man," Warren argued that this is a universal conflict all individuals must face, the examples he provides here are specifically located within the context of the South's desegregation debate. According to Warren, the Southerner faced with the prospect of desegregation may experience a conflict "between his own social idealism and his anger at Yankee Phariseeism . . . between his social views and his fear of the power state . . . between his allegiance to organized labor and his racism . . . between his Christianity and his social prejudice . . . between his sense of democracy and his ingrained attitudes toward the Negro" (53–54). Warren concludes that all of these conflicts, these internal divisions, amount to "a deep intellectual rub, a moral rub, anger at the irremediable self-division, a deep exacerbation at some failure to find identity. That is the reality" (54).

As an example of this sort of failure to find identity, Warren points to people who would hope to resurrect the past and their distorted views of the Old South. Tellingly, his description of this flawed outlook calls to mind the very values he and his fellow Agrarians espoused in *I'll Take My Stand*, values that some such as Donald Davidson still espoused:

> There are other people whose eyes brighten at the thought of the new unity in the South, the new solidarity of resistance. These men are idealists, and they dream of preserving the traditional American values of individualism and localism against the anonymity, irresponsibility and materialism of the power state. . . . *To be Southern again:* to recreate a habitation for the values they would preserve, to achieve in unity some clarity of spirit, to envisage some healed image of their own identity. (*Seg* 55)

In describing these idealists and the things they are willing to fight for—and against—Warren uses words that hark back to the "statement of principles" in *I'll Take My Stand.* But Warren resurrects this myth from his past only to expose what he now regards as its gross deficiencies. After insightfully pointing out that individuals from both sides of the segregation debate may adhere to this myth and consequently adopt a siege mentality toward outside interference, he proceeds to cast a final verdict against those who still cling to such a myth. But his summary judgment against those who would flee to this false image of the past is also a powerful indictment of his own early adherence to the Agrarian myth of the South. He concludes that individuals who cherish this myth place themselves in a paradoxical, untenable, and ultimately irresponsible position:

> in seeking to preserve individualism by taking refuge in the vision of a South redeemed in unity and antique virtue, they are fleeing from the burden of their own individuality—the intellectual rub, the moral rub. To state the matter in another way, by using the argument of *mere* social continuity and the justification by mere *mores,* they think of a world in which circumstances and values are frozen; but the essence of individuality is the willingness to accept the rub which the flux of things provokes, to accept one's fate in time. (*Seg* 55)

With these words, Warren unambiguously dismisses both his early segregationist position and the traditionalist premise behind it. He now accepts the burden of the historical moment and the burden of flux and change. Significantly, this passage also indicates his emerging concern with the construction of individual identity within this flux of time—perhaps the central concern of his later, increasingly autobiographical poetry. As Warren contends in *Segregation,* the inability or unwillingness to accept this flux and uncertainty is in fact a "failure to find identity."

After dismantling such backward-looking justifications for resistance to desegregation, Warren argues through the concluding self-interview that we are not "prisoners of our history" (62); we must accept the burden of our own historical moment:

> Q. Are you for desegregation?
> A. *Yes.*
> Q. When will it come?
> A. Not soon.
> Q. When?
> A. When enough people, in a particular place, a particular county or state, cannot live with themselves any more. Or realize they don't have to.

Q. What do you mean, don't have to?

A. When they realize that desegregation is just one small episode in the long effort for justice. It seems to me that that perspective, suddenly seeing the business as little, is a liberating one. It liberates you from yourself.

Q. Then you think it is a moral problem?

A. Yes, but no moral problem gets solved abstractly. It has to be solved in a context for possible solution.

Q. Can contexts be changed?

A. Sure. We might even try to change them the right way.

Q. Aren't you concerned about possible racial amalgamation?

A. I don't even think about it. We have to deal with the problem our historical moment proposes, the burden of our time. We all live with a thousand unsolved problems of justice all the time. We don't even recognize a lot of them. We have to deal only with those which the moment proposes to us. Anyway, we can't legislate for posterity. All we can do for posterity is to try to plug along in a way to make them think we—the old folks—did the best we could for justice, as we could understand it. (64–65)

As he does in *Brother to Dragons*, Warren in *Segregation* rejects deterministic explanations which would make us "prisoners of our history" and would finally relieve us of individual responsibility; he likewise rejects idealized and uncritical views of the past which necessarily perceive virtue and values as static, unchanging quantities. In both cases Warren departs from the views he espoused in his younger days, whether evidenced in the conservative, traditionalist ideology of his Agrarian beliefs and modernist aesthetic or in the naturalistic impulse behind much of his early verse. But Warren's comments here also reveal an important relationship between his renewed literary investigation into race and his emerging subjectivity.

While Warren's transition from a high modernist formalism to a more subjective, autobiographical poetry certainly reflects more general trends in American poetry following World War II, to say that he was simply following these trends would be reductive. Warren was a poet who was immersed in the contemporary political moment, and his aesthetic transformation reflects his changing political views as much as it reflects these trends in American poetry. Warren's reimmersion in the issue of race coincided with his return to poetry; similarly, his new willingness to place himself in his own poetry corresponded in method with his willingness to deal with race in a frankly personal manner, here in *Segregation* and later in *Who Speaks for the Negro?* In these comments from Warren's self-interview, we can surmise that the emerging subjectivity both in his poetry and in these prose texts was linked to a profound desire to avoid abstract moralizing. As he emphasizes in the self-interview, "no moral problem gets solved abstractly." Warren believed that it is impossible to fully or responsibly address moral issues and questions in a detached, objective manner; instead, he felt we must address them within the concrete contexts of actual human experience. For this reason he increasingly opted to write from specific personal experience, even when dealing with broad-based social issues such as race relations in the United States. Warren's reasoning here is in fact quite similar to comments made by R.P.W. in *Brother to Dragons*. After recounting to Jefferson his earlier attempt to write the poem in ballad form, he explains that the ballad form failed to suit the poem's needs because it was too objective and allowed too much distance: "the action is always and perfectly self-contained" (*BD* 43). This, in turn, would have undermined his theme of complicity; consequently, Warren enters into the poem's action undisguisedly as himself, R.P.W. Along with the traditionalist premise of his early politics and poetry, Warren dismissed the objective formalism he had espoused and practiced as well.

In conclusion, *Segregation* and *Brother to Dragons*, published within three years of each other, are vitally important to understanding Warren's political and poetical transformations. In their racial subject matter, their subjective voice, and their thematic resolutions, they are uniquely complementary texts. Both texts illustrate Warren's emerging reliance upon strategies of synthesis and reconciliation, and through their treatments of race they also reveal the political context and consequences of these strategies which lie at the heart of his Romantic poetry of the 1950s and early 1960s. Taken together, these texts show that Warren's political and poetical conversions occurred in conjunction with one another: his political views on race and his aesthetic views on poetry evolved in a reciprocal and parallel fashion, influencing one another in an ongoing dialogue. The confrontation with his own past views on race and his simultaneous deep engagement with contemporary debates over racial integration became real-life testing grounds for his emerging and solidifying Romantic assumptions. Warren consolidated these aesthetic assumptions in his 1955 essay "Knowledge and the Image of Man" and in his poetry published between *Promises: Poems 1954–1956* and *Selected Poems: New and Old, 1923–1966.* With this transition in mind, in the next chapter I will leave the discussion of race behind for a moment in order to take a closer, more critical look at the interrelated concepts that are new to Warren's poetry of the 1950s and that form the foundation of his Romantic aesthetic.

The Consolidation of Warren's
Romantic Aesthetic, 1955–1966

If poetry does anything for us, it reconciles, by its symbolical reading of experience (for by its very nature it is in itself a myth of the unity of being), the self-devisive internecine malices which arise at the superficial level on which we conduct most of our living.

Robert Penn Warren, "A Poem of Pure Imagination"

In a 1969 interview with Marshall Walker, Robert Penn Warren explained that after he completed *Brother to Dragons* he "felt a whole new sense of poetry" in which he could draw from the "immediate" things of his own life, whether the thing was a current experience or a memory of long ago (Watkins et al. 162–63). As I have noted and as other critics have shown, this new sense of poetry was closely tied to the Romantic tradition with its more subjective forms and its more affirmative themes of reconciliation and synthesis. Significantly, this new sense of poetry represented more of a rejection of his earlier formalist aesthetic than an outgrowth or extension of it, a fact that may be gathered from one of Warren's best late poems, "Red-Tail Hawk and Pyre of Youth." Dedicated to the critic Harold Bloom, "Red-Tail Hawk" is a self-conscious rendering of Bloom's theories of poetic influence, with Warren quite literally dramatizing Bloom's belief that strong poets "wrestle with their strong precursors, even to the death" (*Anxiety of Influence* 5). In the poem, Warren invokes the spirit of Romanticism through a self-conscious rewriting of Coleridge's *Rime of the Ancient Mariner*, with Coleridge's mariner, crossbow, and albatross being replaced by Warren's young boy, rifle, and hawk. At the same time, however, the poem acts out the destruction of Warren's modernist, formalist past. While in Coleridge's poem the shipmates of the Ancient Mariner hang the albatross around his neck as a sign of his guilt, in Warren's poem the narrator places the stuffed hawk he has killed over his bookshelf,

whose contents signify his literary identity as a poet—as Bloom would
have it—by alluding to his primary influences:

> It was regal, perched on its bough-crotch to guard
> Blake and *Lycidas*, Augustine, Hardy and *Hamlet*,
> Baudelaire and Rimbaud, and I knew that the yellow eyes
> Unsleeping, stared as I slept." (*CP* 349)

The climax of the poem occurs when the narrator returns home many
years later. His mother is dead, his father bankrupt, and he feels lost in the
"Meaningless motion of life." In this moment of despair, he feels that the
"yellow eyes" of the bird are somewhere staring at him "in vengeance"
(*CP* 349). He seeks out the remains of the bird in order to destroy them;
importantly, however, he also seeks out and destroys the remnants of his
earlier literary identity:

> And all relevant items I found there: my first book of Milton,
> The *Hamlet*, the yellow, leaf-dropping Rimbaud, and a book
> Of poems friends and I had printed in college, not to mention
> The collection of sexual Japanese prints—strange sex
> Of mechanical sexlessness. And so made a pyre for
> The hawk that, though gasoline-doused and wing-dragging,
> Awaited, with what looked like pride,
> The match. (*CP* 350)

Calvin Bedient has argued that the burning of these books shows that,
"like Yeats, [the narrator] would be content to live it all again—in his case
because shooting the hawk, writing poems, and sexual passion were his
chief share in power and glory, all the life there was" (186). On the con-
trary, the destruction of these items does not represent a willingness to
relive the past; it is an attempt to suppress the past by destroying its re-
mains. The poets named in "Red-Tail Hawk" are among Warren's original
poetic fathers.[1] By destroying them, the poet-narrator frees himself from
both his early influences and his early aesthetic. At the same time, how-
ever, he invokes the spirit of Romanticism and Coleridge, symbolically
one of his new poetic fathers, by rewriting the *Ancient Mariner*. Bedient is
particularly mistaken when he interprets the Japanese sex prints as sug-
gestive of "sexual passion," for the narrator explicitly says they depict
"strange sex / Of mechanical sexlessness." Hardly passionate, these im-
ages are utterly devoid of life. Likewise, the hawk itself, which in life was
described as "the hot blood of the air," is reduced by the narrator's act to a

"chunk of poor wingless red meat" (*CP* 348). Harold Bloom in his own reading of the poem has noted that while the vortex formed by the bird in flight was "the Truth," the stuffed hawk "was merely text" ("Sunset Walk" 205), and this interpretation obviously holds true for the sexual prints as well. But by including his own poems among the items to be destroyed on the hawk's pyre (and the pyre of his poetic youth), Warren distances himself from the aesthetic principles of his early poetry. He essentially equates his early verse with the lifeless forms of the stuffed hawk and the sexual prints. Indeed, his early poetry, with its privileging of form and objectivity, is in many ways devoid of "life"—most particularly the life of the poet. In contrast, Warren's later poetry is defined first and foremost by its more Romantic subjectivity. The dramatic destruction of the bird and the books in "Red-Tail Hawk" implies that Warren came to view his own Romanticism not as an extension of his early modernist aesthetic but as an outright rejection of it. So while critics have often approached Warren's canon of poetry as an organically unified whole, the immolation of his poetic past in this poem suggests that he went through a more tumultuous form of aesthetic conflict and transformation. And as I have attempted to illustrate over the past two chapters, this aesthetic transformation was inextricably linked to his changing political perspectives on the charged issue of race. For the moment, however, I will leave the issue of race behind in order to examine more closely Warren's emerging Romantic aesthetic assumptions as they appear in his important 1955 essay "Knowledge and the Image of Man" and in the poetry that followed.

As mentioned earlier, Warren's work on his 1946 essay on Coleridge's *Ancient Mariner* seems to have provided an early catalyst for his midcareer conversion to a more Romantic aesthetic philosophy.[2] Titled "A Poem of Pure Imagination: An Experiment in Reading," the essay appeared during his ten-year hiatus from poetry and was based upon extensive research into Coleridge and Romantic theory. In true Romantic fashion, Warren in his concluding remarks defines poetry as a "myth of the unity of being" and emphasizes its therapeutic social function (399). This stated ideal of unity of being—which transcends difference and abolishes hierarchies—is one of the central doctrines of all Romantic theory and ideology running from Coleridge and Wordsworth through Emerson and Whitman.[3] Warren in the 1950s appropriated this concept, transforming it into his own theory of an "osmosis of being." While the main features of Warren's theory of an osmosis of being are implicit in the resolution of

Brother to Dragons in 1953, he first articulated the theory in "Knowledge and the Image of Man," an essay that outlines the aesthetic principles upon which his later poetry is founded.[4] Chief among these principles are the Romantic premise of an osmosis of being and a belief in poetry's therapeutic value; this newly espoused theory generates an overall aesthetic that privileges subjectivity and an organic, living form over the detached, impersonal formalism that characterized his early verse. But along with his new subjectivity, Warren articulates a new way of representing the self. In contrast to his early penchant for determinism, which necessarily results in a more limited view of the self, Warren now espouses the Romantic premise and rhetoric of development.

As I mentioned in chapter 5, Clifford Siskin's *The Historicity of Romantic Discourse* shows "development" to be the central strategy and formal feature of Romantic discourse, its characteristic way of representing the self as a mind that grows and develops. With Warren's turn to a more autobiographical voice, the strategy of development becomes his characteristic method of self-representation in his poetry. But while critics have provided numerous explications of Warren's theory of an osmosis of being, they have generally read his newly articulated theory of the developing self as though it were transparent: they accept development as a psychological truth rather than as a formal feature and strategy of Romantic discourse. This oversight is understandable, for as Siskin reveals in his study, development has been so thoroughly naturalized into an accepted truth that critics generally overlook the unique formal features and strategies it entails. In fact, Siskin shows that literary critics tend to reinforce the notion of development in the very frameworks they adopt when approaching an author's oeuvre. In other words, development goes from being the premise and method for writing to the premise and method for reading. This scenario certainly holds true in the field of Warren criticism, as critics have yet to recognize the full implications of Warren's adoption of this strategy of self-representation.[5]

In "Knowledge and the Image of Man" Warren counters deterministic explanations of human behavior by offering his more nuanced theory of an osmosis of being. According to Warren, "man is in the world not as a billiard ball placed on a table, not even as a ship on the ocean with location determinable by latitude and longitude. He is, rather, in the world with continual and intimate interpenetration, an inevitable osmosis of being, which in the end does not deny, but affirms his identity. It affirms it, for out of a progressive understanding of this interpenetration, this texture of relations, man creates new perspectives, discovers new values—that is, a new self—and so the identity is a continually emerging, an unfolding, a self-affirming and, we hope, a self-corrective creation" (186–87). Warren here distinguishes his current position from more deterministic perspectives which reduce human behavior to quantifiable formulas: we are not billiard balls whose capacities and probabilities are determined and limited by rigid physical laws. Instead, the individual possesses the capacity—and responsibility—to develop and to alter his or her destiny, to create a new and better moral identity. Significantly, Warren's use of words and phrases such as "progressive understanding," "continually emerging," "unfolding," and "self-corrective creation" work to naturalize the central technical feature of the Romantic strategy of development, namely *revision*.

Contemporary culture is saturated with the concepts of self-revision, self-improvement, and personal development, but by reading development as a "culture-specific product" rather than as a transparent "psychological truth" or "ahistorical idea," Siskin manages to expose development's persistent technical and formal features, particularly as they appear in literary texts. Of the particular role of revision in literary texts, Siskin writes, "When we take the Romantic subject—that version of the self . . . that invents and is the invention of Literature—to be a text subject to the Romantic logic of vision/revision, then that logic appears in more familiar guise. The insistence upon rewriting to achieve . . . a 'final form' is translated, in that case, into the necessity of change so that potential can be fulfilled; aimed at the human form, the mandatory labor of revision becomes the imperative of development" (95). Siskin demonstrates that this "mandatory labor of revision" entails much more than simply the act of *rewriting*; rather, it encompasses a wide variety of formal relationships within and between texts, poet, and reader—relationships conceptualized in terms of parts and wholes. I will discuss below some of these relationships as they pertain to Warren's poetry, but for the moment it is important to emphasize that Warren's language and metaphors in "Knowledge and the Image of Man" suggest a general acceptance of this view of the self and this method of self-representation. Indeed, the strategy of development as outlined by Siskin becomes Warren's characteristic mode of self-representation in his poetry of this period. However, through his poetry of the late 1960s and early 1970s he will come to question and even undermine this very strategy of development much in the way that Siskin does in his pioneering study of Romantic discourse. In other words, development in Warren's poetry goes from being a relatively transparent method of self-representation to a subject of inquiry in itself. For the moment, however, Warren embraces this strategy both in theory and in practice.

Warren goes on in "Knowledge and the Image of Man" to concede that self-definition through self-knowledge implies a certain degree of separateness: "Despite the osmosis of being to which I have referred, man's process of self-definition means that he . . . disintegrates his primal instinctive sense of unity, he discovers separateness" (187). However, Warren evades any despairing sense of alienation and solipsism—a recurring tendency in his early poetry—by affirming that true self-knowledge restores us to a unity of being with both nature and society. This striving for a deeper unity which both transcends difference and dissolves hierarchies is the ultimate goal of Romantic discourse, and such a strategy certainly carries with it a more egalitarian and democratic emphasis which complements Warren's now more liberal views on racial integration. Continuing in this vein, he claims in the essay that our return to unity through self-knowledge can have progressive social implications and that poetry can provide us with the very knowledge we need. As he explains the premise of his new aesthetic, Warren resurrects the myth of the fortunate fall, which is itself a narrative of development:

> Man can return to his lost unity, and if that return is fitful and precarious, if the foliage and flower of the innocent garden are now somewhat browned by a late season, all is the more precious for the fact, for what has now been achieved has been achieved by a growth of moral awareness. . . . Man eats of the fruit of the Tree of Knowledge, and falls. But if he takes another bite, he may get at least a sort of redemption. And a precious redemption. His unity with nature will not now be that of a drop of water in the ocean; it is, rather, the unity of the lover with the beloved, a unity presupposing separateness. His unity with mankind will not now be the unity of a member of a tribal horde with that pullulating mass; his unity will be that of a member of a sweet society.
>
> I suppose that the ultimate unity of knowledge is in the image of himself that man creates through knowledge, the image of his destiny, the mask he stares at. This would mean that manipulative knowledge, as well as knowledge of vision, calculation as well as con-

ception—to take Shelley's distinction—works toward the creation of
that image. (187–88)

While critics have often discussed this essay, and this particular passage,
they have not considered the fact that Warren is configuring a new strat-
egy for representing and interpreting *himself* in his own poetry. And con-
sidering the context of Warren's recent "conversion" on the issue of race,
his chosen metaphor of the fortunate fall becomes particularly interesting
and suggestive. Indeed, these comments echo the resolution of *Brother to
Dragons* and may perhaps be viewed as a recapitulation, from a more
theoretical aesthetic perspective, of the lessons learned from his immer-
sion in the subject of racial injustice—and his acknowledged complicity in
that injustice.

Considered in the context of this conversion, Warren's adoption of a
Romantic aesthetic—particularly the premise of unity of being and the
strategy of development—seems to have served a variety of perhaps com-
peting functions. On one level, the themes of Romanticism offered him a
more redemptive and hopeful alternative to the dark, often lugubrious
themes of his early poetry. At the same time, these new Romantic prin-
ciples carry a more egalitarian emphasis by positing a unity of being that
transcends difference and dissolves hierarchies. But perhaps more impor-
tant, the Romantic strategy of development, here articulated as a secular
version of the "fortunate fall," allowed Warren to recover and redeem his
past. The premise of development transforms transgression into an asset,
a form of "felix culpa" that leads the self to a higher and, in Warren's
words, "more precious" sense of moral awareness. This in turn restores
the self to a unity of being with both humanity and nature. Such is the
resolution of *Brother to Dragons*, as R.P.W.'s acknowledgment of evil and
complicity allows him to reenter the world full of hope. Indeed, R.P.W.
stands very much as a model of this developing self articulated in "Knowl-
edge and the Image of Man," as his willingness to face the dark potentials
of the self grants him a higher mode of perception and awareness by the
end of the poem and his second trip to Rocky Mount.[6] In a sense, we may
say that Warren in the 1950s reconstructs himself as a much darker ver-
sion of Emerson's (and Whitman's) "Poet." Despite Warren's oft-cited
hostility to Emerson, William Bedford Clark has persuasively outlined
the affinities between the two writers, concluding that the differences be-
tween them are "more a matter of appearance than essence, more superfi-

cial than fundamental" ("In the Shadow of His Smile" 552). According to Emerson, the poet "stands among partial men for the complete man, and apprises us not of his wealth, but of the commonwealth. . . . The poet is the person in whom these powers [of perception] are in balance, the man without impediment, who sees and handles that which others dream of" (218). Warren similarly makes himself representative as one who attempts to see human nature in its fullness. However, rather than revealing our innate divinity as Emerson and Whitman would have it, the completeness Warren reveals is largely contingent upon the acknowledgment of our collective heart of darkness and the individual's unlimited capacity for evil. From Warren's perspective, if we are to handle that which we dream of, we must first face our nightmares, what he refers to in *Brother to Dragons* as "the terror of our condition." But again, the strategy of development finally transforms personal transgressions into meaningful opportunities for growth. In fact, within the Romantic discourse of development, "incompleteness and struggle . . . become evidence of an ongoing state of transcendence" (Siskin 123). In this way, the strategy of development and the premise of a transcendent unity of being become intertwined complements of one another: "the wished-for end of development *and* of Romantic revision is a Unity that transcends difference" (Siskin 108). Furthermore, with this Romantic belief that continual change means continual opportunities for growth, revision becomes imperative—the creative imagination being the tool for carrying out this directive. Warren in "Knowledge and the Image of Man" concurs, explaining his belief that "man creates new perspectives, discovers new values—that is, a new self—and so the identity is a continually emerging, an unfolding, a self-affirming and, we hope, a self-corrective creation" (187).

According to Warren, poetry, as an act of the creative, "manipulative" imagination, provides us with the type of knowledge we need in order to be restored to this unity of being. But it does so only by creating a specular image of ourselves which provides us with what Warren calls "knowledge of form." Tellingly, however, he immediately qualifies this statement by explaining that he is not calling for the detached, objective formalism of his early verse: "By this I mean the furthest thing possible from any doctrine that might go as sheer formalism. I mean the organic relation among all the elements in the work, including, *most emphatically*, those elements drawn from the actual world and charged with the urgencies of actuality, urgencies not to be denied but transmuted. . . . The form is a

vision of experience, but of experience fulfilled and redeemed in knowl-
edge. . . . It is not a thing detached from the world but a thing springing
from the deep engagement of spirit with the world" (191–92). Warren
here argues for poetry based upon the principle of an organic, living form,
and this new principle dictates that true poetry is inherently subjective: it
must be derived from the actualities and specifics of the poet's own expe-
riences. In making this claim, Warren again draws a clear distinction be-
tween his current beliefs and his earlier aesthetic. And while his post–
Brother to Dragons poetry is richly varied, he nonetheless remains quite
steadfast in his Romantic belief in a subjective, living form. For instance,
in *Democracy and Poetry*, published some twenty years after "Knowledge
and the Image of Man," Warren reiterates these same Romantic prin-
ciples. He again asserts that poetry serves a "therapeutic" function in the
modern world and argues that poetry is vital to selfhood, defining the
"self" as "in individuation, the felt principle of significant unity." He goes
on to explain that the "made thing"—in his case, the poem—becomes "a
vital emblem of the struggle toward the achieving of self"; it is "only
insofar as the work establishes and expresses a self [that it] can . . . engage
us. We observe this 'model' of self in its adventures of selfhood" (*Democ-
racy and Poetry* xiii, 69–70).

Following the publication of "Knowledge and the Image of Man" in
1955, a seemingly revitalized Warren put his new Romantic theories into
practice in an outpouring of verse. Between 1956 and 1966, he surpassed
his entire production of poetry from 1923 to 1943; in this ten-year span
he published three new collections: the Pulitzer Prize–winning volume
Promises of 1956, the 1960 volume *You, Emperors, and Others*, and the
1966 collection *Tale of Time*, the "new" poems of *Selected Poems: New
and Old, 1923–1966*. The poems of this period exhibit a variety of new
formal characteristics and thematic emphases. In regard to prosody, War-
ren still often relies on end-rhyme and regular stanzaic patterns, but these
features are commonly offset by irregular line lengths, creating a looser
sense of form than he exhibited in his early poetry. And as Victor
Strandberg has pointed out, by the time Warren published his *Tale of
Time* collection in 1966, he had adopted the more radically open forms of
the New American Poetry.[7] However, trying to divide Warren's career
simply on the basis of these prosodic features has proven exceedingly
troublesome for critics, who have offered numerous opinions regarding
exactly when Warren's prosody changes and how.[8] This is one of the rea-

sons why I have chosen to focus more on the deeper, governing aesthetic principles behind the various changes that occur in Warren's poetry. This is particularly important for the period now under discussion, for while certain formal tendencies in the poetry of 1956–66 seem reminiscent of his early formalism, just as other tendencies seem to anticipate his later, more open forms, the two central Romantic principles I have been discussing—unity of being and the strategy of development—are unmistakably new features which pervade Warren's poetry of this period.

I made the point earlier that critics have tended to repeat Warren's developmental strategies through their approaches to his poetry, and have consequently overlooked the unique formal features of this particular mode of discourse. To illustrate the way in which critics have reinscribed these strategies Warren adopts—and to clarify my own approach—I would like to consider for a moment an analysis offered by Robert S. Koppelman in his book *Robert Penn Warren's Modernist Spirituality*. In his approach to Warren, Koppelman identifies a dialectical process that informs the post-*Promises* poetry. For a more specific example, consider his comments on "To a Little Girl, One Year Old, in a Ruined Fortress," the opening five-poem sequence of *Promises*:

> The five poems dedicated to Rosanna present a dialectical process. We may find three distinct perspectives represented here, all suggesting aspects of the poet's spiritual condition. The first perspective is skeptical: the speaker observing the natural scene and the youthfulness of his daughter and neighboring children with an air of detachment and occasional scorn. The second perspective is that of his daughter (or that which he projects upon his daughter), who is innocent from suffering and disillusion, of whom the speaker says: "you sing as though human need / Were not for perfection." Finally, the spiritual transformation in this section occurs as the poet works through his own cold reserve, comes to participate in the infant girl's joy, and, ultimately, achieves a higher perspective of his own that transcends the apparent limitations of both time and language. It is this perspective, culminated in "Colder Fire," that the poet wants to pass on to his daughter and to readers. . . .
>
> Although Warren invokes no "Great World Spirit," there is a Hegelian dialectic of thesis (speaker's first perspective), antithesis (daughter's and neighbor child's innocence), and synthesis (poet's elevated perspective) at work in the Rosanna section of *Promises*.

> Characteristically, Warren is concerned with the spiritual process and its implications for human consciousness. Final and absolute causes remain a mystery. (43–44)

Significantly, we can see that the strategy of development at work in the poem is repeated here in the critical appraisal of it, for the dialectical process in this instance is presented as a *developmental* process. According to Koppelman's reading, the poem's speaker—Warren himself—revises his perspective and develops to a higher, transcendent state of awareness, but rather than submitting the poem's rhetorical strategies to critical scrutiny, the reading of the poem works to naturalize the Romantic discourse of development into an absolute truth. And just as critics have refrained from considering the formal and strategic implications of Warren's Romantic discourse, they have also overlooked the often startling manner in which he later came to test and even undermine the truth and legitimacy of such strategies. Following on Siskin's analysis of Romantic discourse then, I would like to consider the ways in which development functions as a strategy and formal feature in Warren's poetry, and to illustrate how it is inextricably linked to his newly adopted theory of an osmosis of being.

While I agree with Koppelman that there is an identifiable dialectical process at work in Warren's later poetry, I believe that such a designation in the end illuminates only half of Warren's conceptual framework. For in addition to functioning dialectically, his poetry functions hermeneutically. The conceptual framework for Romantic narratives of transcendence is based neither on principles of addition nor of causation; instead, it is based on "simultaneity: part as whole and whole as part." While an additive principle—or dialectical, for that matter—"posits an unknowable future sum" and a causative principle suggests "an equally unknowable past origin," the hermeneutical framework of Romantic discourse provides "not answers, but a conceptual and temporal rearrangement that obviates any need for them" (Siskin 102–3). We might say that Warren's poems work simultaneously along the diachronic and synchronic axes. Koppelman distinguishes a temporal and chronological progression in the poem, and this may be placed along a diachronic axis. But by exposing the hermeneutical maneuver in Warren's poetry, it becomes clear that he attempts to function concurrently on a synchronic axis. This may help to account for the ongoing distinctions he makes in his later poetry between "time" and "no-time" or "timelessness." To see only a dialectical function in Warren's poetry is to confine it to temporality and to overlook the implications of Warren's interpretative conceptual rearrangement, a rearrangement that alleviates anxiety over both past cause and future closure. John Burt has noticed a simultaneous two-way movement in Warren's poetry, and has also commented on the manner in which his poetry often resists closure. Burt points out that "Warren's characteristic poetic method . . . is a simultaneous evasion and experience of primary truth. Warren attempts, through his alternations of confrontation and retreat, to apprehend a possessing truth without, in turn, becoming possessed by it" (112). This simultaneous movement which resists the need for closure can be traced to the Romantic discourse Warren adopts in his poetry.

As Siskin explains, the Romantic rhetoric of development "assumes and establishes a relationship between parts and wholes that we can . . . define more precisely as interpretative: each part modifies the meaning of the whole while the whole simultaneously modifies the (transcendent) meaning of each part" (104). Within this part/whole framework, the creative habit of the poet "is posited as a continuously modified product of the very experience it processes. To cast the psychological as the revisionary is thus to naturalize the latter while rewriting the former as a means of transcendence" (105). This is exactly the type of revisionary process Warren describes in "Knowledge and the Image of Man." In similar fashion, he claims there that the "ultimate unity of knowledge" is achieved through a creative process of revision, through "manipulative knowledge as well as knowledge of vision, calculation as well as conception—to take Shelley's distinction." Continuing, Warren contends that the psychological "growth" in an individual is a process of continuous, never-ending revision: "Any change of environment—including any making—creates a new relation between man and his world, and other men. Any doing changes the doer. Any seeing changes the see-er. And any knowledge one has of his own being modifies that being, re-creates it, and thus changes the quality of making, doing, seeing" (187–88). As a result of this constant interpenetration and interpretation between parts and wholes, between past and present, the self exists in an ongoing state of transcendence—an "inevitable osmosis of being," as Warren would have it.[9]

To further illustrate this simultaneous part/whole function which alleviates the need for closure, we can return to Koppelman's dialectical reading of the Rosanna sequence of *Promises*. As Koppelman points out, the opening three sections of the poem present the contrasting perspectives of adult skepticism (the poet) and youthful innocence (his daughter). However, section 4, "The Flower," illustrates the hermeneutical, rather than dialectical, nature of the turn that leads to the poet-speaker's "growth" to a higher, transcendent awareness in section 5, "Colder Fire." In "The Flower" the poet describes his daughter's daily ritual of picking a flower on their return walk from the beach.[10] As the season progresses he is struck by the fact that his daughter's pleasure in this ritual is not diminished by the now-withering flowers:

> We give the best one to you.
> It is ruined, but will have to do.
> Somewhat better the blue blossoms fare.
> We find one for your hair,
> And you sing as though human need
> Were not for perfection. (*CP* 106)

This brief recollected moment is immediately followed by the strategic turning point in the poem, a vision of unity that transcends difference and alleviates the implicit sense of loss:

> Let all seasons pace their power,
> As this has paced to this hour.
> Let season and season devise
> Their possibilities.
> Let the future reassess
> All past joy, and past distress,
> Till we know Time's deep intent,
> And the last integument
> Of the past shall be rent
> To show how all things bent
> Their energies to that hour
> When you first demanded your flower.
>
> And in that image let
> Both past and future forget,
> In clasped communal ease,
> Their brute identities. (*CP* 106)

In this particular passage, Warren acknowledges and accepts the inevitability of change ("seasons pace") by placing it within a larger, continuous and unchanging framework (past and future merge into "communal ease"). The sense of difference, separateness, and loss that results from the passing of time becomes a mere "integument" or shell which encases a deeper, unchanging, and unified structure. In this instance, the small part (the image of the daughter demanding her flower) reveals the meaning of the transcendent whole (Time's deep intent), while at the same time the whole reveals the transcendent quality of the particular moment. This single image of the poet's daughter demanding her flower therefore erases the "brute identities" of past and future to reveal a unity transcending such temporal distinctions. Consequently, the turn in the poem functions not according to an additive, dialectical principle (adult perspective plus child's perspective equals higher transcendent perspective) but according to a hermeneutical principle (the part interpenetrates and interprets the whole and vice versa).

This hermeneutical, part/whole relationship is again emphasized in the concluding stanzas of the sequence's last poem, "Colder Fire." This poem places a joyful experience of the present against a recollection from the past, which again suggests the inevitability of change and loss. In the poem's present moment, the poet and his daughter are sitting in the fortress overlooking the sea and enjoying the "whisperless carnival" of butterflies conducting their "ritual carouse" (CP 107). The afternoon brightness ("summer glitter") of the present moment contrasts with the earlier moment the poet recalls: a "sad and white" overcast morning on which he and his wife had ascended a mountain and rested in the "severe shade" of its peak. His eyes now focus on the very same mountain which hangs in the distance, and he recalls "that place I know." The details he recalls of this earlier journey up the mountain seem to forebode the inevitability of change and loss and therefore seem to infect the narrator's present experience with his daughter:

> Now the butterflies dance, time-tattered and disarrayed.
> I watch them. I think how above that far scarp's sunlit wall
> Mist threads in silence the darkness of boughs, and in that shade
> Condensed moisture gathers at needle-tip. It glitters, will fall.
>   (CP 108).

These closing images suggest that the present joyful moment with his daughter will likewise recede into the mist and darkness of the past, and if the poem had ended here, it would seem quite similar in tone to Warren's earlier verse, with its preoccupation with decline and loss. However, in the poem's—and sequence's—last two stanzas Warren again invokes a hermeneutical turn which alleviates the pain resulting from such knowledge of change and loss. Placed in the part/whole conceptual framework, these fragments of memory are transformed from images of loss and separateness into evidence of continuity and an ongoing state of transcendence:

> I cannot interpret for your this collocation
> Of memories. You will live your own life, and contrive
> The language of your own heart, but let that conversation,
> In the last analysis, be always of whatever truth you would live.
>
> For fire flames but in the heart of a colder fire.
> All voice is but echo caught from a soundless voice.
> Height is not deprivation of valley, nor defect of desire,
> But defines, for the fortunate, that joy in which all joys should re-
>   joice. (*CP* 108)

Since the poet does not "interpret" the meaning of these memories, the poem seems to lack a clear sense of closure; there is no stated message or moral. But this absence of interpretation does not result, as one may expect, in frustration and uncertainty.[11] Instead, Warren creates a series of paradoxical images which all posit the sort of part/whole relationship that is central to the strategy of development. To offer a single, conclusive, temporal interpretation of this "collocation / Of memories" would undermine his framework. From Warren's perspective, truth is not arrived at; it is lived in an ongoing state of vision and revision. To borrow from Wordsworth's *Prelude*, there is a sense of "something evermore about to be."[12] And while such a strategy obviates the need for closure, it also invites more writing and rewriting, as each individual poem both stands as an organic whole and integrates itself within the particular sequence and volume in which it appears. The poet's entire oeuvre stands as the final transcendent result of this revisionary labor. In short, there is always a higher unity in mind with Romantic discourse, and Warren's adoption of these strategies provides unique ways for containing, controlling, and finally transforming the darker, more nihilistic impulses that governed the themes of his early poetry.

In contrast to his early poetry's anxiety over change, loss, and uncertainty, Warren now accepts the inevitability of change by creating a higher, continuous, and transcendent order to contain it. Continuous change in fact becomes evidence of an ongoing state of transcendence as the "continually emerging" self is in "continual and intimate interpenetration" with the world. Warren's strategy perhaps may best be seen in the penultimate poem of *Promises*, "Lullaby: A Motion like Sleep." In this poem Warren employs the metaphor of a running stream to convey the absolute continuity of all change, an image he will return to over and over again in his late poetry. The narrator of the poem, addressing his sleeping infant son, links the flow of the stream to the flow of human blood in human veins. In creating this link, Warren again postulates a higher unity of being which subsumes change within continuity:

> Sleep, for sleep and stream and blood-course
> Are a motion with one name,
> And all that flows finds end but in its own source,
> And a circuit of motion like sleep,
> And will go as once it came.
> So, son, now sleep
>
> Till clang of cock-crow, and dawn's rays,
> Summon your heart and hand to deploy
> Their energies and know, in excitement of day-blaze,
> How like a wound, and deep,
> Is Time's irremediable joy.
> So, son, now sleep. (CP 141)

Notice how Warren here admits the consequences of motion and change by describing Time as "irremediable" and "like a wound." But also notice how he diminishes the sense of loss by portraying change as continuous and, in a sense, *unchanging*. As in the Rosanna sequence, he relies on an interpretative strategy of parts and wholes, as each individual part (sleep, stream, and blood-course) reveals the transcendent whole ("a motion with one name") and the whole likewise reflects the transcendent meaning of the particular parts.

Importantly, this new framework allows Warren to continue to address many of the same issues that occupied his early poetry—alienation, solipsism, naturalism, loss, and separateness—without drifting into the despairing nihilism so common in his early poetry. In fact, Warren's theory of an osmosis of being is contingent upon the self's capacity to accept and assimilate these very concerns, as the transcendent and visionary moments of the late poetry often follow closely on the heels of moments of self-doubt, self-loathing, and the acute realization of one's mortal limitations.[13] This may be seen in a poetic sequence such as "Ballad of a Sweet Dream of Peace." Victor Strandberg has described this poem as "Warren's most succinct statement of his osmosis of being vision" (*Poetic Vision* 164). The poem consists of a surreal, often nightmarish dialogue between two voices. The first speaker seems younger, inexperienced, uncertain, while the second speaker, who answers the questions posed by the first, seems confident and all-knowing. Over the course of the dialogue, a variety of disturbing images parade before the first speaker, images from his past which he would rather not acknowledge: the corpse of his grandmother, hogs he had tended to as a boy, and a former sexual partner whom he does not even recognize. He is utterly confounded by these images, but when he protests that these items are irrelevant to his present existence, the second voice definitively replies, "You fool, poor fool, all Time is a dream, and we're all one Flesh, at last" (CP 136). Warren again proposes a unity of being which transcends all disparate levels of life and experience, including our distinctions of time; in this particular instance, however, he underscores our faults, failings, and mortality. The poem's directive is clear: the osmosis of being demands the synthesis of all—the good and the bad, the beautiful and the ugly, or, as Strandberg designates, "the clean and the dirty" (Poetic Vision 121). So while Warren, like Emerson and Whitman, argues a perpetual unity that transcends time and dissolves differences and hierarchies, his emphasis is nonetheless much darker.

But Warren's insistence upon Romantic synthesis finally transforms such encounters with these darker issues into meaningful experiences that lead to a higher, more complete and transcendent understanding. Warren continuously attempts to synthesize a variety of perspectives, at times recalling encounters with figures who are similar to Wordsworth's beggars and leech-gatherers, and who seem to carry a special form of knowledge. Such is the case in "Dark Night of," which appears in Promises. The narrator recalls an incident from his childhood in which he came face to face with an old tramp in the woods bordering his family farm, a scenario that calls to mind the short story "Blackberry Winter." Early in the poem, the boy sees the man skulking across the fields, but later, while out on his family's land rounding up cows, he finds himself face to face with the old man. Warren renders this incident as a fall from innocent unity into separateness and knowledge, although the knowledge comes only many years later upon recollection of the incident:

The cows drift up the lane.
White elder blooms by the lane.
They move in a motion like sleep.
Their jaws make a motion like sleep.
I linger, leaf by leaf.
Dust, pale, powders elder leaf,

And the evening-idle, pale sky
Drains your body light, and dry.
Air moves sweet through pale husk under sky.

But suddenly you are you,
No pale husk the air moves through.
My heart clenched hand-hard as I stood.
The adrenalin tingled my blood.
My lungs made a fish-gasp for air.
Cold prickles ran in my hair.
Beneath elder bloom, the eyes glare. (*CP* 124)

The lyrical repetition of words and phrases in the first of these two stanzas underscores the innocent communion with nature enjoyed by the narrator during childhood. Like Emerson's image of the "transparent eyeball," the boy's very body drains itself into the atmosphere, leaving him a "pale husk" under the summer sky. We may say, however, that this form of innocent unity with nature is, from Warren's perspective, simplistic. In contrast, the second stanza comes across more jarringly and vitally as the narrator, upon meeting the gaze of the tramp, falls into a state of separateness ("suddenly you are you").

In the stanzas that follow, the narrator suggests a common human bond between himself and the old tramp: "And our eyes thread the single thread / Of the human entrapment" (*CP* 124). Yet the narrator apparently did not realize this at the time of the encounter, but only many years later. This may be surmised from the poem's closing stanza, where the narrator explains that while the incident immediately helped him to appreciate the love and care provided by his family, he did not understand the man's intense isolation and desolation. Now older and experienced, the narrator can revisit the scene in memory and sense the man's utter isolation; he can even grant him a form of austere dignity in his isolation:

His head, in the dark air,
Gleams with the absolute and glacial purity of despair.
His head, unbared, moves with the unremitting glory of stars high
    in the night heaven there.
He moves in joy past contumely of stars or insolent indifference of
    the dark air.
May we all at last enter into that awfulness of joy he has found
    there. (*CP* 125)

Through an act of the creative imagination, the narrator here transforms the old tramp into an individual who has bravely accepted and endured his complete isolation and devastating separateness from the world, and is thus able, according to the narrator's vision, to "enter into that awfulness of joy": that love of the world that presupposes separateness.

"Dark Night of" provides a particularly good example of the way memory functions within Warren's concepts of the developing self and the osmosis of being. Through the creative imagination of the poet, memory transforms time into timelessness as later, more knowledgeable feelings are substituted for earlier emotions and reactions, thereby illustrating the self's continuing growth and development. This is the "manipulative knowledge" Warren describes in "Knowledge and the Image of Man," a revisionary labor that "creates new perspectives, discovers new values—that is, a new self—and so the identity is a continually emerging, an unfolding, a self-affirming and, we hope, a self-corrective creation" (186–87). Echoing Faulkner, we may consequently say that for Warren the past is never really past. But instead of feeling utterly and tragically trapped by the past, Warren by his Romantic use of the past ultimately nullifies time ("all Time is a dream"), for each past moment can assume new, transcendent meaning as the self is constantly reborn into a higher, more developed self. This may be seen in a sequence like "Some Quiet, Plain Poems," from *You, Emperors, and Others.* Here the narrator in the poem's present is actually in Italy, but an owl call he hears conjures up a host of images and memories from his childhood in Kentucky. As these memories return, he can now assign new meaning to them, meaning that better represents his "new self." For instance, in part 4, "In Moonlight, Somewhere, They Are Singing," he recalls how as a child he was able to participate in the joy of the song sung by his newlywed aunt and uncle. From his present perspective, however, he can now consider the viewpoint of the other inhabitant of the house at that time, his aging grandfather. The narrator reflects:

> But what of the old man awake there,
> As the voices, like vine, climbed up moonlight?
> What thought did he think of past time as they twined bright in
>   moon-air,
> And veined, with their silver, the moon-flesh of night? (*CP* 162)

Victor Strandberg labels this sequence a "poem of passage" and claims that it portrays an "unqualified sense of loss" (*Poetic Vision* 78). I disagree with this assessment, for while the poem conveys a sense of loss and a tacit desire for lost innocence, it also illustrates the ability of the creative imagination to fashion a new self, a self founded upon manipulative knowledge which recasts and redeems the past. Despite the implicit sense of loss in the sequence—the speaker acknowledges that he has been granted no "absolute" truth—it ends hopefully with the speaker accepting this deficiency, along with the promise of new life and new joy:

> Long since that time I have walked night streets, heel-iron
> Clicking the stone, and in dark in windows have stared.
> Question, quarry, dream—I have vented my ire on
> My own heart that, ignorant and untoward,
> Yearns for an absolute that Time would, I thought, have prepared,
>
> But has not yet. Well, let us debate
> The issue. But under a tight roof, clutching a toy,
> My son now sleeps, and when the hour grows late,
> I shall go forth where the cold constellations deploy
> And lift up my eyes to consider more strictly the appalling logic of
>   joy. (CP 164)

In these concluding lines from the sequence's final poem, "Debate: Question, Quarry, Dream," the speaker can accept the lack of absolute knowledge, for according to the rhetoric of Romanticism, meaning is not arrived at but instead reveals itself in an ongoing process of becoming. The events of the self's past are never exhausted but can continually be renewed through the manipulative knowledge of memory.

These same principles inform the visionary moments in Warren's "Mortmain" and "Tale of Time" sequences, in which he attempts to immortalize the memory of, respectively, his dead father and mother. Even though these poems are elegies, they both end with visionary forms of rebirth: each closes with an imagined encounter with the dead parent as a child. By revisiting and revising the events of the past, Warren uncovers lost possibilities for renewal. "Tale of Time" is a particularly interesting sequence, for the poem's reconciliation of past and present entails a reconciliation between the poet's white and black maternal figures, thus reflecting Warren's own "development" on the issue of race. The opening sections of the sequence focus on the death of Warren's mother and his failed attempt to adequately remember and understand her world. This sense of inadequacy is echoed in the remarkable fourth section of the sequence,

"The Interim." Here the grieving family visit their elderly black nurse, who is herself dying. The woman

> Whom we now sought was old. Was
> Sick. Was dying. Was
> Black. Was.
> *Was:* and was that enough? Is
> Existence the adequate and only target
> For the total reverence of the heart?
>
> We would see her who,
> Also, had held me in her arms.
> She had held me in her arms,
> And I had cried out in the wide
> Day-blaze of the world. But
>
> Now was a time of endings. (*CP* 187)

The family's response to the imminent loss of their dying childhood nurse is hopelessly awkward and inadequate: the father leaves twenty dollars on the table, while the narrator's brother complains that her home smelled of urine. Nonetheless, the narrator, looking back on this event from the past, can infuse it with new meaning—first by simply including it in the sequence. Through his memory, he transforms the real-life situation into a formative moment in which his self comes into being:

> The eyes bubble like hot mud with the expulsion of vision.
>
> I lean, I am the
> Nothingness which she
> Sees.
>
> Her hand rises in the air.
> It rises like revelation.
> It moves but has no motion, and
> Around it the world flows like a dream of drowning.
> The hand touches my cheek.
> The voice says: *you.*
>
> I am myself.
>
> The hand has brought me the gift of myself. (*CP* 188)

The old woman's recognition brings the speaker from a state of nothingness into a state of being and becoming, even if it is also a state of imperfection and inadequacy: like the other members of the family, the speaker cannot make an adequate response to the dying woman. It is interesting and important to note that this knowledge of the self's imperfection comes through an encounter with a black figure, a situation that harkens back to *Brother to Dragons*. This trope is repeated, though in a more humorous fashion, in "Homage to Emerson," where a black figure informs the young Warren of his tainted humanity ("The Wart"), and it also figures prominently in the plot of *Wilderness*, particularly in the interactions between Adam Rosenzweig and Mose Talbutt. For Warren, the subject of race provided a constant reminder of his own imperfections as well as an index of his own capacity for change and growth. The fact that he could reconcile the death of his black nurse with the death of his mother in "Tale of Time" is itself perhaps a possibility that emerged only with the passage of time. Still, the speaker in the sequence finally feels he cannot do justice to either of his maternal figures. As John Burt points out, "The poem leaves us not with accommodation but with a curiously balanced failure to find accommodation. The speaker does not reconcile himself with the dead in their mystery and danger but reconciles himself to his failure to find reconciliation" (83). However, even though the poem ends in failure, it does not end in despair. In contrast to his 1934 elegy to his mother titled "The Return," which does end in a state of pure despair, the rhetoric of Romanticism that Warren now employs allows him to contain this despair and move beyond it.[14] Even though there is no absolute resolution in the poem, as Burt points out, the past is still left open-ended, and this lack of closure contains a seed of hope. As in "Debate: Question, Quarry, Dream," the speaker can accept his failure to arrive at absolute knowledge, for according to the rhetoric of Romanticism, meaning reveals itself in an ongoing process of becoming. Pursuing the Romantic logic of memory, Warren may claim, as he does at the end of "Tale of Time," that the past is as unpredictable as the future. For if we accept Warren's Romantic view that the self is "continually emerging" as a "new self," we may likewise accept that the self's past is continually being recreated as well; consequently, the self exists in a continuing state of renewal and transcendence, as the closing lines of "Tale of Time" promise:

Truth, in the end, can never be spoken aloud,
For the future is always unpredictable.
But so is the past, therefore

At wood's edge I stand, and,
Over the black horizon, heat lightning
Ripples the black sky. After
The lightning, as the eye
Adjusts to the new dark,
The stars are, again, born.

They are born one by one. (*CP* 193)

The Romantic rhetoric of development attempts to document a process of becoming, and its assumptions and strategies render explanations of first and final causes unnecessary. It therefore resists closure while at the same time alleviating anxiety over this lack of closure by providing the promise of "something evermore about to be." In short, Warren's adoption of a Romantic aesthetic—particularly the premise of unity of being and the strategy of development—provided him with a way of controlling and transforming the darker themes that so dominated his early poetry. At the same time, the discourse of development also provided him with a narrative pattern for representing his own conversion on the issue of race, as seen in *Brother to Dragons, Segregation,* and even *Tale of Time.* But Warren does not rest easily upon these Romantic assumptions. Instead, through works like *Who Speaks for the Negro?* and through his poetry that follows in the period 1966–75, he begins to question these very same tenets of Romantic discourse, an endeavor that produces some of his finest poetry and edges him toward an encounter with postmodernism.

Warren in Transition

Who Speaks for the Negro? and *A Plea in Mitigation*

Somewhere in the fable, there is fact. Or do facts, always, strain to flower into fable? And the dreary clichés, do they give us, after all, the fresh, appalling vision of truth?

Robert Penn Warren, *Who Speaks for the Negro?*

Only the new language can let us know the nature of the experience potential in the new world around us—and know the nature of ourselves. In other words, for reader and writer alike, the need for the revolution is a need to discover identity—to locate oneself on the vast and shifting chart of being.

Robert Penn Warren, *A Plea in Mitigation*

In the same year that he published *Selected Poems: New and Old, 1923–1966*, Robert Penn Warren also published a very revealing—though generally overlooked—essay titled *A Plea in Mitigation: Modern Poetry at the End of an Era*. In this essay Warren rings the death knell of both modernism and the New Criticism, while at the same time calling for a new and progressive movement in American poetry. Warren begins *A Plea in Mitigation* by laying to rest the progenitors of high modernism and anticipating the confusion that will follow the end of the regime they helped to create:

> The collected editions are now settled comfortably on the shelves, some, even, gathering a little dust. The authors of some of those books are dead. We are witnessing, in other words, the end of a poetic era, the end of "modernism," that school of which the Founding Fathers were Eliot, Pound, and Yeats.

When a regime falls, there are always, in varying proportions, huzzas of joy, wails of despair, and, even, stout denials of the simple fact. . . . Out of the babble of tongues and the darkening of counsel, after the Kerensky moment—to use a political metaphor—the future gradually emerges. It will probably emerge quite simply, probably unannounced while we are looking the other way. It will emerge from poetry, not from debates about poetry. It may be emerging this very minute, but we do not yet see its shape. (1)

In many ways this essay stands Janus-like, looking back over Warren's own poetic past and anticipating his poetic future. Now at the end of the period 1953 to 1966 in which he moved away from modernism and embraced a Romantic aesthetic, Warren conclusively and unambiguously shuts the door on his modernist past. But at the same time, he also forecasts in this essay an altering direction and emphasis for the poetry he will publish in the years from 1966 to 1975. Consequently, we may say that *A Plea in Mitigation* helps mark another transitional moment in Warren's career as a poet.[1] And though this transition is perhaps more subtle than the one that occurred in the 1950s with his adoption of a subjective, Romantic aesthetic, it is important to note that this moment of change in Warren's poetry once again concurs with his immersion in the issue of race—this time following closely on the heels of his 1965 book *Who Speaks for the Negro?* This wide-ranging book of interview transcripts and personal reflections documents a particularly dynamic moment in the civil rights movement, but it also documents a dynamic moment in Warren's own thinking on issues of self and identity. Throughout *Who Speaks for the Negro?* Warren repeatedly raises certain difficult questions about the nature of self and identity, questions that mark something of a departure from his views expressed in "Knowledge and the Image of Man." These inquiries lead to new and more radical views of self and identity which eventually form a new thematic emphasis for his poetry published from 1966 to 1975.[2]

In this period Warren begins to question and often even undermine the Romantic view of the developing self and the methods of self-representation it entails. In short, development goes from being a method of representation to a subject of inquiry in itself. And for Warren, nowhere were issues of self-representation more charged and complicated than in his public discourse on race. In the 1950s amid the backdrop of the emerging civil rights movement, Warren had immersed himself in the issue of race,

using it as a real-life testing ground for his changing political and aes-
thetic assumptions. Warren continues these meditations on race into the
1960s, but his inquiries increasingly center on the problematic nature of
language. Once again, we can see that Warren's discourse on race and his
poetic themes and theories evolved in a complementary and parallel fash-
ion, as the subtle questions regarding the nature of the self that are raised
in *Who Speaks for the Negro?* take on a more pronounced and radical
form in his subsequent poetry. Significantly, Warren's poetic inquiry into
issues of self-representation ultimately complicates the relationship be-
tween self and language, eventually leading him to the conclusion that the
self is a fictional construct, albeit a necessary one. Warren's adoption of
this new position on the nature of the self will take him to the very
threshold of postmodernism. These issues are most strikingly evident in
his more personal poems about race from this period; however, they are
also evident in an incipient form in both *A Plea in Mitigation* of 1966 and
Who Speaks for the Negro? of 1965.

Perhaps somewhat ironically, Warren's often harsh assessment in *A
Plea in Mitigation* of modernism's failings provides a concise summary of
the main concerns expressed in his own early poetry. According to War-
ren, "The most obvious fact about modern poetry is that it is an alienated
art, and there is no reason for anyone, except a snob or a toady, to be happy
in that fact" (*A Plea in Mitigation* 4). He goes on to explain some of the
cultural and historical forces that contributed to this sense of alienation
and the "self-conscious passion for style" that often resulted in obscurity
and an empty formalism. Later he lists a number of the "programmatic
solutions" offered by various writers, solutions founded variously upon
interests and premises in aestheticism, dandyism, primitivism, and tradi-
tionalism. His comment on the last of these premises clearly recalls the
impulse behind his own early aesthetic: "Some tried to strike back to ear-
lier literature, and earlier notions of society—to take a fresh start or hold
an old stance" (6). At one point he even hints at the sometimes fascistic
political biases of the modernist project:

> A religious yearning, which might focus itself on even Brooklyn
> Bridge, was common, and as often found satisfaction, by love of man-
> kind or by hate of mankind, with Marx or Mussolini as with some
> more established communion. For there was, necessarily, a political
> bias in modernism, and from the Waste Land roads ran as straight to
> Red Square and the Piazza Venezia as to Canterbury. (6)

Considering his early association with the New Criticism, and considering the New Criticism's general bias in favor of apolitical art forms, it is particularly interesting to see Warren now freely admitting modernism's darker political potential. What is perhaps even more surprising is that he goes on to describe the complementary relationship that evolved between modernism and the New Criticism. He at first seems to belittle those who sense a "dark conspiracy" between the two in which the New Criticism functions as the "AGITPROP" of modernism; however, he immediately goes on to admit, "There is some truth in the charge." Warren explains: "As the literature of an age is schematized and labeled, as it is processed for academic distribution, there is always a hardening into orthodoxy, and there is always a certain amount of uncritical parroting in the process of distribution." As a corrective, he calls for "the never-ending revisionism which is the proper academic pursuit" (10). But this, in the end, is a moot point for Warren, because he believes that the New Criticism is as passé as modernism:

> As for what the New Criticism may have done for us, that is now a closed chapter. What was temporarily useful has served its turn and what is permanently sound has been absorbed. What was merely fashionable has become old-fashioned—the formal schematizations, the over-refinement of terms, the hair-splitting of exegesis, the academic mass production of "certified" critics, the dogmatic hardening. But such things always follow as disciples expound a revelation. We are now waiting for a new revelation. (12)

Warren certainly could not have anticipated the "new revelation" that would come with the tumult of 1968 and the emergence of poststructuralism.[3] However, he does make some provocative comments in this essay that indeed seem to forecast the poststructuralist's intensive critique of language—namely, he begins to foreground the uncertain relationships between language, reality, and the self or "subject."[4] Consider, for instance, this passage from near the beginning of the essay, a passage that begins to suggest that both language and the self are unstable and uncertain:

> The fall of the regime of modernism had been in the making a long time. The storm warnings were out. Whenever insight fails, when the fluidity of life puddles and hardens into orthodoxy, when personal styles become period style, then the time is ripe for a change. There is

an organic necessity for revolt, as natural as the rhythm of the seasons. The world changes, the tonality of experience changes, and we seek a language adequate to the new experience. Except for an undefined malaise, we may not even know that language no longer conforms to experience.

No, I should say that the malaise arises because we do not know the nature of our experience. Only the new language can let us know the nature of the experience potential in the new world around us—and know the nature of ourselves. In other words, for reader and writer alike, the need for the revolution is a need to discover identity—to locate oneself on the vast and shifting chart of being. (1–2)

Warren's comments in this passage obviously indicate a continuation of his career-long inquiry into issues of self and identity, and yet we can also sense a shifting emphasis in the nature of this inquiry. Early in his career, Warren had contended that the fragmentation of the individual was symptomatic of the ills of modern society. He felt that if we somehow re-created and maintained a traditional and coherent culture, the individual would be restored to a sense of wholeness and unity. Warren now makes these issues more perplexing by underscoring the gap between language and reality. In short, at this point in his career he is beginning to view the self as *essentially* and *necessarily* fragmented and discontinuous, and he increasingly locates the origins of this inherent fragmentation within language itself. While these assumptions are in nascent form here, Warren's poetry of this later period illustrates over and over again that language never exists in a one-to-one relationship with reality, and since the self attempts to understand itself through language, "true" and complete self-knowledge is impossible. Indeed, the logical end of this line of reasoning, as Warren shows, is that our entire notion of a unitary, stable, and knowable self becomes a fictional construct. These views, which form something of a thematic center for Warren's poetry of this period, are not unlike those espoused by the poststructuralists. However, this is not to say that Warren was in any way *influenced* by poststructuralist critics like Derrida, Lacan, and de Man; instead, his ongoing political and poetic inquiries into the nature of the self and the self's relationship with language eventually led him to confront and generally accept these premises.[5]

To claim that Warren's poetry is in any way similar to poststructuralism may seem ironic considering that Warren is associated with the origins of the New Criticism and that the values of the New Criticism are generally viewed as antithetical to those of poststructuralist theory, particularly deconstruction. Critics have chosen to accentuate these perceived differences in their own approaches to Warren, often as a means of lauding Warren while condemning contemporary critical theory. However, by drawing such sharp polarities, I believe that they have overlooked the more radical implications of Warren's late thematics. Fred Thiemann's discussion of Warren's politics and poetry provides a useful example of the way in which critics have at times attempted to create an artificially inimical relationship between Warren and contemporary theory.[6] Consider the way Thiemann contrasts Warren's supposed humanism with the attitudes and methods of contemporary theorists:

> For Warren, unlike many contemporary theorists, the individual is not simply a "construction" of "discourse" or "ideology," a construction that needs to be "deconstructed." In fact, in much of his writing he explicitly deplores the disintegration (what one might call the "deconstruction" or "de-centering") of the self in modern society. This does not mean that he has a naive view of the self as an isolated, completely autonomous Cartesian *cogito*. He recognizes that human subjectivity is situated socially and historically. He sees that any workable, humane polity must assume that each individual is a responsible moral agent and therefore in some degree unique. But he sees equally the danger to such politics of positing an absolute, isolated, transcendental self.
>
> Whatever disagreements they may have among themselves, poststructuralist thinkers agree that the human self is an illusion created by the structure of language, an illusion which always supports some oppressive power structure. . . . [They] agree that this illusory self should be "deconstructed" or "de-centered." They celebrate the "death of man" as somehow liberating. Destroy the illusion of an integrated self, the reasoning goes, and those who benefit from it are deprived of their power.
>
> Warren has quite a different view of the self and its relation to power and politics. (83–84)[7]

I agree with Thiemann's assessment of Warren's belief that a "humane polity" demands that the individual be viewed as a "responsible moral agent." However, I believe that the contrasts he draws between this belief and the assumptions of poststructuralism are overly simplified and finally limiting. For Warren in his poetry of this period continually foregrounds the very same problematic relationships between self, language, and reality that lie at the heart of contemporary literary theory. While Thiemann here scoffs at the idea that the self is "an illusion created by the structure of language," he overlooks the fact that Warren's late poetry often suggests this very same view of the self. As Warren succinctly puts it in his 1975 poem "Brotherhood in Pain," "You exist only in the delirious illusion of language" (CP 331). While Warren in the 1953 *Brother to Dragons* declares that "isolation is the common lot" of humankind, he now begins to locate the source of this alienation specifically within the human capacity for language. I will discuss these issues as they appear in Warren's poetry more specifically in the chapters that follow; for the moment, however, it is important to emphasize that Warren comes to believe that the responsible moral action Thiemann here describes is possible *only* through constant inquiry into these very relationships between the self, language, and reality.

While Warren in the 1950s and early 1960s adopted a Romantic view of the developing self, development for Warren in the late 1960s and early 1970s goes from being a method of self-representation to a subject of inquiry in itself. For Warren, the autobiographical act was always more the *creating* of a life than the recording of it. But now his poetry begins to foreground the subtle and complex negotiations between memory, language, and the "facts" of the past, showing that the self is indeed an illusory fiction, with self-knowledge being the fictive result of creative activity rather than the discovery of stable and reliable truth. In contrast to Thiemann's assertions, then, I believe Warren does accept the view that the integrated self is an illusion. In his poetry of this period he continually challenges the uncritical and blind acceptance of such notions as ego integrity, the continuity of the self, and autonomous, unitary individualism. He does so by exposing the radical discontinuity of experience and the ultimate uncertainty of any self-knowledge, and by foregrounding the fictive tendencies of self-representation. This is not to suggest that the self is "meaningless" or that personal responsibility is an impossible proposition. On the contrary, Warren's aesthetic requires that in order to achieve responsibility, one must continually engage the limitations of language and the uncertainty of self-knowledge. The sense of an integrated self—a necessary fiction—may be created only through continuous self-inquiry and self-critique, but it is continually displaced and must be recreated over and over again. The result for Warren is that the self, subject to the "vast and shifting chart of being," exists in a state of perpetual flux and contradiction. It should be emphasized that while Warren comes to the conclusion that the self is a fictional construct rather than a unitary, coherent, autonomous, and self-knowable being, he nonetheless affirms the self's capacity for responsible political action. And once again, the political impetus behind Warren's altering aesthetic may be gleaned from his nearly concurrent engagement with the issue of race, *Who Speaks for the Negro?*

Published in May of 1965, *Who Speaks for the Negro?* was researched and written during a period of great social and political change in both the South and the nation as a whole. Ten years earlier, the Montgomery bus boycott of 1955–56 had placed Martin Luther King Jr. in the national spotlight and had engendered an active and aggressive civil rights movement founded upon King's principles of nonviolence and civil disobedience. In the early 1960s, organizations such as the Southern Christian Leadership Council, the Student Nonviolent Coordinating Committee, the Congress of Racial Equality, and the NAACP organized and sponsored demonstrations, sit-ins, freedom rides, voter education campaigns, and legal action to challenge the South's recalcitrant stance on segregation since the Brown decision of 1954.[8] The wide-ranging tactics brought national and international exposure to the civil rights movement, culminating in the 1963 march on Washington and King's being awarded the Nobel Peace Prize in 1964. The efforts likewise brought new legislation such as the Civil Rights Act of 1964 and the Voting Rights Act of 1965. These gains did not come without costs, as they were accompanied by high-profile acts of violence such as the 1963 murder of Medgar Evers, the church bombing later that year in Birmingham, Alabama, which killed four young girls, and the murder of three civil rights workers in Mississippi in the summer of 1964. At the same time, the movement was beginning to show signs of splintering, as a younger generation of black activists began to advocate a more militant, separatist stance; Malcolm X denounced the 1963 march on Washington, calling it a "farce." Undertaken within this dynamic context, *Who Speaks for the Negro?* presents a unique blend of objective reporting and personal reflection. The majority of the text consists of interviews Warren conducted with a wide variety of African-Americans either directly or tangentially connected with the civil rights movement. While the interviews are seamlessly connected with Warren's own narrative and personal reflections, his personal digressions are almost always prompted by comments made by the interviewees; the emphasis of the book, then, is clearly on the African-American perspectives offered in the interviews.[9]

Nonetheless, the personal and confessional aspects of the book are extremely important to our understanding of the way in which Warren's continuing engagement with the issue of race informs his poetry, particularly since his personal digressions are far more direct and revealing than they were in *Segregation*. Nowhere is this more apparent than when he again directly confronts his own past opinions on race and the South.

Warren clusters the bulk of his interviews into chapters focusing variously on major political figures and organizational leaders ("The Big Brass"), successful black professionals and writers, most notably James Baldwin and Ralph Ellison ("Leadership from the Periphery"), and students from black colleges in the South ("The Young"). The book's other chapters include a prelude-like introduction ("The Cleft Stick"), a piece focusing on recent events in Mississippi ("A Mississippi Journal"), and a chapter of Warren's concluding thoughts and reflections ("Conversation Piece"). While some of his interests and interviewing questions may seem dated from today's perspective, the book as a whole provides a fascinating look inside the civil rights movement on the cusp of its transition toward greater militancy. Prompted by the comments of his interviewees, Warren seems very cognizant of this trend to come. In particular, he is often preoccupied by the potential in the movement for violent revolt, and his questions and comments often draw contrasts between the movement's efforts in the rural South and the differing needs and demands of blacks living in urban areas. In these instances, Warren's concerns proved largely prophetic, for some three months after his book was published, the Watts section of Los Angeles erupted into rioting that left thirty-four people dead, and urban race riots would become increasingly common throughout the country in the summers that followed.

Who Speaks for the Negro? is often viewed as a continuation of *Segregation: The Inner Conflict in the South*, but on the whole it delves much more deeply and specifically into the intricacies and subtleties of the politics of race.[10] The result is a much more complete, concrete, and complex book, particularly when Warren confronts his own past opinions, which he does in a more direct and *seemingly* uncompromising manner than he did in *Segregation*. While the book's main purpose is to document the nuances and complexities of the civil rights movement, Warren also explores difficult problems revolving around the more general issues of self and identity. He does so both subjectively, through the confrontation with his own past, and objectively, through his conversations with his interviewees. Warren himself suggests this dual function within the text

of *Who Speaks for the Negro?* In the foreword he claims that he under-
took the book in order "to find out something . . . about the people . . . who
are making the Negro Revolution what it is" (*WSN* ix). Later, when asked
by an interviewee why he is writing the book, Warren adds that he also
wanted to explore his "own feelings" (*WSN* 232).[11] This latter goal, how-
ever, necessarily involved a direct confrontation with his early views on
race—particularly his defense of segregation in "The Briar Patch"—and
in the first chapter, "The Cleft Stick," Warren launches into a lengthy
digression on the subject of his early segregationist views.[12] His represen-
tation of his past, however, is often perplexing and at times perhaps even
unconvincing. Describing his "Briar Patch" essay as a "cogent and hu-
mane defense of segregation," Warren claims to have felt "some vague
discomfort" and "self-consciousness" even while he was writing it in En-
gland. Interestingly, he attributes these feelings to "an awareness that in
the real world I was trying to write about, there existed a segregation that
was not humane" (*WSN* 11). Warren generally ascribes his early segre-
gationist views to his environment, particularly his sense of the South's
"massive immobility . . . an image of the unchangeable human condition,
beautiful, sad, tragic" (*WSN* 12). But by blaming his environment for
his early opinions, Warren seems to contradict the conclusions he draws
in both *Brother to Dragons* and *Segregation*: we are not "prisoners of
history" and we must assume responsibility for our actions. Perhaps the
most questionable moment of this confessional section occurs when he
seems to suggest that he was actually more progressive than the Supreme
Court and the country as a whole: "But to return to my essay, the hu-
maneness was self-conscious because even then, thirty-five years ago, I
uncomfortably suspected, despite the prevailing attitude of the Supreme
Court and of the overwhelming majority of the population of the United
States, that no segregation was, in the end, humane" (*WSN* 12). This
statement makes Warren sound like a solitary soul struggling against the
tide of human history, a depiction that certainly provides fodder for those
critics who continue to suggest that he was never *really* arguing for segre-
gation. Such a representation of his past is not entirely persuasive if we
recall the specific details of "The Briar Patch," or poems like "Tryst on
Vinegar Hill," or his 1932 letter to Allen Tate complaining of a "nigger-
loving" colleague at Vanderbilt, written in the wake of the Supreme
Court's overturning of the Scottsboro convictions.

Warren goes on to explain that his sense of the South's "massive im-
mobility" was altered upon his return to the region, and with it his views

on race and segregation. Echoing the conclusion he draws in *Segregation*, he again asserts that individuality is achieved only through the acceptance of the change and flux generated by time. Interestingly, the portrayal of his "conversion" echoes "Knowledge and the Image of Man" and its use of the fortunate fall metaphor:

> When I actually got back to the South, the "unchangeable human condition" had changed. The Depression was there, and conversation always turned on the question of what could be done to claw out of that desperation; but that meant to "change" things, even if for some people the change desired was to change things back to their old unchangeableness. But that would be a kind of change, too. So there was no way to avoid the notion of change: you had to take a bite of the apple from the mysterious tree that had sprung up in the Confederate—no, the old American—garden. The apple might, incidentally, have given some knowledge of good and evil; but it certainly gave a knowledge of more profound consequence, the knowledge of the inevitability of change. (*WSN* 12)

Once again, we see the strategy of development at work, as Warren is able to recuperate even the negative aspects of his personal past, transforming them into meaningful opportunities for growth and awareness. However, Warren's late poems on race often undermine this very strategy of development.

Representing his early views on race and the South is clearly no simple task for Warren, yet he nonetheless resurrects these ghosts over and over again in *Who Speaks for the Negro?* For instance, he asks interviewees on more than one occasion if they can understand why a white Southerner may misguidedly defend segregation as a "necessary aspect to his cultural identity" (*WSN* 69).[13] When we consider the argument of "The Briar Patch," particularly his belief at that time that the goal of the South should be to maintain the "integrity" and "dignity" of its Agrarian lifestyle—"to preserve its essential structure intact"—these questions make it seem as though Warren is now seeking understanding and perhaps even some form of forgiveness for his early opinions. At another point, when he reflects upon the possible reasons why "whites cling to the 'myth' of Negro sexuality" and "animality," a reader familiar with his early poetry may be reminded of his early representations of race in "Tryst on Vinegar Hill" and "Pondy Woods," racial representations that uncritically evoke these very myths (*WSN* 294). Later, after an interviewee mentions the name of John Brown, Warren embarks on a long series of questions about Brown's historical legacy, followed by personal reflections on his first published book, *John Brown: The Making of a Martyr*. Looking back upon his past, he now notes, "It is far from the book I would write now, for that book was shot through with Southern defensiveness, and in my ignorance the psychological picture of the hero was presented far too schematically. But even so, the work on the book was my real introduction into some awareness of the dark and tangled problem of motives and values" (*WSN* 320).[14]

Of *Who Speaks for the Negro?* James Justus has said, "On a purely personal level this book is (and undoubtedly was intended to be) a tangible sign of its author's capacity for growth" (*Achievement* 150). I agree in a general sense with this view of Warren's purposeful representation of his own self-development; however, I also believe that in many passages we can see that he is already raising questions that will eventually compromise any strict belief in an autonomous, developing self, even though elsewhere in the text he incorporates developmental strategies of self-representation. Indeed, the overall view of the self that emerges in *Who Speaks for the Negro?* often undermines the assumption of the self's orderly and purposeful development; in many instances, Warren seems headed toward the conclusion that the self is necessarily fragmentary, disordered, and contradictory, and that the unitary and integrated self is a fictional construct. To return to Warren's comments on John Brown, perhaps the most interesting moment of this digression occurs when Warren shifts abruptly and offers a jarringly sudden transition to the world of poetry; here he suggests that the poem may stand as an emblem of order despite the inherent disorder of the poet's life:

> John Brown was, indeed, mad, and not always nobly mad—he was arrogant, sometimes unscrupulous, sometimes contemptuous of the truth, ambitious, angry, blood-obsessed; but, in the end, he spoke and died nobly. What do we make of a poet who, out of the ruck of a confused and obsessed life, creates the beautiful poem? (*WSN* 321)

As mentioned above, Warren early in his career contended that the "fragmentation" of the individual was a symptom of the ills of modern society. He felt that if we somehow maintained or recreated a traditional and coherent culture, the individual would be restored to a sense of wholeness and unity. At this point in his career, however, Warren is beginning to view the self as necessarily and essentially fragmented, and according to his comments in *Who Speaks for the Negro?* we must first acknowledge and accept this disorder and flux if we are to create an orderly, integrated self—a necessary fiction through which we may achieve a standard of morality, value, and personal responsibility.

Warren announces the interrelated themes of self and identity at the very start of *Who Speaks for the Negro?* During an interview from early in the text, Dr. Felton Clark, president of Southern University, mentions that he sees the "Negro Revolution" as a "movement for freedom, for a sense of identity" (*WSN* 17). Clark's comments prompt this digression from Warren:

> I seize the word *identity*. It is a key word. You hear it over and over again. On this word will focus, around this word will coagulate, a dozen issues, shifting, shading into each other. Alienated from the world to which he is born and from the country of which he is a citizen, yet surrounded by the successful values of that world, and country, how can the Negro define himself? There is the extreme act of withdrawing as completely as possible from that white world. There is the other extreme of "self-hatred," of repudiating the self— and one's own group. Clearly, neither extreme offers a happy solution. Yet there is no simple solution of half-and-half, for the soul doesn't operate with that arithmetical tidiness. (*WSN* 17)

Warren here portrays the individual as a complex combination of conditioned response, outright determinism, willed—though often blind—action, and, *importantly*, the perceptions of others. This particular passage reveals some of Warren's important emerging assumptions on the issues of self and identity. Notice that Warren shifts freely and rather ambiguously among three terms: identity, self, and soul. While he never offers a clear definition of these terms, his professed agnosticism would obviously rule out the possibility that the last of these terms is being used in any traditional religious sense. Despite the general lack of clarity in his use of these terms, I do believe we can draw some important conclusions from the fact that he makes a clear distinction between self and identity: they are not synonymous terms here. Significantly, Warren implies *both* a necessary split and a necessary connection between self and identity, and he also suggests that self and identity are mutually unstable.[15] To clarify, we may say that the self is a subject's consciousness of itself as a separate, unique entity. Part of this sense of self—what we can term identity—is contingent upon the perceptions of other people, or, to be more accurate, what the self believes other people perceive it to be. In other words, there is always the possibility (or probability) of a misinterpretation or gap between self and identity. Moreover, it is even questionable whether the self can objectively perceive itself as a distinct and separate being, whether it can ever be fully and wholly conscious of itself.[16] Consequently, there is always a gap or a split in the self, a gap that—Warren increasingly demonstrates—is caused by and exacerbated by the instability of language. The notion of a stable, integrated, and holistic self, then, is a fiction.

Because of what he perceives to be the self's general instability, Warren comes to believe that we must constantly question our sense of "truth" and the system of values that is founded upon this truth. In *Who Speaks for the Negro?* we can see that he is beginning to challenge the blind acceptance of supposed "universal" truths, and to suggest instead that meaning is always provisional, local, and contingent. Consider, for example, the impression Warren creates in his description of Martin Luther King Jr., whom he obviously admires:

> Even if it is a question that you know he has heard a hundred times before, there is a withdrawing inward, a slight veiling of the face as it were. There is the impression that for an answer for even that old stale question he must look inward to find a real answer, not just the answer he gave yesterday, which today may no longer be meaningful to him. It is a remarkable trait—if my reading is correct: the need to go inward to test the truth that has already been tested, perhaps over and over again, in the world outside. (*WSN* 210)

Warren's portrayal of King's "fluidity" of self may be contrasted with his earlier interview with Charles Evers, brother of the slain NAACP representative Medgar Evers. At one point early in the interview, Evers recalls a formative moment in his youth when he and Medgar—prompted by remarks of Senator Theodore Bilbo—made a pact to commit themselves to the struggle for equality. Warren reports that he felt

> something contrived, arranged about the narrative . . . something false in the language. . . . It all ran like a piece of fiction tediously conventional, a tissue of echoes.
>
> Memory and rhetoric and unconscious contriving—the freezing of facts in public repetition that can only become less and less true as language hardens—have, undoubtedly, played some odd, sad tricks here. Charles Evers, age fifteen, and Medgar, age twelve, never talked as they are reported to have talked. (*WSN* 108)

Warren's description here of language hardening and diverging from truth recalls the passage cited earlier from *A Plea in Mitigation* in which he described how language no longer conforms to experience.[17] It would seem, then, that Warren simply prefers King's willingness to test his own sense of truth over the seemingly contrived anecdote offered by Evers. However, even though Warren here senses something fictitious in Evers's anecdote from childhood, he goes on to subvert his initial interpretation by offering yet another possible alternative, one that raises profound questions and forecasts future dilemmas Warren will face regarding the nature of self-representation:

> But does this scene correspond to something that did happen? For they did come back and work in voter registration, they could have prospered and "lived in richness," they did accept persecution, Medgar Evers was indeed shot down in the dark, Charles Evers does walk, day and night, knowing that an eye stares through a telescopic sight, at his back.
>
> Somewhere in the fable, there is fact. Or do facts, always, strain to flower into fable? And the dreary clichés, do they give us, after all, the fresh, appalling vision of truth? (*WSN* 108)

In this remarkable passage, Warren first seems suspicious of what Evers portrays as the "facts" of his past; he thinks Evers has simply fabricated or at the least embellished an event from his youth. However, Warren goes on to call into question the entire notion of *ever* perceiving truth in the personal past. Still, he does suggest that the fiction created in recollection, while not factual, nonetheless may contain a truth that did not necessarily inhere within the facts themselves. If this is the case, the balance of power in the construction of self shifts decidedly away from the "facts" of the self's life and toward the fictions the self creates. Significantly, Warren's suspicions about the patness of Evers' anecdote may just as well be raised regarding his own representation in written texts and in interviews of his early views on race and the writing of "The Briar Patch."[18] In any case, his comments here call to mind the last section of "Tale of Time," where he concludes that the past is as "unpredictable" as the future. While these ideas exist in a nascent form in *Who Speaks for the Negro?*, we can see in this text that Warren is beginning to entertain new assumptions regarding the nature of the self, assumptions he will explore in a more radical manner through his autobiographical poetry.[19]

In *Who Speaks for the Negro?* some of the most interesting and pro-
vocative comments on these issues occur during Warren's interview with
James Baldwin.[20] Warren begins his section on Baldwin by subtly raising
questions about the nature and definition of the self. After pointing out
that Baldwin has been labeled a "voice" for a variety of groups, attitudes,
and phenomena, he goes on: "He has not been called the one thing he
really . . . is: *the voice of himself*. What is that self?" (*WSN* 277). Warren
first answers this question by listing in a brief biographical sketch the
main facts of Baldwin's life. However, he immediately dismisses the sig-
nificance of these strictly objective details:

> So much for the objective version of the career. But Baldwin has
> written that "the interior life is a real life," and the interior life, with
> no shadowy screen of fiction or sociological analysis, is sometimes
> presented almost nakedly and painfully. (*WSN* 278)

The distinction Warren draws here between the objective, factual life and
the "interior life" develops the questions he had raised regarding Charles
Evers's anecdote. Interestingly, by the end of his section on Baldwin, War-
ren will argue that the "interior life" that forms the basis of self is itself a
fiction.

Critics have contended that it is obvious from his counterpointing in
chapter 4 of Baldwin and Ralph Ellison that Warren prefers the views of
Ellison to those of Baldwin, just as he prefers King to Malcolm X in chap-
ter 3.[21] However, this tendency to view Baldwin simply as a foil for Ellison
has prevented critics from seeing the way in which Warren's comments
on Baldwin actually inform his own aesthetic preferences. Warren clearly
respects Baldwin and seems genuinely intrigued by what he sees as the
dilemmas and contradictions in Baldwin's various comments and opin-
ions. Near the end of his section on Baldwin, Warren recalls how an earlier
interviewee, Wyatt Tee Walker, disagreed with a statement of Baldwin's
that Warren had recalled. Walker responded, "James Baldwin can speak
for James Baldwin . . . but that does not make him the architect of expres-
sion for the Negro community" (*WSN* 296). To this assessment Warren
offers a rebuttal of sorts:

> Walker is right, in one perspective. But he is wrong if he thinks that
> the fact that Baldwin speaks for himself is a limitation. It is, rather,
> the source of Baldwin's power. Whatever is vague, blurred, or self-

contradictory in his utterances somehow testifies to the magisterial
authenticity of the utterance—it is the dramatic image of a man
struggling to make sense of the relation of personal tensions to the
tensions of the race issue. In his various shiftings of ground in treat-
ing the race issue he merely dramatizes the fact that the race issue
does permeate all things, all levels; and in the constantly presented
drama of the interpretation of his personal story with the race issue
he gives the issue a frightening—and fascinating—immediacy. It is
his story we finally listen to, in all its complexity of precise and
shocking image, and shadowy allusiveness. (*WSN* 296)

Blurred, contradictory, shifting, complex, and shadowy: these are the sorts
of terms Warren now uses to describe the self as it actually exists. Accord-
ing to his current perspective, the self is indeed fragmentary, and our be-
lief in a stable, integrated self is an illusion, a necessary fictional construct.
We can also see in this passage that Warren still values the role of subjec-
tivity in art, confirming the views expressed in "Knowledge and the Im-
age of Man" a decade earlier.

From here, Warren goes on to compare Baldwin's subjective art with
Faulkner's objective art. Tellingly, Warren seems to believe that Baldwin's
subjectivity is more powerful and effective. However, he begins by argu-
ing that the two are, in at least one sense, very similar, as

both are concerned with "truth" as lived, are concerned with the den-
sity of experience and the inevitable paradoxicality of feeling, with
the shifting depth of being. Both are willing to recognize the tearing
self-division that may be implicit in experience, to recognize that the
logic of experience is multiphase and contradictory; and are yet will-
ing to submit themselves, without reservation, to this risk of experi-
ence. (*WSN* 296–97)

But this is where the similarity ends. According to Warren, Faulkner exer-
cises this drama of self-division objectively in his fictions, while Baldwin
exhibits it subjectively—clearly running the greater risk. Since "Faulkner
remains taciturn, enigmatic, sealed, his reality absorbed into the objective
thing created," his occasional personal comments on race seem "thin, or
contradictory" (*WSN* 297). In contrast, Warren lauds Baldwin for his
greater subjectivity and authenticity. However, in a particularly revealing
moment, he claims that this, too, is a form of fiction:

The drama in which Baldwin seeks his knowledge is, on the contrary, subjective. When we mention the name Baldwin, there is no parade of characters speaking and gesticulating as they swing across the mind, the fictions created. What appears is the face of James Baldwin, a fiction too, for what Baldwin has most powerfully created is a self. That is his rare and difficult work of art. (*WSN* 297)

This then, is the view of the self that emerges in *Who Speaks for the Negro?* and will come to inform Warren's poetry of the period to follow: the self is naturally and essentially fragmented, and the order we create as an integrated, developing self is a fiction created through language. Warren here investigates these issues objectively through the figure of James Baldwin, but through his subjective, autobiographical poetry he will begin to wrestle with the more radical implications of these newly articulated assumptions. Indeed, Warren's adopted subjectivity in his poetry leads him quite naturally to confront the vexed and elusive relationships among self, language, and reality.

As mentioned above, critics have contended that Warren prefers Ellison's aesthetic to that of Baldwin, for Ellison, according to Warren, has found the "*basic unity of human experience*" (*WSN* 351, emphasis in original). But I believe that Warren's allegiance is perhaps more torn between these two writers. In fact, the tension or division between Baldwin and Ellison serves as something of a metaphor for Warren's altering thematic interests and aesthetic principles. Warren still posits a unity of human experience, as his comments on Ellison make clear, but this is not some form of typical, universalist assumption. Instead, he is careful to guard against such an interpretation, pointing out that Ellison's view of the American experience insists on "diversity and a pluralistic society" (*WSN* 351). Interestingly, Warren in *Who Speaks for the Negro?* actually forecasts the central point of debate for the "culture wars" that are currently taking place in America, asking at one point, "Are we to think of a culture in a unitary or a pluralistic way?" (415). Warren never explicitly answers this question, perhaps because he seems to want it both ways. He certainly wants it both ways in terms of his aesthetic approach, lauding on the one hand Baldwin's subjectivity and his authentic portrait of the self's contradiction and complexity, and on the other hand Ellison's vision of a "basic unity of human experience." In the end, perhaps the unity of human experience Warren sees *is* that of self-division. In other words, the one thing that we all have in common and that thus binds us is this internal fragmentation, along with our individual attempts to construct a unified and integrated version of the self through language. But as I have attempted to illustrate above, Warren now accepts that such a version of the self is a fiction. For Warren, to be a responsible moral agent requires that we willingly and continually confront these stark limitations of self and language, an agenda he pursues to great effect in his poetry of the years to follow.

Reinterpreting the Personal Past

Race in Warren's Later Poetry

The past must be studied, worked at—in short, created. For the past, like the present, is fluid. . . . There is no absolute, positive past available to us, no matter how rigorously we strive to determine it—as strive we must. Inevitably, the past, so far as we know it, is an inference, a creation, and this, without being paradoxical, can be said to be its chief value for us. In creating the image of the past, we create ourselves, and without the task of creating the past we might be said scarcely to exist. Without it, we sink to the level of protoplasmic swarm.

Robert Penn Warren, "The Use of the Past"

When one considers the scope of Robert Penn Warren's writings on race—writings that include every genre and span every decade of his career—what may appear most striking is the fact that he kept returning to the subject well after his published conversion to an integrationist position in *Segregation: The Inner Conflict in the South*. In light of his early segregationist position, one can read *Segregation* as a public attempt to correct a mistake of the past and perhaps assuage some personal guilt. However, if this was Warren's purpose, there would be no need to return to the subject again. In *Who Speaks for the Negro?* we can sense that Warren genuinely set out to gain a deeper understanding of the civil rights movement as well as a deeper knowledge of himself. Race, for Warren, served as a testing ground for his own changing assumptions on issues such as self, identity, politics, and aesthetics; it also provided an index for measuring and understanding these changes. To get a sense of how much Warren's views on race changed—of how he developed a sense of the issue's deeper complexities—one need only compare his early poems "Pondy Woods" and "Tryst on Vinegar Hill" with late poems such as "Ballad of Mister Dutcher and the Last Lynching in Gupton" and "News Photo." But in addition to revealing Warren's changing attitudes on race, his poems addressing racial subjects can also reveal the complexity of his poetry's changing assumptions and themes. This is especially true in poems where Warren addresses racial subjects through a personal, autobiographical voice. "Ballad of Mister Dutcher" and "News Photo" are told through a more objective voice, and while they readily reveal his changing views on race, more seems to be at stake when Warren confronts race through a more personal voice. For when he does, he is not only confronting his own past views on race, he is also confronting the subtle complexities of the autobiographical act.

As Warren turned to a more personal voice at the midpoint of his career in the 1950s with *Brother to Dragons* and *Promises,* the facts of his past increasingly became the fodder for his poetry. As he explained in an interview, his late poems are "really autobiographical—things that really happened" (Watkins et al. 332). Elsewhere, however, he qualifies this statement by explaining that while in his late poetry he is "drawing more and more on memory," it is "Memory reinterpreted of course; not memory literally taken" (Watkins et al. 372). While Warren contemplated the nuances and complexities of memory throughout his canon, his late poetry increasingly foregrounds the view that truth cannot be discovered from historical facts—that even our memories are *interpretations* of factual events, not the events themselves. And this shift in emphasis in turn alters the way we define the self. In a similar fashion, contemporary critics such as Paul de Man, James Olney, and Paul John Eakin, who have attempted to theorize the autobiographical act in literature, have become increasingly doubtful about the significance of the factual events we believe constitute the "truth" of an individual's existence; instead, these critics and others have argued that the construction of meaning in an individual's life *necessarily* involves the forfeiture of historical accuracy. As Elaine M. Kauvar concisely explains,

> To make . . . facts meaningful . . . is to sacrifice accuracy for the narrative aspects of an interpretation. From that perspective, memories are not factual events; . . . . the process of recollection is itself a mental construction and selfhood is a product of invention, language [being] the agent for fashioning a self. It follows that authentic truth can be found only in narrative; for only in fiction do writers report with precision on what takes place in their imaginations, . . . fantasies are given the free rein necessary to recount the psychical reality that constitutes genuine selfhood. (413)

Considering his comments in the epigraph to this chapter, Warren would seem to concur with such an assessment. Similarly, in explaining that his 1980 volume *Being Here* is a "shadowy autobiography. . . . a fusion of fiction and fact," he concludes that "fiction may often be more deeply significant than fact. Indeed, it may be said that our lives are our own supreme fiction" (*CP* 441). This statement clearly echoes and extends Wallace Stevens's claim that poetry is the supreme fiction, but critics have failed to acknowledge or even consider the more radical implications of Warren's equating of life with fiction.

These perplexing issues in Warren's poetry become especially interesting and powerful when he considers from a confessional perspective the most controversial aspect of his career as a writer: his early association with the Agrarian group and the racist, pro-segregation argument of his 1930 essay "The Briar Patch." The often startling implications of Warren's confessional voice in his late poems on race have been overlooked by critics, and I would like to examine three poems that show Warren struggling in various ways with the fact of his own past views on race: the "Internal Injuries" sequence from the 1968 volume *Incarnations: Poems 1966–1968*; "Forever O'Clock," first published in the 1974 volume *Or Else: Poem / Poems 1968–1974*; and "Old Nigger on One-Mule Cart Encountered Late at Night When Driving Home from Party in the Back Country," from *Selected Poems: 1923–1975*. All three of these poems were written many years after Warren had publicly repudiated his pro-segregation position and adopted a more liberal stance on race, but the fact that he keeps returning through his poetry to the subject of race suggests the extent to which he felt uncertainty, anxiety, and guilt over the implications of his earlier beliefs. To his credit, Warren refused to simply evade the past through silence as Paul de Man did; instead, like the Ancient Mariner who must relive the guilt of his crime whenever he repeats his tale, Warren felt compelled to confront the specter of his early views on race over and over again. Interestingly, each of these poems seems to reach a different conclusion regarding the relationship between the facts of the past and an individual's constructed sense of self. In "Internal Injuries" Warren essentially undermines the strategy of development by exposing the potential abuses of self-serving and self-constructed developmental narratives. Development in this poem becomes little more than an artificial means to escape the awful reality of the self's transgressions and failings. In contrast, "Forever O'Clock" and "Old Nigger on One-Mule Cart" together illustrate that the self's construction of personal narratives is necessary and can lead to meaningful forms of self-knowledge and self-actualization. In "Forever O'Clock" Warren presents a narrator who is reluctant to truly consider the full implications of this past, and consequently the poem lacks a clear sense of closure; it seems locked in a moment of stasis. On the other hand, "Old Nigger on One-Mule Cart" presents something of a penitential conversion narrative. Here Warren more directly confronts the past, reinterpreting it with narrative meaning and projecting himself into a vision of the future. Like Heidegger, Warren seems to believe that in "retrieving" or "presencing" the past, we may uncover lost possibilities and thereby construct meaningful visions of the future.[1] As Warren himself explains in "I Am Dreaming of a White Christmas: The Natural History of a Vision," another poem of 1974, "This / Is the process whereby pain of the past in its pastness / May be converted into the future tense // Of joy" (CP 281). But at the same time, Warren in "Old Nigger on One-Mule Cart" acknowledges that such narratives are indeed self-constructed fictions and that self-knowledge is created rather than discovered. In short, he illustrates the need for these strategies of self-invention and incorporates them in his own poetry, even as he shows that these same strategies result in fictions that must be constantly interrogated. Taken together, then, these three poems show Warren confronting a veritable conundrum of self-representation as he foregrounds the inherent, necessary tension between the facts of the past and the desire to create meaningful, narrative interpretations of the self.

Warren's "Internal Injuries" sequence from Incarnations is certainly among his most disturbing poems, and it is also one of his most frequently misunderstood. The situation of the poem is this: An old African-American woman has been struck by a car in the street outside Penn Station in New York city. She lies bleeding and screaming in the street, and the narrator, sitting in a taxicab stuck in the resulting traffic tie-up, becomes a reluctant witness to her suffering. Critics have tended to approach this poem by focusing on the figure of the woman who is the victim of the accident, but I believe the poem actually centers on the narrator's varied responses to the woman. Indeed, "Internal Injuries" is a disturbing psychological study of the effects of racism on one who perpetuates it. In this sense, the title refers not so much to the physical trauma suffered by the woman as to the psychological trauma suffered by the poem's narrator at the knowledge of his own inhumanity. And this raises an important question regarding how we approach this poem: To what extent is this poem "confessional" or autobiographical? Is the incident here described drawn specifically from Warren's own life, representing something that "really happened"? Or is it perhaps symbolically representing a recollected state of mind or way of thinking? Critics are generally eager to draw links between Warren and the personae of his late poems,[2] but what about a sequence such as "Internal Injuries"? Can this be located in Warren's past, either literally or metaphorically? As I will illustrate below in my discussion of "Old Nigger on One-Mule Cart," Warren's blurring of the line between fact and fiction may ultimately make this a moot issue.

The "Internal Injuries" sequence opens with a disturbingly callous response on the part of the narrator. Perhaps seeking to distance himself from the reality of the woman's suffering, he responds through a series of racial epithets and stereotypes:

> *Nigger:* as if it were not
> Enough to be old, and a woman, to be
> Poor, having a sizeable hole (as
> I can plainly see, you being flat on the ground) in
> The sole of a shoe (the right one), enough to be
>
> Alone (your daughter off in
> Detroit, in three years no letter, your son
> Upriver, at least now you know
> Where he is, and no friends), enough to be
>
> Fired (as you have just today
> Been, and unfair to boot, for
> That durn Jew-lady—there wasn't no way
> To know it was you that opened that there durn
> Purse, just picking on you on account of
> Your complexion) (*CP* 242)

Hugh Ruppersburg contends that this woman is "the unluckiest of the unlucky: she is black, old, female, and alone. . . . Moreover, she has just been fired from her job." He goes on to conclude that she represents the "ultimate social outcast, the prime urban *misérable*" (108). What Ruppersburg fails to recognize is that the details upon which he is making this interpretation have no basis in reality. Instead, all of the information regarding the woman's life has been created in the narrator's mind, formed from negative racial stereotypes. Warren italicizes the word "Nigger" in order to draw the reader's attention to the immense, alienating power of this signifier. What follows is a chain of signification that, almost like a natural chemical reaction, crystallizes in the narrator's mind: the woman is black; therefore she *must* be a thief, *must* come from a dysfunctional family, *must* have a son in the state penitentiary. All of these assumptions emerge from and cling to the one signifier "*Nigger.*" This is an extremely important, though generally overlooked, aspect of the poem.[3] The narrator has fabricated for this woman an identity and a history that separate his life and experience from hers. She is denied her own existence and reality, becoming instead a figment of the narrator's imagination.

As the opening poem concludes, the narrator's tone shifts as he tries to imagine the woman contemplating the details of her current situation:

Merely to be—Jesus,
Wouldn't just *being* be enough without
Having to have the pee (quite
Literally) knocked out of
You by a 1957 yellow Cadillac driven by
A spic, and him
From New Jersey?

Why couldn't it of at least been a white man? (*CP* 242)

The narrator imagines that insult has been added to injury: she's been struck not by a white New Yorker but by a New Jersey "spic." He imagines that the woman feels she deserves better. This crude attempt at humor may be seen as another ploy to distance himself from the woman's suffering, but considering the context of the situation it is a particularly troubling reaction. An early typescript draft of the sequence among the Robert Penn Warren Papers contains an additional poem which may have been another attempt at humor: a parody of Blake's poem "The Tyger" titled "Nigger, Nigger, Burning Bright."[4] Happily, Warren chose not to include it in the published sequence.

Whether relying on racist stereotypes or base humor, the narrator's efforts to suppress from his mind the reality of the woman's pain and suffering are ultimately useless. He is stuck in traffic, and her screams, which are as "regular / As a metronome," cannot be blocked out (*CP* 243). Frustrated by his momentary loss of autonomy, he desires an escape. He first feebly attempts to let his mind wander away from the scene, asking himself, "How long since last I heard birdsong in the flowery hedgerows of France?" (*CP* 245). But before he can continue the thought, he senses the woman's gaze upon him:

Just now, when I looked at you, I had the distinct impression that
    you were staring me straight in the eye, and
Who wants to be a piece of white paper filed for eternity on the
    sharp point of a filing spindle?
. . .
Nobody wants to be a piece of white paper filed in the dark on the
    point of a black-enameled spindle forever (*CP* 245).

This moment in the poem is reminiscent of the repeated scenes from
Brother to Dragons in which white characters interpret the black gaze as a
sign of rebuke for their own complicity in racial injustice. Unlike Lacan's
concept of the gaze—through which a subject imagines itself to be an
integrated, holistic self—Warren's image of the black gaze is an accusa-
tion which exposes disturbing cracks and fissures in the speaker's facade
of propriety: "I, // . . . / Am no Peeping Tom with my // Own face pressed
directly to the / Window of your pain" (*CP* 243). Perhaps growing un-
comfortable with his own responses to the woman's suffering, the nar-
rator's desire for escape intensifies:

I must hurry, I must go somewhere
Where you are not, where you
Will never be, I
Must go somewhere where
Nothing is real, for only
Nothingness is real and is
A sea of light.
. . .

                —Oh driver!
For God's sake catch that light, for

There comes a time for us all when we want to begin a new life.

All mythologies recognize that fact. (*CP* 246)

Victor Strandberg has pointed out that the narrator is here "rationalizing
his flight reflex" (*Poetic Vision* 104), but what exactly does Warren mean
by saying that "all mythologies" recognize this need to be born again? In
many ways, the Romantic strategy of development that Warren adopted
in his poetry promises just this sort of new life which the narrator so
desperately desires. Romantic development has the potential to free us
from the past through its promise of something evermore about to be.

Moreover, Warren often equated poetry with myth, which raises the interesting possibility that in this poem he is somehow commenting upon the validity of his own art form, pointing out the potential pitfalls and shortcomings of this Romantic promise of development. In the case of this narrator, these "mythologies" of rebirth and renewal are portrayed as little more than convenient escapes from the pressures of reality; they are reduced to tenuous, self-constructed methods for evading truth.

But the poem's final section illustrates the dubious nature of this self-constructed form of escapism, for even as the narrator is making his getaway, reality continues to impinge upon him and he is forced to confront, at least momentarily, the horror of his own inner nature:

> Driver, driver, hurry now—
> Yes, driver, listen now, I
> Must change the address, I want to go to
>
> A place where nothing is the same.
> My guts are full of chyme and chyle, of Time and bile, my head
> Of visions
> . . .
> The traffic begins to move, and that fool ambulance at last,
>
> Screaming, screaming, now arrives.
> Jack-hammers are trying, trying they
> Are trying to tell me something, they speak in code.
> . . .
>   my head is full of
> The code, like Truth or a migraine, and those men in orange hel-
>   mets,
>
> They must know it, they must know,
> . . .
>   must know the message, know the secret names and all the
>   slithery functions of
>
> All those fat slick slimy things that
> Are so like a tub full of those things you
> Would find in a vat in the back room of a butcher shop, but
>   wouldn't eat, but
>
> Are not that, for they are you.
> Driver, do you truly, truly,

Know what flesh is, and if it is, as some people say, really sacred?

Driver, there's an awful glitter in the air. What is the weather fore-
cast? (*CP* 246–47)

This is perhaps one of the most disturbing moments in Warren's poetry,
both for the imagery used to convey the narrator's sense of self and for
the manner in which the narrator attempts to segue to another subject
after this brief and ugly moment of self-awareness. His ability to change
the subject in such a superficial manner hints that perhaps this strategy of
escape works for him after all and he will be able to forget the incident.

In contrast, Warren's 1974 poem "Forever O'Clock" illustrates the
axiom that the past may never be left behind, or, as he elsewhere puts it,
"nothing is ever lost." Warren in this poem portrays a moment at which
he appears unwilling to truly confront his past in all its implications; sig-
nificantly, the poem clearly indicates that the past he is concerned with is
his Agrarian defense of segregation. The poem's autobiographical basis is
actually much clearer than in "Internal Injuries," particularly when we
consider Warren's own explanation of the poem, which I will discuss be-
low. In the first, brief section, the narrator describes a clock that "is getting
ready to strike forever o'clock," but the sound the clock makes is "purely
metaphysical," a sound "you hear in your bloodstream and not your ear"
(*CP* 288).

The poem shifts abruptly with its long second section. As the narrator
waits for the clock to strike, he has time to think of what he portrays as a
meaningless image from his memory, though for the reader it is clear that
the memory is anything but meaningless, particularly since the narrator
goes into such minute detail in describing it:

The clock is taking time to make up its mind and that is why I have
    time
To think of some things that are not important but simply are.

A little two-year-old Negro girl-baby, with hair tied up in spindly
    little tits with strings of red rag,
Sits in the red dust. Except for some kind of rag around her middle,
    she is naked, and black as a ripe plum in the sunshine.

Behind the child is a gray board shack, and from the mud-chimney
    a twist of blue smoke is motionless against the blue sky.
The fields go on forever, and whatever had been planted there is
    not there now. The drouth does not see fit to stop even now.

The pin-oak in the yard has been dead for years. The boughs are
    black stubs against the blue sky.
Nothing alive is here but the child and a dominecker hen, flattened
    puff-belly down, under the non-shade of the pin-oak.

Inside the gray feathers, the body of the hen pants with the heat.
The yellow beak of the hen is open, and the flattened string-thin
    tongue looks black and dry and sharp as a pin.

The naked child with plum-black skin is intensely occupied.
From a rusted tin snuff can in the right hand, the child pours red
    dust over the spread fingers of the left hand held out prone in
    the bright air.

The child stares at the slow-falling red dust. Some red dust piles
    precariously up on the back of the little black fingers thrust out.
    Some does not.
The sun blazes down on the naked child in the mathematical center
    of the world. The sky glitters like brass.

A beat-up old 1931 Studebaker, of a kind you are too young ever to
    have seen, has recently passed down the dirt road, and a plume
    of red dust now trails it toward the horizon.
I watch the car that I know I am the man driving as it recedes into
    distance and approaches the horizon. (*CP* 289)

This second section begins with what seems to be the makings of a quaint,
picturesque pastoral scene of the South. One may be reminded of the
grandmother from Flannery O'Connor's "A Good Man Is Hard to Find"
who, upon witnessing such a scene, delightedly exclaims, "Oh look at the
cute little pickaninny! . . . Wouldn't that make a picture, now?" (12). But
the accumulating details quickly force any such sentimental notion to col-
lapse under their weight. The scene as it is described presents a disturbing
contrast to Warren's idyllic portrayal in "The Briar Patch" of the life and
opportunities available for African-Americans living in the rural South.
There, he had determined that the "Southern Negro" is "a creature of the
small town and farm . . . who is likely to find in agricultural and domestic
pursuits the happiness that his good nature and easy ways incline him to
as an ordinary function of his being" (260–61). This poem presents the
dismal reality blacks faced in the rural South, a reality Warren evaded in
his "Briar Patch" essay. But this is a reality that the narrator in retrospect

cannot deny: the stark images of the child in poverty loom up from his memory and become the "mathematical center" of the world. With this line, the remembered image from the past effectively displaces the narrator's sense of self.

As if to emphasize the autobiographical reference to his 1930 "Briar Patch" essay, Warren concludes the poem's second section by shifting his focus to the 1931 Studebaker that has just driven by the scene, which he of course is driving. Warren implicates himself within the stark landscape and all it represents; one can even imagine the dust plume trailing from his car sifting its minute particles down over the figure of the little girl. While the narrator has suggested that this memory is "not important," it is apparent to the reader that it is important to him, for the long second section which describes the memory of the child in excruciating detail dominates the poem.

Warren in interviews and in his prose offered a series of confessions, apologies, and rationalizations for his early stance on segregation, and his comments were at times perplexing or even contradictory. One may recall, for instance, his claim in *Who Speaks for the Negro?* that even while he was writing "The Briar Patch" he "uncomfortably suspected . . . that no segregation was, in the end, humane" (12). While his various explanations at times may seem evasive, the extent of Warren's sense of guilt and anxiety over his early views can be acutely felt in his poetic texts. Indeed, it is the contradiction and conflict within Warren's writings on race that make them seem an authentic portrayal of individual struggle and change. In the brief final section of "Forever O'Clock," the narrator again attempts to claim that the memory is "not important"; despite this claim, he seems on the verge of a painful realization. As he wonders if the car will ever reach the horizon, he confesses: "The wondering throbs like a bruise inside my head. / Perhaps it throbs because I do not want to know the answer to my wondering" (*CP* 289). The narrator appears reluctant to face the fact of his past in all its implications, and as a result the poem lacks a clear sense of closure, for in refusing to face the fact of the past, he refuses to face the possibility of the future as well. The narrator seems stuck in time, and in the poem's last line we are informed that the clock still has not struck.

Warren's own comments explaining this poem suggest the inherent tension that exists between the facts of our past and our desire to construct meaning from that past. The Robert Penn Warren Papers at Yale include a particularly revealing exchange of letters from 1973 between

Warren and Howard Moss, who at the time was poetry editor at *The New Yorker*. Warren originally submitted the poem to *The New Yorker*, but while Moss in a letter of October 5 described the poem as powerful, he also expressed confusion over what it meant in the end. At one point, Moss pointedly asked if the poem was about a white Southerner's guilt over his ability to flee the South while a poor black child cannot. Warren responded to Moss's queries with a two-page, single-spaced typewritten letter dated October 10. He begins his long explanation of the poem with this overview, which includes a peculiarly interesting aside in which Warren seems exasperated by the word "identity":

> The poem is, in the most general way, about time, or rather, about kinds of time and their relations and about identity (how I loathe that word now!) Involved in this background (and in the poem) is the notion of two kinds of memory—or two views of time. The first kind of "sequential," the second "archetypal." (I don't mean this to have any connection with Jung, just my special label.) (RPW Papers)

Warren goes on to explain that sequential memory is the manner in which we reconstruct chronologies and locate the events of our lives as they actually happened in time: "In sequential meaning we see, of course, a long flow leading to the present moment and the present self." That is, Warren's sequential time corresponds with our objective concept of clock time. In contrast, Warren's concept of archetypal memory exists outside of time and outside of sequence; in short, it is the meaning-making form of memory, that which assigns personal significance to the object, person, or scene recollected. Importantly, Warren suggests that an intrinsic tension exists between sequential and archetypal memory, between the facts of the past and the desire to create meaningful interpretations of those facts. Consider, for example, these comments on archetypal memory:

> Archetypal memory is the kind involved when, for instance, I say, "I remember my mother"—or whoever. I don't see a story. I see a face, for instance, in some characteristic way, a characteristic expression, at a characteristic time (do I see the face as young or old?), a way that summarizes, is typical of, the meaning, for me, of the person remembered. (Or place or whatever.) This image is not in time, in sequence. And our sense of the past exists in fact in a peculiar tension between sequential memory and archetypal memory—and this tension, I should say, represents the essential quality of experience. For in-

stance, to turn to the poem, the "meaning" of the old green Stude-
baker moving through a certain landscape with me at the wheel (age
26 or 27) is sequential. The "I" of that moment is moving toward the
"I" of the time of the writing of the poem. And this raises a complex
of feelings for the writer of the poem.

Interestingly enough, Warren in this letter to Moss suggests that his
"complex of feelings" did not include the issues of race or the South. In
response to Moss's suggestion that the poem seemed to be about a white
Southerner's guilty conscience, Warren cagily offers a parenthetical aside:
"(I'll stop here to say that neither "the South," nor "race" necessarily
enters in the matter. The image might well have been of an old decrepit
white man by a cabin door in the mountains of Wyoming. Just, I happen
to be me.)" As is often the case when he is asked a direct and personal
question on the importance of race in his work, Warren seems to hedge in
his response. But on second thought, perhaps he is not hedging after all,
for while he contends that race is not necessary to the poem's meaning,
his admission that "I happen to be me" makes race necessary to *his* mean-
ing—in other words, to his constructed sense of self. Warren's explanation
to Moss of how the image of the black baby functions in the poem would
seem to confirm this possibility. He describes the way an archetypal
memory, "detached from all context, [begins] to assume a 'meaning' that
exists in a void, to become portentous in a mysterious fashion, to have an
immanence of identity unspecified." Warren in "Forever O'Clock" cap-
tures this particular moment of mystery, uncertainty, and portentousness
in which a memory seems to have "an immanence of identity unspeci-
fied." But since the identity or "meaning" has not been specified, the nar-
rator cannot move forward in time; at the end of the poem, the clock is still
waiting to strike.

Like "Forever O'Clock," Warren's 1975 poem "Old Nigger on One-
Mule Cart" illustrates the inherent tension between the facts of the past
and meaningful narrative interpretations, or the tension Warren describes
between sequential and archetypal memory. But it also offers significant
points of contrast, for here Warren does specify the significance of the
portentous memory, and consequently he is able to construct a meaning-
ful vision of the future. Moreover, while he contended that race was not
necessary to the meaning of "Forever O'Clock," Warren in this poem
foregrounds race in an undeniable way. Interestingly, the poem also sug-
gests the parallel manner in which his views on race and his views on

poetry changed. Nowhere are the dilemmas of Warren's adopted subjectivity clearer than in "Old Nigger on One-Mule Cart." The poem is a two-part narrative focusing on a distant memory of a brief encounter the younger Warren had with a black man hauling a cart of junk down a dirt road at night; Warren in interviews has emphasized the authenticity of the poem's recollection, claiming that the incident described in the poem "really happened" (Watkins et al. 332). However, a closer look at the poem, along with evidence from the Robert Penn Warren Papers, shows that the poem is in fact an exercise in self-invention; Warren privileges fiction over fact as he rewrites and reinterprets an event from his past in order to offer a retrospective narrative of his changing views on race—and poetry. While the narrated incident foregrounds the issue of race, the poem is also very much about the act of writing poetry—and the self.

The poem first focuses on the remembered incident from the narrator's distant past: while driving home drunk from a party, he narrowly avoids a deadly collision with the black man and his junk cart. Even though the narrator is driving "too fast" and under the influence, he blames the near collision on the black man:

> At the sharp right turn,
> Hedge-blind, which you take too fast,
> There it is: death-trap.
>
> On the fool-nigger, ass-hole wrong side of
> The road, naturally. (*CP* 333)

The narrator's response to the situation is guided automatically by racist stereotypes. He assumes that the black man, "naturally," must be at fault; ironically, he admits to driving drunk and to taking the turn too fast. Later that same night, the narrator wakes from a fitful sleep and imagines the black man's face hovering over him, a vision that strangely enough prompts him to attempt a sonnet; tellingly, even this vision that floats up from his unconscious calls to mind the degrading images of the blackface minstrel shows:

> I wake to see
> Floating in darkness above the bed the
> Black face, eyes white-bulging, mouth shaped like an *O*, and so
> Get up, get paper and pencil, and whittle away at
> The poem. Give up. Back to bed. And remember
> Now only the couplet of what

Had aimed to be—Jesus Christ—a sonnet:
> One of those who gather junk and wire to use
> For purposes that we cannot peruse.

As I said, Jesus Christ. (*CP* 334)

It is the recollection of this disastrous couplet from his failed attempt at a poem that suddenly shifts the scene back to the present moment—and the completed poem, which in form is the antithesis of a sonnet—where the aging narrator has again awakened in the middle of the night. It is significant to note that the sonnet Warren here describes has been discovered by John Burt among the Robert Penn Warren Papers at Yale, and it appears to have been written during the ten-year hiatus when Warren published no new poems. The existence of the sonnet would seem to support Warren's claim of authentic referentiality—that the incident described in the poem "really happened." Moreover, Warren's recollection of the closing couplet is accurate. Warren recalls the couplet as, "One of those who gather junk and wire to use / For purposes that we cannot peruse." The original version among the Robert Penn Warren Papers reads, "One of the poor with a cart of junk to use / For purposes which we cannot peruse" (*CP* 813). On the surface, then, it would appear that Warren is accurately recalling and representing a verifiable fact from his past.

However, there is no indication in the original sonnet that the old man is black, and this absence raises interesting questions regarding Warren's view of the autobiographical act in his poetry. In particular, the fact that the original poem does not distinguish the man as black—let alone as either an "ass-hole" or a "nigger"—brings to mind at least two possible scenarios, both of which suggest the extent to which Warren's extended dialogue with race affected him as an individual and as a poet. First, the old man from the real-life incident may have been white and, as the original line suggests, poor. If this is the case, the earlier sonnet would have been, to some degree, about class differences. Warren's revising of the poem's scenario would then constitute an effort to better represent his early, racist views. This in turn would suggest the extent to which Warren came to view the issue of race as a determining factor in his career as a writer, for "Old Nigger on One Mule Cart" is in many ways a poem about writing poetry. The second possibility is that the man in the real-life incident was indeed black. This would imply that at the time Warren wrote the poem, race was not the central issue it eventually became for him. As he reattempts the poem many years later—in a very different form—the issue of race is placed squarely in the foreground of the poem. In either case, the poem becomes an exercise in self-invention, as Warren privileges fiction over fact, rewriting an event from his past in order to offer a retrospective narrative of the self's growth and development, one that relates Warren's parallel conversion experiences on race and poetry.

In the second half of the poem, the scene suddenly shifts forward many years to the present. The aging narrator is awake in the middle of the night, looking out over a wintry, mountainous landscape under stars. Confronted by the permanence of this natural setting, he contemplates the flux and uncertainty of his own life, asking,

> In the lyrical logic and nightmare astuteness that
> Is God's name, by what magnet, I demand,
> Are the iron and out-flung filings of our lives, on
> A sheet of paper, blind-blank as Time, snapped
> Into a polarized pattern—and I see,
> By a bare field that yearns pale in starlight, the askew
> Shack. He arrives there. (CP 335)

Almost as an answer to his question, the image of the black man comes to his mind; in his imagination he sees the old man arriving home to an unlit shack in the middle of the night. The black man, however, is no longer simply a racist stereotype; the narrator, humbled by his own past transgressions, addresses the reconstructed image of the old black man, asking,

> Brother, Rebuker, my Philosopher past all
> Casuistry, will you be with me when
> I arrive and leave my own cart of junk
> Unfended from the storm of starlight and
> The howl, like wind, of the world's monstrous blessedness,
> To enter, by a bare field, a shack unlit?
> Entering into that darkness to fumble
> My way to a place to lie down, but holding,
> I trust, in my hand, a name—
> Like a shell, a dry flower, a worn stone, a toy—merely
> A hard-won something that may, while Time
> Backward unblooms out of time toward peace, utter
> Its small, sober, and inestimable
> Glow, trophy of truth.
>
> Can I see Arcturus from where I stand? (CP 335)

The narrator here confronts the past and seems genuinely humbled by it. Bringing forth this image of the past, he transforms it into a vision of the future in which, like the black man, he enters his own unlit shack with a "hard-won something." This moment of identification, which borders on the sentimental, seems to lead to self-knowledge, self-restoration, and self-transcendence, particularly with the narrator's final look to the stars, which echoes his vision of the black man, whom he imagines gazing at the stars. However, Warren's own explanation of the poem's ending subverts such a reading in an important and revealing way. In response to a request from Howard Moss, poetry editor of *The New Yorker*, that the poem's last line be dropped, Warren offered this explanation of the poem and its conclusion:

> The literal scene is the speaker up in the middle of the night staring out on the snowy woods and mountain and starlit sky. Stated as short-hand, and very crudely, he is trying to make sense of history, his relation to it and to the world. In the midst of this specific scene, the "old nigger" arriving home to his shack reappears in his mind and he seizes on this as an image of his common humanity, and as an image of what he may save from his load of "junk." What he may carry with him into his darkness. Now the poem may end here, and in my first version did end here. But two things set in—or rather two impulses. This original end is so long that the reader forgets that the fantasy springs from staring at the night sky and is related to that contextual fact. Second, the "limited" "down-beatish" ending I do not want felt as less than what the man is straining for in the literal scene. What I want to convey is that the small inward thing is not a half-a-loaf but the whole loaf. That the look to the bright star and the look to the inward, downward "shack" grave, etc. are the same. The small must fuse with the big, the downward . . . look with the lifting of the eyes outward, upward.[5]

Significantly, Warren's comments on the image of the black man suggest that he came to view his own career-long struggle with the issue of race as one of the things he could salvage from his "load of 'junk.'" However, his explanation of the poem's ending undermines any sense of supernal transcendence as he is careful to emphasize death and privation ("the inward, downward 'shack' grave"). This more austere interpretation of the poem's conclusion may perhaps be understood if we consider Paul de Man's analysis of the autobiographical act in literature.

De Man argues that it is impossible for autobiographical texts to contain "reliable self-knowledge" (71). We tend to assume that autobiography is drawn from actual and verifiable events in the author's life, and that there is a clear, one-to-one correspondence between the life and the text. In other words, we believe the life *creates* the text as a natural consequence. But de Man shows that it works in just the opposite way: the conventions of the textual endeavor guide, govern, and determine the representation of the life. Moreover, the seemingly simple referential basis that forms our belief in the verity of autobiography is in fact an illusion which reveals itself as such. According to de Man,

> the specular moment is not primarily a situation or an event that can be located in a history, . . . it is the manifestation, on the level of the referent, of a linguistic structure. The specular moment that is part of all understanding reveals the tropological structure that underlies all cognitions, including the knowledge of the self. The interest of autobiography, then, is not that it reveals reliable self-knowledge—it does not—but that it demonstrates in a striking way the impossibility of closure and of totalization (that is the impossibility of coming into being) of all textual systems made up of tropological substitutions. (70–71)

We may say that this assessment of the referential instability in autobiography is confirmed in Warren's own fictionalizing of an incident that works to underscore the issue of race in a way that does not seem readily apparent in the historical evidence of that incident. Furthermore, we may say that Warren in the poem openly acknowledges that this specular image is in fact a self-constructed fiction. The poem's central image of the magnet, which throws the "iron and out-flung filings of our lives" into a definable pattern, functions as a metaphor for the autobiographical act itself. The force of this magnet is not divine providence; it is the force of the poetic, autobiographical imagination. Only in retrospect are the random dots of our experience connected into a pattern of development and growth, making autobiography a self-constructed, secularized form of providence.

As Paul John Eakin points out, with de Man's analysis, "The balance of power in the relation between self and language shifts decisively to the side of language" (189).[6] And de Man explains, "To the extent that language is figure (or metaphor, or prosopopeia) it is indeed not the thing itself but the representation, the picture of the thing and, as such, it is silent, mute as pictures are mute. Language, as trope, is always privative. . . . To the extent that, in writing, we are dependent on this language we are all . . . deaf and mute. . . eternally deprived of voice and condemned to muteness." With this displacement, we find ourselves in a "linguistic predicament," and, de Man concludes, "Death is a displaced name for a linguistic predicament" (80, 81). Warren's closing images in the poem, along with his comments to Moss, seem to concur with de Man's emphasis on silence and death: Warren imagines his name as a shell, a dry flower, a worn stone, as something that utters *not a sound but a glow*.

In "Old Nigger on One-Mule Cart," we see that the Romantic subjectivity Warren adopts creates a number of questions and dilemmas regarding the politics of self-representation. As the self becomes the primary subject of inquiry in Warren's poetry, so too does the representation of his past. And considering Warren's early views on segregation, this is no simple matter, for he at times offered conflicting interpretations on this aspect of his past. Interestingly, Warren in his later poetry willingly confronts this conundrum of self-representation and the problems it raises regarding the nature of identity and the pursuit of self-knowledge. In fact, this issue becomes one of the primary themes of his later poetry. Often in his later poems, Warren questions and undermines the tropes by which we connect the past to the present and construct narratives of growth and development. Similarly, in the "Afterthought" of his 1980 volume *Being Here*, Warren reflects on the autobiographical nature of his poetry and concludes that "our lives are our own supreme fiction" (*CP* 441). In making such a statement, Warren seems to acknowledge the hidden assumptions on which Romantic discourse is grounded, assumptions that have been exposed by critics such as Clifford Siskin and Paul de Man.

Warren's Romantic subjectivity becomes a strategy designed to question the formation of self and identity on both individual and, by extension, national levels. Warren's early, misguided views on race and segregation—largely the result of adherence to the Agrarian myth of the South—left him both conscious and wary of the seductive powers of totalizing cultural narratives, and Warren late in his career seems just as wary of the potentially self-serving functions of the Romantic concept of the self's organic development. As a result, Warren ends by invoking Romanticism with a substantial amount of skepticism; he knows and accepts that development is a self-constructed rhetorical strategy. In fact, he often employs traditional Romantic themes and methods in order to delineate Romanticism's boundaries and expose its failings. By foregrounding the limitations of his own poetry, Warren finally concludes that "true" self-knowledge is indeterminate; we can only hope that the specular image the individual makes is "a self-corrective creation" ("Knowledge and the Image of Man" 187).

Toward the Self as Fiction

Language, Time, and Identity in Warren's Poetry, 1966–1975

> You exist only in the delirious illusion of language.
>
> Robert Penn Warren, "Brotherhood in Pain"

Most critics agree that Warren entered his greatest phase as a poet with his work of the late 1960s, especially *Audubon: A Vision* and, to a lesser extent, *Incarnations*. Calvin Bedient, perhaps the most adamant admirer of Warren's late poetry, goes so far as to claim that Warren's "greatness as a writer" began with *Audubon* and a seemingly new "determination to concentrate on poetry as the extreme resource of language-knowledge, language-being." According to Bedient, "*Audubon* rose above his previous volumes like a curiously abrupt, grand escarpment, a repudiation of the scrub country of uncertain poetic purpose" (3). I agree that Warren's late poetry is his best, but what Bedient calls his Grand Last Phase did not emerge like the sudden geological accident Bedient here uses as a metaphor. Instead, the great late period of Warren's poetic career came about only after his continuous reevaluation and recasting of himself as a poet. And as I have attempted to illustrate throughout this study, his aesthetic refashioning did not take place in a vacuum. Warren was not some detached aesthete standing apart from or above the world of society and politics; rather, his evolution as a poet responded to the pressures of social and political change—which for a white Southerner of Warren's era were felt most personally and profoundly within the context of race politics.

Returning to the subject of race over and over again, Warren willingly submitted himself to these overt political pressures as a way of testing and understanding his own changing ideological, political, and aesthetic assumptions—and as a way of knowing himself. In short, Warren lived the examined life. He constantly modified his own assumptions, both political and aesthetic, and these two aspects of his being became increasingly indistinguishable as his career progressed, culminating in his 1975 book *Democracy and Poetry*, which ardently argues for poetry's relevance as both a diagnostic and a therapeutic social agent. While the question of whether Warren's politics were more responsible for his aesthetics or vice versa will always amount to a chicken-or-egg dilemma, it is still worthwhile to trace the parallel evolutions of his politics and poetry.[1] This is especially the case when we consider what Bedient terms the Grand Last Phase of Warren's poetic career. Just as Warren in the 1960s develops a more subtle and complex appreciation of the arbitrary yet real power race holds in determining identity, he also becomes more keenly aware of the intricacies of the autobiographical act as well as the limitations *and* potentials of language. These issues take on more dramatic and radical dimensions in his poetry of the late 1960s and the 1970s, as Warren offers his most pointed critique of self, identity, language, and the construction of knowledge—a critique that has political antecedents and consequences. While the view of language as a fixed and stable medium supports the construction of rigid ideologies and hierarchies, Warren increasingly sees language as a flexible medium which allows for greater personal and social change.

Between 1966 and 1975 Warren in his poetry adopts perspectives on the issue of selfhood that are more radical than critics have heretofore acknowledged, and these altering perspectives take him up to the very borders of postmodernism. Critics agree that the late Warren is a deeply philosophical poet, and they have variously described his poetic ruminations on selfhood as "tragic," "heroic," "existential," "Romantic," and "sublime."[2] But at the same time, critics have yet to consider fully the very assumptions regarding the nature of the self that Warren now expresses, assumptions that both form the basis of and inform the appealing complexity of his poetry of the period. In brief, Warren in his later poetry explores the fundamental gaps in the self, especially the gaps that necessarily arise from the self's existence in language and time. Warren now accepts the "linguistic predicament": we must rely on language to create order and understanding both of the world around us and of ourselves, yet language is an imperfect filter for reality since there is always a gap between the signifier and the signified. Language separates us from the world and even from ourselves. Warren's thematic obsession with time is inextricably linked to these views on language and further exposes and exacerbates the void between language and reality. His own conceptual categories of sequential time and archetypal time, described in chapter 9, acknowledge the inherent gaps between the facts of the past (which exist in sequential time) and the meaning-making function of personal memories (which exist in archetypal time as linguistic and narrative interpretations of those facts). Warren describes the "tension" that arises between the facts of the past and the narrative interpretations of those facts as the "essential quality" of human experience. Proceeding from these assumptions regarding language and time, Warren in his poetry shows that the self exists within a network of gaps, displacements, and absences; any sense of unity, wholeness, and presence we may perceive is in fact a fiction, nothing more than a "delirious illusion."

In addition to destabilizing our belief in an integrated, autonomous self, these thematic concerns lead to a general sense of uncertainty and instability which ultimately compromises our entire notion of truth—if by "truth" we mean some absolutely verifiable, objective, and universal truth. This does not mean that Warren does not write *of* truth and believe in the human need for truth; rather, it means that he believes that our concept of truth, a linguistic construct superimposed on reality, is always inadequate and must be continually interrogated, reshaped, and extended. Similarly, Warren views the self as a necessary fiction—a willed construction worthy of both praise and blame—which must be continually questioned, reexamined, and reconstructed. Importantly, even though he sees time and language as having a destabilizing and alienating effect on the self, Warren still believes that memory and our linguistic representations of it provide the only mediums through which a responsible moral self may be created. While language and memory are both imperfect mediums and can easily be used for self-deception and self-evasion, they nonetheless have the potential to restore and redeem the self, to organize and direct an individual toward meaningful change and responsible action.

The drastic implications of Warren's views of language are sketched out in two poems published in 1975, "Trying to Tell You Something" and "Brotherhood in Pain." These poems appear consecutively in Warren's 1975 *Selected Poems*, and together they illustrate that our sense of truth, dependent upon language, is in fact an artificial human construct which does not exist in a one-to-one relationship with reality—a fact with profound consequences on the way we define the self. "Trying to Tell You Something" opens with lines that immediately suggest the inadequacy of language to articulate the whole of reality: "All things lean at you, and some are / Trying to tell you something, though of some // The heart is too full for speech" (*CP* 330). This statement echoes Warren's earlier claim in *A Plea in Mitigation* that language does not conform to experience, but in these two poems Warren explores the more radical implications of such a premise. From these opening lines and their suggestion of language's inadequacy, Warren shifts abruptly into a long description of an ancient oak tree:

On a hill, the oak,
Immense, older than Jamestown or God, splitting

With its own weight at the great inverted
Crotch, air-spread and ice-hung, ringed with iron

Like barrel-hoops, only heavier, massive rods
Running through and bolted, and higher, the cables,

Which in summer are hidden by green leaves—the oak,
It is trying to tell you something. It wants,

In its fullness of years, to describe to you
What happens on a December night when

It stands alone in a world of snowy whiteness. (*CP* 330)

Warren's description sharply contrasts the natural world with the human world: the natural tendencies of the tree to split and fall are countered by the artificial and hopelessly human efforts to defy those tendencies. As the poem continues, Warren associates the iron hoops and cables with human truth itself—suggesting that this uniquely human concept of truth, constructed from language, is not commensurate with reality but is instead artificially imposed upon reality. Consider the way in which the cables and hoops take on an almost sinister quality as Warren continues:

It is ten below zero, and the iron
Of hoops and reinforcement rods is continuing to contract.

There is the rhythm of a slow throb, like pain. The wind,
Northwest, is steady, and in the wind, the cables,

In a thin-honed and disinfectant purity, like
A dentist's drill, sing. They sing

Of truth, and its beauty. (*CP* 330)

It is important to notice that it is the man-made cables, not the tree, that are singing of truth—and that Warren emphasizes the constrictive and unnatural quality of these hoops and cables which, like human truth, are placed artificially upon reality in an effort to contain and control it. The tree is simply "trying to tell" of its own reality, its natural being, but the cables—singing of human truth—are in fact working against this reality and not with it. As Calvin Bedient has pointed out, Warren here is revising Keats's famous dictum from "Ode on a Grecian Urn," but unlike Keats, his stance on truth and beauty is marked by a "cold-snap severity" (122). And what are the implications of such a view of human truth? How does this affect our definition of the self and the self's relationship to the world? Warren's poem ends with a note of ambiguous portent as these questions are hinted at but, for the moment, unanswered:

> The oak
> Wants to declare this to you, so that you
>
> Will not be unprepared when, some December night,
> You stand on a hill, in a world of whiteness, and
>
> Stare into the crackling absoluteness of the sky. The oak
> Wants to tell you because, at that moment,
>
> In your own head, the cables will sing
> With a thin-honed and disinfectant purity,
>
> And no one can predict the consequences. (CP 330)

The winter setting echoes other important moments of revelation in Warren's poetry. Both *Brother to Dragons* and "Old Nigger on One-Mule Cart" come to mind—and, tellingly, Warren at one point instructed his editor Albert Erskine to place this poem immediately before "Old Nigger on One-Mule Cart."[3] Certainly one can see why Warren considered placing "Trying to Tell You Something" before that poem, for these closing lines would have provided an excellent segue into both its theme and its setting, with the narrator staring out into the stars hanging over a snow-covered landscape as he tries to make sense of his past. While "Trying to Tell You Something" shows that human truth is imposed upon and constricts reality, "Old Nigger on One-Mule Cart" reveals that truth is contemplated and created only in retrospect: it is always constructed after the facts and imposed over those facts as interpretation, interpretation that may actually be at odds with the facts of the past. This may help explain the profound sense of uncertainty in the closing lines of "Trying to Tell You Something." In any case, "Trying to Tell You Something" works equally well with "Brotherhood in Pain," a poem that may help to explain those closing lines.

In "Brotherhood in Pain" Warren takes the premise of the previous poem—that human truth, constructed from language, is not commensurate with reality—and draws the logical and seemingly inevitable conclusion that the self exists in a linguistic predicament that irrevocably separates it from reality. He begins this poem by instructing the reader, "Fix your eyes on any chance object" (a falling leaf, a piece of chewing gum, a black sock, a pebble), or perhaps "Whirl around three times . . . with eyes shut // Then fix on the first thing seen when they open" (CP 331). The conclusion Warren draws from this little experiment links the human capacity for language with a solipsistic condition. On the one hand he suggests that we create the world in the act of naming it, and on the other hand he contends that our reliance upon language to create that world separates us from reality:

> In any case, you will suddenly observe an object in the obscene
>   moment of birth.
>
> It does not know its own name. The matrix from which it is torn
> Bleeds profusely. It has not yet begun to breathe. Its experience
>
> Is too terrible to recount. Only when it has completely forgotten
> Everything, will it smile shyly, and try to love you,
>
> For somehow it knows that you are lonely, too.
> It pityingly knows that you are more lonely that it is, for
>
> You exist only in the delirious illusion of language. (CP 331)

Warren here portrays us as irreparably cut off from reality, trapped in the illusory realm of language. While we obviously must rely on language to name the world around us, there is always a gap between the signifier and the signified. And since we also order and define ourselves through this imperfect medium of language, these gaps extend even to our construction of self-knowledge. Any sense of unity, wholeness, and presence we may perceive is in fact a fiction, nothing more than a "delirious illusion." Warren further exposes and exacerbates these inherent gaps between language and reality through his all-consuming thematic interest in time; his poetic texts continually venture forth into the voids which exist between past and present, and between fact and memory. In a sense then, Warren portrays the self as being twice-removed from reality: first by language and secondly by time.

But despite the inherent uncertainty that arises from these thematic concerns, Warren's late poetry is anything but despairing. Indeed, even though he portrays language as a flawed medium, he nonetheless celebrates the fact that it provides the means by which we connect the past to the present and project ourselves into the future through the construction of meaningful interpretive narratives. In summary, Warren now views the self as necessarily and essentially fragmented, and he believes that we must first acknowledge and accept this fact if we are to create a responsible version of an integrated self—a necessary fiction by which we may construct standards of value and responsibility. These intertwined relationships between time, language, and the construction of self provide the central focal points for Warren's poetry of this period. He does not provide any definitive answers on these subjects; rather, he accepts the necessary tension of human experience, and as a result, the conclusions he draws are always provisional, contingent, and temporary.[4]

The tension that necessarily arises between Warren's concepts of sequential time and archetypal time forms the thematic center of his 1974 volume *Or Else*. The poems oscillate back and forth between the unforgiving world of sequential time and the potentially redeeming realm of archetypal time. Often in *Or Else*, sequential time is portrayed as an unrelenting, even violent force which threatens to annihilate the individual. This view of time is introduced in the volume's opening poem, "The Nature of a Mirror," where we are told that "The sky has murder in the eye" as the sun sets (*CP* 271). As both days and seasons pass us by ("The solstice of summer has sagged"), we are reminded of our basic weakness under time's inevitable progression, and the sun becomes an increasingly menacing image as it sets beyond a hill:

> soon now, even before
> The change from Daylight Saving Time, the sun,
> Beyond the western ridge of black-burnt pine stubs like
> A snaggery of rotten shark teeth, sinks
> Lower, larger, more blank, and redder than
> A mother's rage, as though
> F.D.R. had never run for office even, or the first vagina
> Had not had the texture of dream. Time
>
> Is the mirror into which you stare. (*CP* 271)

The mentioning of Daylight Saving Time is an ironic reminder of our feeble attempts to cope with time's constant progression. The present is continually devoured by the past and reduced to a seeming state of nonexistence; as historical events and personal memories recede further into the past, they similarly dissolve into nothingness. Moreover, the closing lines, which claim that "Time // Is the mirror" in which we perceive ourselves, threaten likewise to reduce our entire sense of identity to nothingness. But Warren immediately qualifies and complicates the matter in the very brief, three-line poem that follows, "Interjection #1: The Need for Re-evaluation":

> *Is this really me?* Of course not, for Time
> Is only a mirror in the fun-house.
>
> You must re-evaluate the whole question. (*CP* 271)

While the first poem, "The Nature of a Mirror," describes time as the mirror we stare at, we are now told that the reflection we see is anything but representational of reality; instead, the image of ourselves we discern is a distortion of reality. As Warren explains in his essay "The Use of the Past," "There is no absolute, positive past available to us, no matter how rigorously we strive to determine it—as strive we must. Inevitably, the past, so far as we know it, is an inference, a creation" (51). There is an inherent gap between the objective facts of the past, which exist in se-quential time, and our subjective memories of those facts, which exist in archetypal time as linguistic and narrative interpretations. Warren would contend that we are indeed twice-removed from reality: we exist in the "delirious illusion" of language, staring at the fun-house mirror that is time.

The friction between Warren's categories of sequential time and arche-typal time runs throughout *Or Else*—and indeed is an ongoing concern in his late poetry. Images of the relentlessness of sequential time always seem to lurk in the background, as in "Ballad of Mister Dutcher and the Last Lynching in Gupton," where time is described as "that howling or-thodoxy of / darkness that, like speed-hurled rain on / glass, streams past us" (*CP* 285). A more menacing image is seen in "Chain Saw at Dawn in Vermont in Time of Drouth." There the perpetual passage of time as-sumes the violent characteristics of the Chain Saw: "the saw / Sings: *now!* Sings: / *Now, now, now,* in the / Lash and blood-lust of an eternal present, the present / Murders the past, the nerve shrieks" (*CP* 285). As Richard Jackson explains, this series of repeated "nows," rather than representing the "eternal present," actually exposes an "abyss" of gaps or discontinui-sties which illustrate "the impossible irony of a temporal 'eternal present'" (14). Jackson has provided what is certainly the most extensive and thought-provoking study of Warren's views of time and rightly refers to him as "perhaps the most time conscious poet of this century" (2). His approach to Warren, informed primarily by Heidegger and Derrida, demonstrates that Warren's reevaluation of time is in fact a reevaluation both of the self and of language's role in defining the self. Our notion of the self's stability is inevitably linked to our belief in time's continuity, and therefore whenever Warren exposes the discontinuity of time—as he does in "Chain Saw at Dawn"—he also exposes the discontinuous, fragmentary nature of the self. As Jackson points out, Warren's claim in "Interjection #1" that time is like a "mirror in the fun-house" undermines the idea of simple self-referentiality and raises a number of fundamental questions regarding the nature of the self: "What abyss lurks here beneath the distorting mirror of simple presence, and even in absence that the referentiality of presence seems to veil? What does this calling into question mean for the structure of the moment of presence . . . ? What does it mean for the self whose stability seems so bound with the continuity of time?" (12).

But it is out of just this sort of strain and uncertainty that Warren believes selfhood must be responsibly constructed. In the poem "There's a Grandfather's Clock in the Hall," Warren portrays the relationship between sequential memory and archetypal memory ("Time" and "no-Time") in sexual terms and suggests that a self-procreative process emerges from the self's conflicting feelings of its own continuity and discontinuity. The poem contains subtly contrasting images of death and sexuality—of endings and potential beginnings—and thus implies that time offers both the threat of self-annihilation and the promise of self-procreation: the self is always dying away even as it is coming into being. The poem is comprised of a series of frozen moments or, as Warren might describe them, archetypal memories:

> There's a grandfather's clock in the hall, watch it closely. The
>   minute hand stands still, then it jumps, and in between jumps
>   there is no-Time,
> And you are a child again watching the reflection of early morning
>   sunlight on the ceiling above your bed,
>
> Or perhaps you are fifteen feet under water and holding your
>   breath as you struggle with a rock-snagged anchor, or holding
>   your breath just long enough for one more long, slow thrust to
>   make the orgasm really intolerable,

Or you are wondering why you do not really give a damn, as they
  trundle you off to the operating room,

Or your mother is standing up to get married and is very pretty
  and excited and is a virgin, and your heart overflows, and you
  watch her with tears in your eyes, or
She is the one in the hospital room and she is really dying. (*CP*
  309–10)

This memory of his mother on her deathbed becomes the developing fo-
cus for the next four stanzas, with Warren at one point painfully recalling
her question about his suit, which "in its murderous triviality, is the last
thing she will ever say to you" (*CP* 310). But despite the obvious pain
associated with this memory of personal loss, he insists that we must con-
tinually revisit the past, even its pain, if we are to create the self of the
future. This is the poem's "truth":

Nor do you know the truth, which is: *Seize the nettle of innocence*
  in both your hands, for this is the only way, and every
Ulcer in love's lazaret may, like a dawn-stung gem, sing—or even
  burst into whoops of, perhaps, holiness. (*CP* 310)

Here Warren suggests that the past, with its complete record of our defi-
ciencies, weaknesses, and failings, still holds a promise of renewal, regen-
eration, and self-procreation. By retrieving our memories of the past—by
"presencing" the past, as Heidegger says—we may recover lost possibili-
ties and thereby project ourselves into the future. In the closing stanza,
Warren returns to sexual imagery to convey these procreative powers
that emerge from time's passing:

But, in any case, watch the clock closely. Hold your breath and
  wait.
Nothing happens, nothing happens, then suddenly, quick as a wink,
  and slick as a mink's prick, Time thrusts through the time of no-
  Time. (*CP* 310)

Commenting on these lines, Richard Jackson describes the "thrusting
through" as an attempt to establish "a structure of consciousness, a veil,
across the abyss" of the self's discontinuity in time. Importantly, language
is the material from which this veil across the abyss is created. Drawing
from Heidegger, Jackson explains:

It is the poet who manipulates language best, who makes of it a "span" which crosses the abyss. For Heidegger, all works of art create and fill this abyss; the poem itself is its own "cleft" marking the difference between Time and "no-Time," engaging the utter emptiness of that abyss, its utter loss of referentiality, loss of relation to the self—but also remaking that self, that Time in recentering the moment. (17)

The self's conflicting perceptions of its own continuity and discontinuity are played out in two poems that appear consecutively in *Or Else*, "Interjection #2: Caveat" and "I Am Dreaming of a White Christmas: The Natural History of a Vision." In the former, Warren at first states:

Necessarily, we must think of the
world as continuous, for

. . . .

if it were not so, you wouldn't know
you are in the world, or even that the
world exists at all— (*CP* 274)

Warren here suggests that we must think of the world as continuous if we are to conceive of the self as a "development in time" capable of purposeful and meaningful action. But just as he had done in "Interjection #1," he quickly qualifies this statement and complicates the whole matter:

but only, oh, on-
ly, in discontinuity, do we
know that we exist, or that, in the deep-
est sense, the existence of anything
signifies more than the fact that it is
continuous with the world. (*CP* 274)

Warren here argues that the human capacity for self-consciousness presupposes a sense of the self's separateness and discontinuity. At the same time, though, he believes that we cannot simply accept the discontinuity of our existence, for that would reduce us to a state of chaos and meaninglessness. We therefore must view the world and the self as continuous if we are to create meaning through narrative. Warren's poetry often suggests, however, that we must be careful in the narratives of continuity we construct, for as seen in the "Internal Injuries" sequence, the continually emerging self of Romantic development is capable of terrible acts of self-evasion and self-deception. Likewise, Richard Jackson points out that the return to the past which is necessary to the construction of such narratives always carries the danger of solipsistic nostalgia.

In the poem that follows, "I Am Dreaming of a White Christmas: The Natural History of a Vision," Warren considers both the rewards and the pitfalls of our efforts to construct the self in time, to span the abyss of our own discontinuity with meaningful narrative representation. This is a particularly confusing poetic sequence which moves simultaneously toward two different conclusions. On the one hand, Warren here contends that we must view the world as continuous if we are to order our experiences and assess our lives, and yet the form of the poem calls this belief in continuity into question. The poem is comprised of a dozen sections, the majority of which recount a dream which the narrator has had in which he encounters the decaying corpses of his parents sitting in his boyhood home, which also contains the remains of a family Christmas celebration. The first seven sections compile details of this dream that becomes continually clearer despite the narrator's initial reluctance to enter into its surreal dreamscape:

> *No, not that door—never!* But,
> Entering, saw. Through
> Air brown as an old daguerreotype fading. Through
> Air that, though dust to the tongue, yet—
> Like the inward, brown-glimmering twilight of water—
> Swayed. Through brown air, dust-dry, saw. Saw
> It.
>
> The bed.
>
> Where it had
> Been. Now was. Of all
> Covering stripped, the mattress
> Bare but for old newspapers spread.
> Curled edges. Yellow. On yellow paper dust,
> The dust yellow. No! Do not.
>
> Do not lean to
> Look at that date. Do not touch
> That silken and yellow perfection of Time that
> Dust is, for

There is no Time. I,
Entering, see.

        I,
Standing here, breathe the dry air. (*CP* 275)

The scene grows clearer and clearer over the next seven sections, with the narrator alternately focusing on the decayed corpses of his parents, the bare Christmas tree, and, perhaps most important, three unopened Christmas presents, one for each of the children in his family: "Each with red bow, and under / The ribbon, a sprig of holly. // But look! // The holly / Is, clearly, fresh" (*CP* 278). The importance of this image of the unopened Christmas present cannot be overestimated. The entire poem up to this point has underscored the ravages of time with its detailed descriptions of the decaying corpses of the narrator's parents; however, the sprig of fresh holly on the unopened Christmas present playfully indicates that this time-ravaged past still offers some new gift to the narrator: this memory of the past contains the "present" of his future self. In other words, this riddlelike image functions on the view of the future as an *unopened* present moment. Through this image Warren again illustrates Heidegger's belief that by "presencing" the past we project ourselves into the future.[5] Moreover, the poem illustrates Warren's dualistic view of time in which the ravages of sequential time contrast with the self-restorative power of archetypal memory, through which we construct meaning. A similar duality is expressed in "Reading Late at Night, Thermometer Falling," where the past is described as "great / Eater of dreams, secrets, and random data," but also as "Refrigerator of truth" (*CP* 314).

In "I Am Dreaming of a White Christmas" the truth is never revealed—the present of the future is left unopened. Just as the narrator seems to be on the threshold of revelation, he abruptly awakens from his reverie to find himself standing in Times Square toward sunset:

        Where I was
Am not. Now am
Where the blunt crowd thrusts, nudges, jerks, jostles,
And the eye is inimical. Then,
Of a sudden, know:

        Times Square, the season
Late summer and the hour sunset, with fumes
In throat and smog-glitter at sky-height, where

A jet, silver and ectoplasmic, spooks through
The sustaining light, which
Is yellow as acid. (CP 279)

The unnatural color of the sky is matched by Warren's detailed scene of
urban depravity and social decay; it is a scene of psychopathology, false
hope, sexual depravity, and alienation:

What year it is, I can't, for the life of me,
Guess, but know that,
Far off, south-eastward, in Bellevue,
In a bare room with windows barred, a woman,
Supine on an iron cot, legs spread, each ankle
Shackled to the cot-frame,
Screams.

She keeps on screaming because it is sunset.

Her hair has been hacked short.

    [10]

Clerks now go home, night watchmen wake up, and the heart
Of the taxi-driver, just coming on shift,
Leaps with hope.

All is not in vain.

Old men come out from the hard-core movies.
They wish they had waited till later.

They stand on the pavement and stare up at the sky.
Their drawers are drying stiff at the crotch, and
The sky dies wide. The sky
Is far above the first hysteria of neon.

Soon they will want to go and get something to eat. (CP 280)

But these disturbing meditations end as abruptly as they began, as the
poem shifts its focus yet again. The narrator, perhaps overwhelmed by the
urban scenes before him, momentarily retreats or escapes into his memo-
ries of the Montana wilderness in snowfall:

In any case,
I stand here and think of snow falling. But am
Not here. Am

Otherwhere, for already,
This early and summer not over, in West Montana—
Or is it Idaho?—in
The Nez Percé Pass, tonight
It will be snowing.

The Nez Percé is more than 7,000 feet, and I
Have been there. (*CP* 281)

It should be remembered that the narrator is still standing in Times Square as he retreats into this more peaceful, pleasant memory, and so there is a dubious quality to this form of escape. In contrast to the sharply detailed urban scene, the narrator is not even certain what state he is remembering. Moreover, while the surreal memories of his family are self-reflective and carry the potential for the construction of self-knowledge, this memory of the vacant natural landscape does not. The sequence at this point has deteriorated into a seemingly perplexing clutter of surreal dream, troubling reality, and pleasant nostalgia.

But the last section of the poem offers yet another abrupt transition to the sequence. This one is final; order and control are definitively imposed on all the experiences detailed throughout the poem—the memory of the dream, the present scenes of New York, and the memories of Montana (or was it Idaho?). The poet-narrator intrudes from the actual present—the writing of the poem—in an attempt to construct from these disparate fragments a narrative of self-continuity and self-development, language being the medium:

All items listed above belong in the world
In which all things are continuous,
And are parts of the original dream which
I am now trying to discover the logic of. This
Is the process whereby pain of the past in its pastness
May be converted into the future tense

Of joy. (*CP* 281)

Victor Strandberg sees this effort to connect the past with the future as one of Warren's "grandest conceptions" of mysticism, "rendering the oneness of time and flesh on a scale that binds together the living with the dead, family members with total strangers, densely compacted city-scape with vastly vacant countryside, summer heat and winter snow, past and present" (*Poetic Vision* 225). From this perspective, Warren's strategy seems very similar to the transcendent, unifying moments of his poetry of the 1950s; the passage becomes simply another articulation of the Romantic "osmosis" or "unity" of being. But to what extent has any "binding"—particularly with the cityscape—taken place? Has the narrator made himself one flesh with the taxi drivers and the old men coming out of the pornographic movie houses? Or is the narrator's retreat into his memory a convenient method of avoiding the disturbing urban reality with which he is faced? The answers to these questions are by no means clear, but what is clear is the strategy of the twelfth and final section. Warren—or the poet-narrator—attempts to encapsulate the variety of experiences detailed in the poem within a larger construct of reality; he subsumes these dissimilar events within a developmental narrative, a self-made linguistic construction based upon the premise of time's continuity. However, the conspicuously prosaic tone of this last section almost calls into question the sincerity of the statement, particularly since it is so unlike the moments of synthesis that occur in poems such as *Brother to Dragons*, with its incantatory rhythms, and "Old Nigger on One-Mule Cart" with its evocative and deeply poetic imagery. In contrast, these closing lines sound as if they are from an owner's manual or how-to book. The narrator is essentially claiming, "The world is continuous because I say it is!"—and the reader is simply supposed to accept his claim.

Then again, perhaps we are not simply supposed to accept it, for the logic of this claim—or lack thereof—seems to refer back quite specifically to the preceding poem, "Interjection #2: Caveat," where the narrator states, "Necessarily, we must think of the / world as continuous, for if it were / not so I would have told you" (*CP* 274). Such statements are hardly meant to be persuasive, so we may conclude Warren is articulating this assumption of continuity in a way that naturally inclines the reader to question it. Furthermore, the poem's fragile final assertion of continuity has already been undermined by the radically fragmented and discontinuous form of the sequence itself, particularly its abrupt transitions in time and place. In short, the reader experiences the narrator's discontinuity and likewise experiences the narrator's exasperating efforts to trace some logic amid these disparate fragments.[6] Warren ends the sequence with a moment of ironic tension in which he boldly asserts continuity while at the same time illustrating the impossibility of such a claim. He is sincere when he states that "This / Is the process whereby pain of the past in its pastness / May be converted into the future tense // Of joy." However, he is also tying to illustrate that this holistic and integrated sense of self is a fiction, a necessary illusion which we construct from language. So while Warren in the 1950s and early 1960s uncritically adopts and accepts the Romantic concept of the developing self, he now interrogates this concept even as he employs its strategies. A strict adherence to or belief in development would suggest that there is some pre-existing logic or pattern that may be *discovered*. Now, however, Warren more often than not admits that any such logic is *created* rather than discovered; it is created through an act of the imagination which, like the image of the magnet in "Old Nigger on One-Mule Cart," thrusts the "iron and out-flung filings of our lives" into a discernible pattern of development. In Warren's view, if we hope to create ourselves as responsible moral agents, we first must be aware of the perplexing and paradoxical nature of the self, and second, we must be willing to submit ourselves to continuous scrutiny and questioning.

Warren's intertwined themes of time, language, and self merge most affirmatively and powerfully in what is perhaps his most celebrated poem, *Audubon: A Vision*. My purpose here is not to offer another exhaustive reading of the poem, for it has already been the focus of many excellent studies. As critics have argued, *Audubon* is a poem of mythic qualities, a poem that both affirms the individual's struggle for a meaningful sense of selfhood and celebrates the power of the imagination to create timeless and sustaining visions of experience.[7] However, I would like to focus for a moment on an important though neglected aspect of the poem: the human dilemma of referentiality. Warren's views on the self's existence in language and time underscore the impossibility of achieving a pure and unadulterated referentiality, a clear correspondence between ourselves and reality. Can we ever hope to capture the essence of reality and represent it through images, as in Audubon's art, or words, as in Warren's? Can we ever hope to adequately represent the self through language, even to ourselves? Warren's answer to these closely related questions would be quite simply "no." Warren sees us as twice-removed from reality—defining ourselves through the "delirious illusion" of language as we stare into the distorting mirror of time. Similarly, his *Audubon: A Vision* demonstrates that any representation, whether in painting or poetry or even in the case of self-representation, is always a diminishment, or constriction, of the world's reality—like the iron hoops on the ancient oak tree in "Trying to Tell You Something." Warren illustrates in the poem that the human act of creation always carries with it a sense of estrangement or separateness, whether the thing being created is painting, poem, or self. But *Audubon* similarly posits that even in the face of this estrangement, the creative imagination nonetheless has the power to sustain us: through it the fiction of the self is created, and through its narrative constructions the self may be guided toward meaningful, visionary action.

Importantly, Warren's two epigraphs for the *Audubon* sequence both point to the inherent problems of representation:

> Thou tellest my wanderings: put thou my tears into thy bottle: are they not in thy book?
>
> Psalms 56:8

> I caught at his strict shadow and the shadow
> released itself with neither haste nor anger. But
> he remained silent.
>
> Carlos Drummond de Andrade:
> "Travelling in the Family"
> Translated by Elizabeth Bishop (*CP* 251)

While the first of these epigraphs might seem to suggest that pure representation is possible—with the tears being literally in the book—it should be noted that this verse from the Book of Psalms is a lamentation directed to God: the psalmist, persecuted by enemies, takes comfort in his belief that God is keeping a perfect record of his suffering and will surely make amends. In contrast, the second epigraph suggests the inherent deficiencies in human efforts at representation and seems to be directed specifically toward Warren's representation of Audubon, which, as critics have often pointed out, is anything but strict and accurate.[8] But this second epigraph also reflects Audubon's own art which, as Warren illustrates in the penultimate section of the poem, was dependent upon the destruction of his subjects. Consequently, both Warren's poetic vision of Audubon and Audubon's paintings of the birds are merely shadows of the life they strive to represent. Indeed, this image of the shadow releasing itself perhaps may best be understood through Heidegger's image of the trace. Drawing again from Heidegger, Richard Jackson explains that "Being and Time are given metonymically in poetry. They must always be talked around, traced, recentered. It is the poet's task, Heidegger says in 'What Are Poets For?,' to recover some of the 'traces' from the abyss. Rather than a statically centered, purely referential moment, a moment of clear origins, there is instead the moment of traces, of re-beginnings in the shadow of the abyss" (21).

But these epigraphs also tie in with the sequence's entire theme of identity, for if we cannot adequately represent the other, are we ever capable of adequately representing the self in a moment of strict and pure referentiality? Again, because we define and represent the self through language, Warren would answer negatively. Our reliance upon the imperfect medium of language to define ourselves results in gaps and displacements. We feel separated and alienated even from ourselves. Moreover, a similar separation exists between self and identity. As seen in *Who Speaks for the Negro?*, Warren acknowledges that there is always a gap between self and identity, and he highlights this gap in his portrayal of the naturalist painter. As the preface to the sequence points out, Audubon "was early instructed in the official version of his identity" to avoid the embarrassment of being known as a bastard: "By the age of ten Audubon knew the true story, but prompted, it would seem, by a variety of impulses, including some sound practical ones, he encouraged the other version, along with a number of flattering embellishments. He was, indeed, a fantasist of talent, but even without his help legends accreted about him" (*CP* 253). Warren opens the sequence by dismantling one of these legends—that Audubon was the lost dauphin of France:

> Was not the lost dauphin, though handsome was only
> Base-born and not even able
> To make a decent living, was only
> Himself, Jean Jacques, and his passion—what
> Is man but his passion? (*CP* 254)

As John Burt points out, these opening lines "have the air of clearing away the unessential, of listing the matters that will not be of concern" (93). Warren here privileges the concept of self over identity, but over the course of the poem, it becomes clear that he sees selfhood, like identity, as a fictional construction, with language being the tool from which the self is created.

The undercurrent of separateness that runs throughout the poem, particularly through Warren's counterpointing of the human world with the world of nature, can also be traced to the issue of language and its inherent problems of referentiality and representation.[9] As section 1 of the sequence unfolds, Audubon watches the silhouette of a heron move across the blood red horizon of sunrise. Like Adam, he names the world around him, but this act of naming results in tension and an awareness of the gap between subject and object, namer and named:

And the large bird,
Long neck outthrust, wings crooked to scull air, moved
In a slow calligraphy, crank, flat, and black against
The color of God's blood spilt, as though
Pulled by a string.

        Saw
It proceed across the inflamed distance.

Moccasins set in hoar frost, eyes fixed on the bird,
Thought: "On that sky it is black."
Thought: "In my mind it is white."
Thinking: "*Ardea occidentalis*, heron, the great one."

Dawn: his heart shook in the tension of the world.

Dawn: and what is your passion? (*CP* 254)

Warren here represents the inherent and necessary tension of the self as it exists in both time and language. The repetition "Thought . . . Thought . . . Thinking" functions much like the series of "*nows*" in "Chain Saw at Dawn," which ironically expose an abyss of gaps and illustrate the impossibility of a temporal eternal present. Moreover, Audubon's naming of the bird, rather than uniting him with it, makes him more acutely aware of his separateness from it, and as this opening section concludes, he reflects on the "thin . . . membrane between himself and the world" (*CP* 255).

While at this point in the poem Audubon seems very like a Romantic hero in the Emersonian tradition—with the "thin membrane" here described being reminiscent of Emerson's division of the world into the "me" and the "not-me"—Warren once again complicates matters with his focus on language and the fragmentation of the self. Ironically, while Audubon in section 1 is able to name the heron with some degree of confidence, in section 4 he is unable to name himself. So while section 1 shows Audubon's separateness from the world, section 4E reveals his sense of estrangement from himself. This self-division is again linked to the uniquely human problem of language and referentiality. In the opening lines of this section Warren writes: "The world declares itself. That voice / Is vaulted in—oh, arch on arch—redundancy of joy, its end / Is its beginning" (*CP* 263). With this statement he portrays the world's reality as a unity or wholeness that is beyond the problem of referentiality; it is pure, unadulterated being. Unfortunately, this sort of pure, unmediated existence is foreign to humans, for we must rely on language to mediate our experiences; even our innermost thoughts and feelings present themselves in words. But as Warren points out in the lines that follow, language is an imperfect filter for experience: truth is "the only thing that cannot / Be spoken" (CP 263). Since there is always a gap between signifier and signified, we never achieve a moment of strict and pure referentiality, a moment of absolute being and wholeness; instead, we feel separate from the world and even ourselves, as seen in the figure of Audubon: "he stood, // At dusk, in the street of the raw settlement, ... and did not know / What he was. Thought: 'I do not know my own name'" (CP 263). This moment of the sequence clearly refers back to the "Thought ... Thought ... Thinking" passage of section 1 in which Audubon names the bird. But while the earlier passage results in an awareness of the split between himself and the world, between the namer and the named, this passage reveals the necessary and inherent fragmentation of the self that exists in time and language.

Just as he does in "I Am Dreaming of a White Christmas," Warren again contrasts the inherent discontinuity of our existence with the need to construct continuity, order, and meaning in our lives. We accomplish this through the medium of language, which is used to span the gaps of time and create "timeless" visions of both the self and the world around us. Language, then, is presented in two very different lights in the sequence, as both a cause of alienation and a source for restoration. In a passage that is strategically similar to the closing lines of "I Am Dreaming of a White Christmas," Warren imagines Audubon aligning his past and present in an effort to construct a narrative of continuity and project himself into the future:

> The blessedness!—

> To wake in some dawn and see,
> As though down a rifle barrel, lined up
> Like sights, the self that was, the self that is, and there,
> Far off but in range, completing that alignment, your fate.

> Hold your breath, let the trigger-squeeze be slow and steady.

> The quarry lifts, in the halo of gold leaves, its noble head.

> This is not a dimension of Time. (CP 261)

But even as Warren represents such a timeless vision of continuity, he also hints at the necessary problem of referentiality and the separateness it entails. The image of the rifle in this passage reminds us of Audubon's own efforts at representation, for in order to act out his fate—to create from his passion his magnificent *Birds of America*—he was required to destroy the objects of his passion: he was an excellent marksman who slaughtered thousands of birds for specimens. Similarly, the poet may be said to destroy in order to create since, according to Lacan, to invoke language is to murder the thing. And yet this destruction is necessary if we are to give permanence to our otherwise fleeting perceptions. This tension between the continuity of life and the stasis of the word is also echoed in the poem's counterpointing of narrative and lyric. As John Burt explains, the poem's form allows Warren "to face the central conflict between truth and life, between value and humanity, by posing it as a conflict between lyric and narrative, between the stopped time in which meaning reveals itself and the progressing time in which life is to be lived" (111).

Warren returns to Audubon's ironic separateness from his passion in section 6, "Love and Knowledge." The section opens with a beautiful linguistic portrait of the birds that were the subjects of Audubon's art:

> Their footless dance
> Is of the beautiful liability of their nature.
> Their eyes are round, boldly convex, bright as a jewel,
> And merciless. They do not know
> Compassion, and if they did,
> We should not be worthy of it. They fly
> In air that glitters like fluent crystal
> And is hard as perfectly transparent iron, they cleave it
> With no effort. They cry
> In a tongue multitudinous, often like music. (*CP* 266)

The section shifts abruptly with the next lines, however, as Warren illustrates that the creative act of representation is an ironically destructive act since it is always a diminishment of the reality being represented:

> He slew them, at surprising distances, with his gun.
> Over a body held in his hand, his head was bowed low,
> But not in grief.

He put them where they are, and there we see them:
In our imagination.

What is love?

One name for it is knowledge. (*CP* 266)

The human act of creation—whether the thing being created is a painting, a poem, or a self—always carries with it a sense of estrangement or separateness. Audubon's timeless paintings are not the birds themselves but representations and, in the end, are silent.

Significantly, Warren suggests that his own poetic vision of Audubon is similarly silent. Consider, for example, section 5C, where he self-reflexively describes his own vision of Audubon, which exists in a timeless "dream / Of a season past all seasons":

In such a dream the wild-grape cluster,
High-hung, exposed in the gold light,
Unripening, ripens.

Stained, the lip with wetness gleams.

I see your lip, undrying, gleam in the bright wind.

I cannot hear the sound of that wind. (*CP* 265)

While the majority of these lines work toward the creation of a timeless vision of Audubon in language, the last line underscores the silence of this vision and points again to de Man's portrayal of the linguistic predicament: "To the extent that language is figure . . . it is indeed not the thing itself but the representation, the picture of the thing and, as such, it is silent, mute as pictures are mute" (80). Like Audubon's paintings of the birds, Warren acknowledges that his own poetic vision of Audubon is mute, as both the second epigraph (where the shadow remains silent) and this last quoted line show.

However, even amid the poem's undercurrents of separateness and silence, *Audubon* still celebrates the uniquely human capacity to create, whether the thing being created is the art object or the self. Indeed, *Audubon* is perhaps Warren's most celebratory and affirmative poem. The poem's affirmative vision is constructed as a delicate balance, in which he celebrates our capacity for vision and creation while at the same time interrogating the nature of these endeavors and exposing their inherent contradictions and limitations. As the closing lines of the poem's final section, "Tell Me a Story," indicate, Warren believes that we need narrative fictions if we are to construct meaning in our lives:

Tell me a story.

In this century, and moment, of mania,
Tell me a story.

Make it a story of great distances, and starlight.

The name of the story will be Time,
But you must not pronounce its name.

Tell me a story of deep delight. (CP 267)

Here we can see more evidence of the delicate balance Warren attempts to achieve in *Audubon*, a balance in which he both celebrates and interrogates the nature of the creative imagination and the role it plays in the construction of the self. Even in this final plea for a narrative that will construct meaning in our lives, he still points to the referential limitations of such a narrative, for the phrase "you must not pronounce its name" reminds us of his earlier claim that truth is "the only thing that cannot / Be spoken" (CP 263). For Warren, language is incapable of capturing the essence of reality, and consequently our concept of truth, a linguistic construction, is always a diminishment or even destruction of the reality being represented. And yet at the same time, Warren shows that these linguistic constructions have the power to guide the self toward action, action that is essentially a new reality unto itself. In summary, then, while Warren's thematics show that language cannot apprehend reality, he does point out that it nonetheless can alter and create new realities. As Warren goes on to explain in the passage just cited, truth "can only be enacted, and that in dream, / Or in the dream become, as though unconsciously, action" (CP 263).

Earlier I argued that *Who Speaks for the Negro?* is a transitional text in which Warren, writing subjectively within an explicitly political context, begins to raise difficult and complex questions regarding self, identity, and language. While it would be reductive and foolish to claim that his racial texts are responsible for his poetic texts, I believe—as I have argued throughout this book—that an important relationship nonetheless exists between the two. This is certainly the case in *Who Speaks for the Negro?*

and in the poetry of the period that followed. Through his reimmersion in the race issue and his writing of that book, Warren became more intensely aware of both the problems and the possibilities of language and the role it plays in defining the self and the world. On the one hand, language may be viewed as a fixed or rigid medium—a view that supports the construction of ideologies. On the other hand, language may be viewed as a pliable, flexible medium—a view that allows for and promotes personal and social change. Many critics have commented on Warren's use of the dialogic method in both his prose and poetry, and most recently Karen Ramsay Johnson has demonstrated that Warren's use of this method in *Who Speaks for the Negro?* is evidence of his awareness that both personal and social change are contingent upon this flexibility of language. As I have attempted to show in this chapter, Warren's later poetry similarly attempts to foreground the flexibility of language, and while his poetry usually lacks the clearly political referents of his nonfiction writings on race, it was not written in a vacuum and is not without political consequences. By raising such fundamental questions regarding the nature of the self as it exists in language and time, Warren prompts the reader to question his or her own self (as may be seen when the narrator directly addresses the reader in section 1) and to open up the possibilities for meaningful change and action. This is particularly important to the way we read *Audubon*, for the underlying message of the poem becomes clearer when we consider the context in which it was written. Warren's *Audubon* emerged from the wake of the turmoil of 1968—the assassinations of King and Robert Kennedy, the violence at the Democratic National Convention, and the social unrest, racial strife, and rioting in urban centers and on college campuses across the country.[10] *Brother to Dragons* may have been intended as a warning against the complacent culture of the 1950s, but *Audubon* was intended as a sober statement of hope amid the turmoil of the late 1960s. While the story of Audubon had first interested Warren some twenty years earlier, the poem was actually written in an intense and relatively short span of time, in late 1968 and early 1969. At this particular moment—this "moment of mania"—Warren felt the need to construct a poetic vision of the past that actually celebrated our capacity to alter the future. Explaining the poem's ending in a letter to Howard Moss dated March 24, 1969, Warren stated that the poem "gets beyond what the birds 'mean' to what Audubon (the 'story' we need to hear) means in this moment of 'mania': a vision of man's faith in his own possibilities" (RPW Papers). Warren believed that it is only through language that we create these visions of the future, but he similarly believed that in order to create meaningful and effective visions of the future, we must always be aware that language is a flexible rather than a frozen medium. It is only from the free play between language, memory, and the imagination that meaningful fictions of the self are created.

Conclusion

Warren at the "Inevitable Frontier"
of Postmodernism, 1975–1985

For remember now, this is the frontier
Where words coming out of a mouth are always upside-

Down, and all tongues are sloppily cubical, and shadows of nothing are,
Whatever the hour, always something, and tend to bleed.

Robert Penn Warren, "Inevitable Frontier"

Over the last decade of his career, Warren continued to produce new po-
ems at an incredibly rapid rate, publishing between 1975 and 1985 four
new collections along with a new version of *Brother to Dragons*. While
Warren's poems of this last period are less formally adventurous than his
poetry of the late 1960s and early 1970s, they are oftentimes more aus-
tere, particularly in their views of language. Warren's late poetry returns
again and again to the sublime sentiment in which the poet—the gener-
ally accepted arbiter of language—attempts to present an experience that
is unpresentable; over and over again, he is left to retreat to a statement of
his own—and language's—inadequacy in the face of the world's reality.[1]
Consider, for example, "Mountain Plateau," from *Now and Then:*

At the center of acres of snow-whiteness
The snag-oak reared, black and old, boughs
Crank. Topmost twigs—pen-strokes, tangle, or stub—fretted
The ice-blue of sky. A crow,
On the highest black, frail, and sky-thrust support,

Uttered

Its cry to the immense distance.

I hear the cry across the immense distance
Of the landscape of my heart.

That landscape now reduplicates, snow-white, the one
In which I once stood. At its center, too, the
Black snag stands.

A crow gleams there up-thrust against the blue sky.

I can make no answer
To the cry from the immense distance,

My eyes fill with tears. I have lived
Long without being able
To make adequate communication. (*CP* 351)

As is the case with much of Warren's late verse, this is a poem about language—*and* about poetry. On the surface the poem is quite simple: the poet recalls a scene in which a crow calls from a black tree which sits in the center of a snowy landscape, and then the poet reflects on this recollection. But notice that in the third line Warren describes the twigs of the oak as "pen strokes"—an image that deflects the reader away from the concept of the referent (the "real" scene from which the memory derives) and back toward the words on the page. By comparing the twigs to pen strokes, he subtly reminds the reader of the "linguistic predicament," of the gap between the signifier and the signified, between the word and the world. Notice also how he isolates the word "Uttered" amid the blank white space of the page. At first it would seem that the word's placement attempts to visually repeat, or visually "present," the scene, becoming—like the tree and crow themselves—black images in the "snow-whiteness" of the page. But instead of the words of the poem becoming the tree and crow, what has actually happened is the "real" objects have been reduced to mere words; this is the source of the poet's pain, his sense of inadequacy. It is at the point of attempted "utterance"—that moment in which we attempt to *present* the *conceived of*—that we sense the way in which language alienates us from the world. Even though the scene "reduplicates" in the poet's heart, complete with the crow's cry, he claims that he "can make no answer" because the reality he seeks to present is in fact unpresentable. But this particular claim is at least partly false, for he has made an answer through the text of the poem itself—though unfortu-

nately it is an answer that cannot escape the text of the page. Conse-
quently, the closing three lines are a summary not so much of a single,
isolated experience as they are of the poet's entire creative endeavor: "I
have lived / Long without being able / To make adequate communica-
tion." He is left finally with only a "Black snag" at the center of his heart's
landscape, a snag that is nothing more than words. These words in the
heart in turn become pen strokes, which in turn become the typed charac-
ters of the text that the poem's reader sees, a text that finally fails to make
visible the real scene. This being a poem that expresses the sublime senti-
ment, the poet's closing reflection imparts no definitive knowledge or
truth; instead, the poet can only reflect on his own inability to make his
recollection wholly present through language—a reflection that, of course,
is also subject to the vagaries of language. With this sublime sentiment
in mind, it is interesting to note that the poem focuses on the mundane
image of a crow rather than the more stately image of the soaring hawk so
often seen in Warren's poetry. Much has been made of Warren's hawk
imagery: critics such as Victor Strandberg, Harold Bloom, and John Burt
have claimed that these hawk images represent everything from total
knowledge and merciless truth to poetic power and necessity of being.[2]
But in "Mountain Plateau" it is the utterly ordinary image of a crow, not
the more regal hawk, that provokes the feeling of the unpresentable—a
fact that further underscores the inadequacy of language, and of Warren's
own poetic effort.[3]

Warren in his last four volumes returns again and again to statements
that point to the sublime sentiment and the acute awareness of language's
inadequacy in the face of the world's reality.[4] These statements directly
challenge our belief in an attainable, universal truth; in making them,
Warren attempts to combat the complacency of our assumptions by re-
turning us to a vigorous inquiry into the complexity and uncertainty of
our own experience in all of its irony and limitation. These recurring
statements on the inadequacy of language prompt the reader to rethink
exactly what is meant by words like "truth" and "reality," and to explore
the enormous assumptions contained therein. This is the focus of the
poem "The Whole Question," which opens innocuously enough with
"You'll have to rethink the whole question. This / Getting born business
is not as simple as it seemed" (CP 566). But the complexity Warren details
goes beyond what the clichéd opening lines would indicate, as he again
links the uncertainty in our lives to the fundamental issue of language

and the inevitable failure of words and names to convey or capture what is real. Almost like Lacan, Warren in this poem portrays the acquisition of language as the central alienating moment in an individual's life:

> You had not, for instance, previsioned the terrible thing called love,
> Which began with a strange, sweet taste and bulbed softness while
> Two orbs of tender light leaned there above.
> Sometimes your face got twisted. They called it a smile.
>
> You noticed how faces from outer vastness might twist, too.
> But sometimes different twists, with names unknown,
> And there were noises with no names you knew,
> And times of dark silence when you seemed nothing—or gone.
>
> Years passed, but sometimes seemed nothing except the same.
> You knew more words, but they were words only, only—
> Metaphysical midges that plunged at the single flame
> That centered the infinite dark of your skull; or lonely,
>
> You woke in the dark of real night to hear the breath
> That seemed to promise reality in the vacuum
> Of the sleepless dream beginning when underneath
> The curtain dawn seeps, and on wet asphalt wet tires hum.
>
> Yes, you must try to rethink what is real. Perhaps
> It is only a matter of language that traps you. You
> May yet find a new one in which experience overlaps
> Words. Or find some words to make the Truth come true. (CP 566)

Writing of this poem, Robert Koppelman states that "the persona seems to possess a capacity for Truth, but the language of society has corrupted Truth to the point where genuine meaning is accessible only through dreams" (91). Unlike Koppelman, I do not believe Warren is locating the problem of meaning in the corruption of society; he is locating the problem in the very nature of language itself, which traps us in its prison of self-referentiality ("You knew more words, but they were words only, only— / Metaphysical midges"). The poem's final stanza points again to the gap between signifier and signified, ending with an understated paradox: How are we to make the Truth true?

This linguistic dilemma is never resolved in Warren's late poetry, but that does not mean he accepts a world without meaning. Instead, he achieves a curious balance, continually approaching the "Inevitable Frontier" at which language fails, and returning to a sober acceptance that we must nonetheless have faith in language if we are to construct any form of meaning and value in our lives. The point is that this meaning is anything but stable and must be constantly interrogated and reshaped. As Warren states in "Unless,"

> All will be in vain unless—unless what? Unless
> You realize that what you think is Truth is only
>
> A husk for something else. Which might,
> Shall we say, be called energy, as good a word as any. (CP 356)

The poet's hesitation here over replacing the word "Truth" with "energy" points, on the one hand, to the arbitrary nature of the sign and, on the other hand, to our inability to communicate without *some* sign. In other words, Warren accepts that we must rely on language, but he constantly reminds the reader to not become complacent in this reliance on an unstable and arbitrary system. These views on language have profound implications and take Warren, philosophically and thematically at least, to the boundary line of postmodernism—a line, however, that he refuses to entirely cross.[5]

"Postmodernism" is a particularly nebulous and slippery term, and critics have applied the postmodern label to Warren's later poetry in a variety of ways.[6] Perhaps the links between postmodernism and Warren's late poetic inquiry into the flawed medium of language can best be approached, as John Van Dyke has argued, through the theories outlined by Jean-François Lyotard in his influential 1979 book *The Postmodern Condition: A Report on Knowledge*. It is important to emphasize, however, that Warren did not come to these often radical conclusions regarding the self and language through the influence of theorists and philosophers; instead, his arrival at the "inevitable frontier" of postmodernism came about through his own life experience, particularly through his willingness to engage the complex social and political issues of his day in a deeply personal and self-reflective manner. Lyotard extends the poststructuralists' critique of language by attacking the notion of holistic, universal truth, an approach that clears the way for a greater diversity or heterogeneity of truth-claims and, ideally at least, for a more pluralistic democracy. According to Lyotard, the simplest definition of postmodernism is "incredulity toward metanarratives" (xxiv). By "metanarratives" he means the grand narratives that serve as the totalizing and legitimating myths forming the foundation for Western culture in the modern age. Of these, Lyotard singles out and dismantles the belief in continuing human liberation through progress in science and technology, as well as the assumption that we can achieve a valid form of universal knowledge. Lyotard undermines both of these myths by dismissing the traditional hierarchies of knowledge that have developed in Western culture, placing the heretofore privileged realm of "scientific knowledge" on the same plane as "narrative knowledge." Indeed, according to Lyotard, all forms of knowledge may be reduced to a matter of "language games," each of which operates under its own system of ground rules and standards for proof. In other words, the "truths" of one field of knowledge are not necessarily translatable to another, and so, Lyotard claims, there can be no "universal" knowledge. Instead, meaning can be determined only locally, provisionally, and temporarily, and the health of a society depends largely upon its ability to maintain a multiplicity or variety of such language games.

Warren's 1975 book of criticism *Democracy and Poetry* expresses concerns and views remarkably similar to those outlined by Lyotard, as do many of his late poems which illustrate his evolved views on language and the "unpresentable." *Democracy and Poetry* is Warren's most extensive statement on the social significance of poetry in contemporary culture and society, and it is often cited and discussed by critics. Significantly, the same sense of uncertainty regarding the self that informs Warren's late poetry—an uncertainty he increasingly locates in the arbitrary nature of language—also informs his comments in *Democracy and Poetry* regarding science, technology, rationalism, and progress. While the book's first essay, "America and the Diminished Self," documents poetry's "diagnostic" function, the second of the essays, "Poetry and Selfhood," attempts to argue that poetry may also serve a "therapeutic" role in contemporary society, particularly within the context of what Warren refers to as the Technetronic Age (*DP* 42).[7] It might seem tempting to view Warren's complaints against the world of "science, technology, and big organization" as simply a recapitulation of his early Agrarian principles, but this would be a severe distortion of his position. In addition to responding to a very different cultural context, Warren now has a very different view of the self, and he therefore has a very different justification for his argument in support of poetry's social value. Warren's Agrarian views held that the individual in the modern age had been cut off from the sustaining cultural traditions of the past, and he desired a rapprochement with the past and its stable, static values. Now, however, Warren accepts uncertainty, flux, and fragmentation as the self's natural state. And instead of calling for a recovery of tradition that would restore the self to a sense of wholeness, he now calls for poetry that both acknowledges and documents the enormous complexity and uncertainty of the self. As Warren explains near the end of *Democracy and Poetry,* poetry cannot "give definitions and certainties. But it can help us to ponder on what Saint Augustine meant when he said that he was a question to himself" (92). He explains that such a question is itself an indication of our "divided nature," the necessary result of our capacity for "self-consciousness" (93). Warren's comments make it clear that he sees self-division as the natural and inevitable state, and not as simply the consequence of modernity:

> On that day when the hairless ape felt the first flicker of self-consciousness and self-criticism, and was first aware that something inside him was looking at something else inside him, he was doomed, as we are doomed, to live, both in the flesh and in society, in the bright irony and long anguish of the machine and the vision—for that is what we are, machines capable of vision. (*DP* 93)

For Warren, poetry can serve a therapeutic function by reminding us of these ironies and complexities of the divided self. In short, he conceives of poetry as an antidote to the myths of rationalism and positivism, which offer false promises of certainty and upon which science, technology, and progress all feed. Warren, like Lyotard, is very much concerned about the privileged status achieved by science and technology in the modern age. And Warren, again like Lyotard, attempts to undermine this hierarchy by arguing that there are other forms of knowledge which have equal claims to legitimacy—claims that science, operating under different rules, cannot delegitimate. Warren asks, "Even though overwhelmed by the grandeur and apparent inevitability of the scientific project, does man, nevertheless, still yearn for other kinds of knowledge? Not in place of, but in addition to, scientific knowledge, in order to make a world more humanly habitable?" (*DP* 47). He at first places this question within a continuing humanistic tradition, alluding to thinkers as diverse as Vico, Kierkegaard, and Bertrand Russell. But his commentary is not simply the restatement of traditional humanist desires. Instead, his comments on multiple forms of knowledge are informed by the postmodern condition and the acute awareness of language's central and problematic role in the construction of *any* form of knowledge. Tellingly, Warren expresses a certain amount of hope for the "sequel" to the "Cartesian epoch"—quantum physics—particularly for the radical uncertainty that accompanied its cultural as-

cendancy. He even notes optimistically that some scientists "began refer-
ring to artists as brother symbolists with merely a different kind of net for
snaring 'reality'" (*DP* 51). This potential promise of equality between the
truth-claims of science and those of art suggests exactly the sort of het-
erogeneous view of knowledge described by Lyotard. But unfortunately,
as Warren points out, "the kind of technology we have does not seem to
derive from the more open-ended and inclusive views which rumor in-
structs me are to be found in current scientific thought" (*DP* 52).

This being the case at the time he entered into his last decade of writ-
ing, Warren set out in his poetry to expose the limitations of language and
its problematic role in the construction of any truth-claim. Over and over
again, Warren's late poems return the reader to the sense that language is
finally incapable of "snaring" reality—a fact that alters our view of both
scientific knowledge and narrative knowledge. Indeed, this sensation of
language's inadequacy becomes something of a refrain in Warren's last
four collections of poems—*Now and Then: Poems 1976–1978; Being
Here: Poetry 1977–1980; Rumor Verified: Poems 1979–1980;* and "Alti-
tudes and Extensions," the "new" poems within Warren's *New and Se-
lected Poems: 1923–1985.* This refrain of language's inadequacy not only
calls attention self-reflexively to the limitations of Warren's own art—as
in "Mountain Plateau"—but, perhaps more important, it calls into ques-
tion the concept of universal truth.[8] In this way, the later Warren may be
compared to the contemporary poets discussed by Lynn Keller in *Re-
Making It New,* who "strive on the one hand, to bring art close to life in all
its fluid non-order, and on the other, to bring life closer to art by underlin-
ing the fictionality of all perceptual, conceptual, and verbal structures"
(259).[9]

The poem "Fear and Trembling," which serves as a "coda" for the vol-
ume *Rumor Verified,* provides what is perhaps the best illustration of the
balance Warren attempts to achieve in his inquiry into language. The first
thing to be mentioned about this poem is the title's allusion to Søren
Kierkegaard's *Fear and Trembling,* a text that attempts to illuminate the
cold, stark, and austere nature of true faith. Through a creative analysis of
the Genesis account of Abraham's dilemma following God's command
that he sacrifice his son Isaac, Kierkegaard argues that true faith exists "by
virtue of the absurd": "it is not an immediate instinct of the heart, but is
the paradox of life and existence" (57–58). For Kierkegaard, the "knight of
faith" has the "passion" necessary to "plunge confidently into the ab-
surd" (44). Warren similarly sees our existence as a paradox that requires

a leap of faith, but for him, the paradox forms around the issue of language and the problem of meaning.[10] In the poem "Fear and Trembling," he again reminds us of the arbitrary nature of language, while at the same time asking if meaning is possible *without* words:

> The sun now angles downward, and southward.
> The summer, that is, approaches its final fulfillment.
> The forest is silent, no wind-stir, bird-note, or word.
> It is time to meditate on what the season has meant.
>
> But what is the meaningful language for such meditation?
> What is a word but wind through the tube of the throat?
> Who defines the relation between the word *sun* and the sun?
> What word has glittered on whitecap? Or lured blossom out?
>
> Walk deeper, foot soundless, into the forest.
> Stop, breath bated. Look southward, and up, where high leaves
> Against sun, in vernal translucence, yet glow with the freshest
> Young tint of the lost spring. Here now nothing grieves.
>
> Can one, in fact, meditate in the heart, rapt and wordless?
> Or find his own voice in the towering gust now from northward?
> When boughs toss—is it in joy or pain and madness?
> The gold leaf—is it whirled in anguish or ecstasy skyward?
>
> Can the heart's meditation wake us from life's long sleep,
> And instruct us how foolish and fond was our labor spent—
> Us who now know that only at death of ambition does the deep
> Energy crack crust, spurt forth, and leap
>
> From grottoes, dark—and from the caverned enchainment?
>   (CP 487)

The poem opens simply enough with a series of declarative statements describing the decline of the season, but as soon as the issue of meaning is introduced in the fourth line, the direct statements dissolve into questions and uncertainty, with the second stanza again illustrating the arbitrary nature of the signifier and its irrevocable separateness from reality ("Who defines the relation between the word *sun* and the sun?"). But at the same time as he questions language's ability to capture reality, Warren also asks in the fourth stanza whether or not we can meditate on meaning without language. Can meaning and knowledge exist in a "wordless" form? Warren never answers this question in the poem; in fact, he can only ask more and more questions as the poem moves toward its "conclu-sion"—itself in the form of a question. This poem suggests that when we consider language's central yet elusive role in the creation of meaning, any meaning we create is reduced to interpretation (do the boughs and leaves move in "joy" and "ecstasy" or "pain" and "anguish"?). And if this is the case, we can never locate an absolute form of universal truth. Per-haps Warren is saying that it is only by facing this dark linguistic paradox that the "deep energy" of our potential is allowed to "crack crust, spurt forth, and leap" into being. The construction of meaning requires a leap of faith in the face of this absurd linguistic predicament; the only other op-tion would be silence.

But then again, there is another option—an option that Lyotard claims distinguishes the *truly* postmodern art form from the modern, an option that finally distinguishes Warren from the more typically postmodern, from such contemporary American poets as John Ashbery or the Lan-guage poets. Lyotard distinguishes modern aesthetics from postmodern aesthetics as follows:

> Here, then, lies the difference: modern aesthetics is an aesthetics of the sublime, though a nostalgic one. It allows the unpresentable to be put forward only as the missing contents; but the form, because of recognizable consistency, continues to offer to the reader or viewer matter for solace and pleasure. Yet these sentiments do not constitute the real sublime sentiment, which is an intrinsic combination of plea-sure and pain: the pleasure that reason should exceed all presenta-tion, the pain that imagination or sensibility should not be equal to the concept.
>
> The postmodern would be that which, in the modern, puts forward the unpresentable in presentation itself; that which denies itself the solace of good forms, the consensus of a taste which would make it possible to share collectively the nostalgia for the unattainable; that which searches for new presentations, not in order to enjoy them but in order to impart a stronger sense of the unpresentable. A postmod-ern artist or writer is in the position of a philosopher: the text he writes, the work he produces are not in principle governed by prees-tablished rules, and they cannot be judged according to a determining judgment, by applying familiar categories to the text or to the work. Those rules and categories are what the work of art itself is looking for. (81)

This, then, is exactly where we would have to draw the line between War-ren and the postmodern. According to Lyotard's distinctions, we would have to place Warren in the former, not the latter, category. Even though Warren articulates postmodern linguistic dilemmas in a very direct man-ner throughout his late poetry, his texts do not exhibit the more radical features of presentation that we have come to associate with someone like John Ashbery on the one hand or the Language poets on the other. Ashbery is perhaps the most acclaimed and prominent poet writing in America since the death of Warren in 1989—deservedly so, I think—and in *A Map of Misreading* Harold Bloom correctly sees a link between Ashbery and Warren, describing them both as post-Stevens inheritors of the American Sublime. Yet Warren was ambivalent about Ashbery's po-etry, as may be gleaned from correspondence from Bloom among the Robert Penn Warren Papers.[11] Perhaps Warren felt that a poetry such as Ashbery's *gave in* too much to the "language barrier," or perhaps he felt that his opaque style of writing was creating a new form of elitism remi-niscent of the antidemocratic tendencies of high modernism. If this is the case, we can only imagine what he might think of contemporary Lan-guage poets such as Charles Bernstein, Ron Silliman, and Susan Howe, whose textual effects deliberately confound the reader and are reminis-cent of Gertrude Stein's *Tender Buttons*, one of their literary precursors. Despite Language poetry's self-proclaimed revolutionary politics, even such an advocate of the avant-garde as Marjorie Perloff has suggested some of it might be "no more than a mandarin game designed to entertain an elite coterie" (quoted in Gelpi 537). If so, Albert Gelpi responds, the distinction between the mandarins and the poets "lies in the degree to which one yields to language a devouring self-reflexivity that denies both subject and object by refusing to mediate between them" (537). Gelpi goes on to explain that the "increasing inclination" to detach the text of the poem from, on the one hand, "a consciousness" and, on the other, "a world" distinguishes this contemporary avant-garde from the "earlier Postmodern experiments" of Lowell, Creeley, and Ashbery (537, 538).[12] It is interesting to note that Warren's last four volumes, published over the same years that this new avant-garde was ascending, contain what is ar-guably his most accessible poetry, as he retreats from the more daring and challenging formal methods found in sequences such as *Audubon* and *Or Else*.[13] Warren refrains from illustrating the breakdown of language and meaning in his forms, because he still believes that faith in language is essential to the possibility of an evolving democratic community. He continually approaches the "Inevitable Frontier" at which language collapses upon itself, but he always returns to a chastened faith in the word.

The surreal, nightmarish landscape Warren describes in his poem "Inevitable Frontier" seems in fact to point to what could result if we were to entirely lose faith in the word, if we were finally to give in to the vagaries of language:

Be careful! Slow and careful, for you now approach
The frontier where the password is difficult to utter—or grasp.

Echo among chert peaks and perilously balanced boulders
Has something to do with it, not to mention your early rearing,
    with

Its naïve logic. For remember now, this is the frontier
Where words coming out of a mouth are always upside-

Down, and all tongues are sloppily cubical, and shadows of nothing
    are,
Whatever the hour, always something, and tend to bleed

If stepped on—oh, do keep mindful how
Slick the blood of shadow can be, especially

If the shadow is of nothing. As a corollary,
The shadow of something, yourself for instance,

Provides its own peculiar hazards. You may trip
On it, and start falling upward, screaming,

Screaming for somebody to grab you before you are out
Of reach. Your eyes, too, must be readjusted, for

Here people, owl-like, see only by dark, and grope by day. Here,
People eat in shamefaced privacy, but the great Public Square,

Sparsely planted, is full, in daylight, of gut-wheeze and littered
    with feces
Till the carts come, and later, à l'heure sexuelle, at noon, waiters
    wheel out

To the café terraces divans of ingeniously provocative designs,
While clients, now clad in filmy robes, emerge from locker-rooms,
    laughing

Like children at tag. Food is, of course, forbidden, but scented
   drinks,
And coffee, are served under awnings. Another item:

Criminality is rare, but those convicted,
Mystically deprived of the memory of their names, are exiled

To the Isles of the Blest, where they usually end by swallowing
   their tongues,
This from boredom, for in their language *bliss* and *boredom*

Have the same linguistic root. Yes, many things
Are different here, and to be happy and well-adjusted, you

Must put out of mind much you have been taught. Among others,
   the names
Of Plato, St. Paul, Spinoza, Pascal and Freud must not be spoken,
   and when,

Without warning, by day or night, the appalling
White blaze of God's Great Eye sweeps the sky, History

Turns tail and scuttles back to its burrow
Like a groundhog caught in a speeding sportscar's headlight. (*CP*
   369–70)

For Warren, to lose faith entirely in language is to accept a world in which
nothing is as it seems, and everything collapses into nothing. As our col-
lective faith in language fails, so too must our belief in meaning; responsi-
bility, ethics, value, and history all become void, while community and
democracy give way to a solipsistic pursuit of personal pleasure. But in the
world here described, even this pleasure loses its luster, for without a con-
structed sense of value, everything is the same and bliss becomes boring.
In order for us to have a meaningful democratic community, Warren be-
lieves that we must maintain our faith in the positive power of the word,
and in *Democracy and Poetry* he argues that poetry can indeed play a vital
role in creating such a democratic community. But as his poetic state-
ments make clear, we must not be complacent in our faith in language; we
must instead recognize that language is a flexible rather than a frozen
medium. While this flexibility can at times be terrifying, it also makes
possible what Warren describes as one of the "most precious heritages" of
democracy: "The will to change" (*DP* 79). Importantly, this will to change

is finally contingent upon one's willingness to plunge into the absurdity of the linguistic predicament, for just as history is recorded in language, so too is the future anticipated in language.

Yet Warren also knows that this "will to change" cannot bring us to definitive resolutions, and he arrived at this inevitable frontier of post-modernism only by continually scrutinizing, testing, and modifying his own assumptions over the course of his career. While Warren in his poetry may provide—to borrow Lyotard's phrase—the "solace of good forms," he refuses himself the solace of closure. Warren throughout his career investigated the complicated and, for him, increasingly interrelated issues of selfhood, democracy, aesthetics, and race, yet he never achieved a definitive sense of resolution on any of these issues. Nowhere is this more apparent than in his writings on race, which illustrate that he never rested easily upon any resolutions he may have momentarily achieved. Warren could never leave the issue of race behind him because he understood that we can never achieve closure on such a complex issue—neither individually nor as a nation. The poems "Last Meeting" and "Last Night Train," published in Warren's final collection when he was eighty years old, both give a sense of the incompleteness he felt in his own lifelong personal struggle with race. The poems describe chance encounters with black women, one a former childhood nurse, the other a total stranger. For the narrator of the poems, the chance meetings both end in a failure "to make adequate communication"—a failure to bridge the gap of racial difference.

The typescript draft of "Last Meeting" was dedicated to Geraldine Carr, who was hired as a nurse by the Warren family following the birth of Robert Penn in 1905.[14] In the poem, Warren recalls a chance meeting with his former nurse during one of his visits back to his hometown "some forty years" earlier. The opening stanzas set the context for the meeting by hinting at the segregated social rituals that still governed life in the small Southern town. The narrator and his former nurse momentarily cross these social boundaries as they meet and embrace on a crowded public street, but his recollected response to the situation betrays the awkward self-consciousness he felt at the moment of the encounter. When the woman asks that he always remember her, he fails to respond: "I tried to say 'I couldn't forget,' / But the words wouldn't come, and I felt how frail // Were the vertebrae I clasped" (*CP* 563). As they say goodbye to one another, the narrator notices "eyes staring at us / And laughter in some corner, somewhere" (*CP* 564). If we can trust the narrator's recollection of the memory, the meeting would have taken place sometime in the 1940s. The poem's last three stanzas shift to the present time as the narrator reflects on his own failures to pay his former nurse proper homage:

> All's changed. The faces on the street
> Are changed. I'm rarely back. But once
> I tried to find her grave, and failed.
> Next time I'll promise adequate time.
>
> And find it. I might take store-bought flowers
> (Though not a florist in twenty miles),
> But a fruit jar full of local zinnias
> Might look even better with jimson weed.
>
> It's nigh half a lifetime I haven't managed,
> But there must be enough time left for that. (CP 564)

The narrator desires to pay appropriate homage as a means of achieving some sense of closure, yet the concluding stanzas suggest that the only closure afforded to us occurs in death. The narrator's search for the grave of his former nurse—an effort that ends in failure—prefigures the eventual journey he will make to his own grave. The narrator here is like the narrator of "Old Nigger on One-Mule Cart," who hopes to take to his grave "A hard-won something." The poem itself is perhaps an image of this hard-won thing because it involves an honest confrontation with the speaker's own failings and limitations; however, "Last Meeting," unlike "Old Nigger on One-Mule Cart," lacks any sense of transcendental unity and redemption. The poem shows that the past is always capable of rebuking us, that self-knowledge is, perhaps more often than not, a melancholy meeting with our own failures and inadequacies. Still, this knowledge is worth the effort. As in the case of "Forever O'Clock," there is always an "immanence of identity unspecified" hovering on the horizon of our past, and by confronting it we may project ourselves into the horizon of our future. This is the ongoing process through which the self is constructed in time—a process that resists closure and can offer no definitive meanings. Instead, any meaning we construct is provisional and temporary.

The lack of closure in "Last Meeting" is repeated in "Last Night Train." In this poem, the narrator is on a late-night commuter train traveling from New York City through the Connecticut suburbs and on to Bridgeport. As the train hurtles past deserted platforms, the narrator fixes his gaze on the only other passenger in the car, a middle-aged black woman who has fallen asleep: "a hundred and eighty pounds of / Flesh, black, female, middle-aged, / Unconsciously flung by roadbed jerks to wallow, / Unshaped, unhinged, in / A purple dress" (CP 577). As he continues to study the woman, he seems to be trying to empathize with her and can slowly begin to feel her weariness. However, as he arrives at his station— probably Fairfield—he finds himself faced with a dilemma: "My station at last. I look back once. / Is she missing hers? I hesitate to ask, and the snore / Is suddenly snatched into eternity" (CP 577). The narrator is faced with what seems like a mundane and relatively minor dilemma, but for Warren, whenever the issue of race is involved, things quickly become complicated. There's a sense of uncertainty and inadequacy in the narrator's voice, as though he cannot gather himself to momentarily cross the boundaries of race and gender—and even class. The narrator has gotten off of the train in what is probably a prosperous suburb, and the train has continued on toward the poorer urban area of Bridgeport. As the narrator watches the train receding into the distance, his indecisiveness takes on a larger significance; he reflects on this momentary failure in a way that suddenly begins to consume his entire life:

> The last red light fades into distance and darkness like
> A wandering star. Where the brief roar just now was,
> A last cricket is audible. That lost
> Sound makes me think, with quickly suppressed
> Nostalgia, of
> A country lane, late night, late autumn—and there,
> Alone, again I stand, part of all.
> Alone, I now stand under the green station light,
> Part of nothing but years. (CP 577)

Following his inability to address the woman, the narrator experiences two successive and very distinct emotional reactions. He first experiences a nostalgic mood, drawing upon a pastoral memory to romanticize the encounter with the black woman—a strategy that calls to mind "Tryst on Vinegar Hill" and even "Old Nigger on One-Mule Cart." But the narrator self-consciously suppresses this emotion, perhaps aware that such a response runs the risk of condescension.[15] It is also important to note that the accompanying sense of feeling "part of all" roughly corresponds to Warren's high Romantic assumption of a transcendental unity that reconciles all differences. Now, however, the poet-narrator suppresses this strategic turn even though it could help to alleviate his apprehension by obviating the need for closure. By holding these initial responses in check, the narrator in the final two lines of the stanza is left in a far more austere position: he accepts that he is utterly alone, "Part of nothing but years." This refusal to invoke the Romantic strategy of synthesis is also evident in Warren's 1979 revised version of *Brother to Dragons*, particularly in his startling deletion of the 1953 version's climactic, visionary moment of transcendent unity.[16] In "Last Night Train" the narrator, feeling both insignificant and inadequate, next expresses a desire to free himself from the world's complexities ("I think of swimming, naked and seaward, / In starlight forever"), but he finally turns to face—belatedly—the reality that prompted this sense of inadequacy:

> But I look up the track toward Bridgeport. I feel
> Like blessing the unconscious wallow of flesh-heap
> And white sandals unstrapped at bulging of instep.
>
> I hear my heels crunch on gravel, making
> My way to a parked car. (*CP* 578)

In a conclusion that contrasts sharply with that of "Old Nigger on One-Mule Cart," the poet-narrator refrains from offering the blessing he yearns to impart. He states his desire to offer a blessing, yet he also knows that the actual articulation of a blessing—the molding of the desire into language—would fall short of the mark. Perhaps he also senses that to offer the blessing would somehow be a form of evasion, providing him with a false sense of reconciliation and absolution. The poet-narrator instead accepts his failure "to make adequate communication," and somewhat ruefully he admits his separateness from the woman. The poet is acutely aware of the language barrier; he knows that language cannot apprehend the world's complexities, or even his own.

The lack of closure in these two late poems attests to the compelling authenticity of Warren's writings on race, an authenticity that makes him especially relevant today. Like his altering aesthetic assumptions, Warren's writings on race are anything but consistent; rather, they readily reveal his own conflicts and shortcomings. Certainly one could cite numerous examples from Warren's canon that do not pass today's heightened standards of racial awareness and understanding;[17] nonetheless, his writings on race, like his poetry, chronicle his sincere efforts to gain a greater understanding of himself and the world in which he lived. Such an endeavor can never be irrelevant, even if it provides no definitive answers. Warren's complex career-long engagement with the politically charged issue of race demonstrates the fact that there can be no closure, no easy resolutions on such an issue. The failure to make reparations in "Last Meeting" reflects the incompleteness not only of Warren's personal struggle with the issue but also of the nation's. The failure to reach, even momentarily, across the boundaries of race and class in "Last Night Train" speaks not only of an individual's sense of inadequacy but also of the nation's. It is this open display of internal conflict and incompleteness that perhaps makes Warren's texts seem most real—and most relevant. Indeed, the words Warren used to describe the source of power in James Baldwin's works (*WSN* 296) might just as well be used to describe his own:

> Whatever is vague, blurred, or self-contradictory in his utterances somehow testifies to the magisterial authenticity of the utterance—it is the dramatic image of a man struggling to make sense of the relation of personal tensions to the tensions of the race issue. In his various shiftings of ground in treating the race issue he merely dramatizes the fact that the race issue does permeate all things, all levels; and in the constantly presented drama of the interpenetration of his personal story with the race issue he gives the issue a frightening—and fascinating—immediacy. It is *his* story we finally listen to, in all its complexity of precise and shocking image, and shadowy allusiveness.

Notes

Introduction: Robert Penn Warren's Political and Poetic Transformations

1. William Faulkner of course also comes to mind; however, Warren, unlike Faulkner, often addressed the subject in a personal manner through both his nonfiction prose and his poetry. In chapter 4, I discuss Warren's own comments on Faulkner's more detached treatment of race in his fiction.

2. For other, similar appraisals of Warren's canon, see Justus, *Achievement*, 49–50, and Bedient, *Heart's Last Kingdom*, 3–21. My comments on the concept and strategy of development are greatly influenced by Clifford Siskin's *The Historicity of Romantic Discourse*.

3. While high modernists such as Eliot and Pound often cast themselves in opposition to the aesthetics and philosophy of Romanticism, critics have persuasively shown that the epistemology of modernist poetics—and particularly the way in which the modern poet's imagination attempts to create order from disorder—is often more of a continuation or condensation of Romanticism than a contradiction of it. Most notably, see Harold Bloom's *A Map of Misreading* and Albert Gelpi's *A Coherent Splendor*. Still, despite the fact that moderns and Romantics may be confronting the very same epistemological issues, the emphasis in their responses to these issues remains distinct.

4. In *Poems of Pure Imagination*, Corrigan persuasively demonstrates Warren's affinities with the Romantic tradition; however, she argues that there is even more "continuity of development" in Warren's career than previous critics have shown (24). I see much more conflict in Warren's canon, conflict that becomes abundantly clear when his poetic canon is considered in light of his changing political perspectives.

5. See Warren's comments in Watkins et al., 130, 162, and 239. Critics recently have become increasingly speculative regarding this hiatus from poetry. See, for example, Mark D. Miller, "Faith in Good Works," and James A. Perkins, "Racism and the Personal Past."

6. Gelpi's "The Genealogy of Postmodernism" offers an excellent, concise over-view of the conflicts and continuities between the various trends of modernism, Romanticism, and postmodernism in American poetry. The distinctions I draw be-low in the introduction regarding Warren's modernism and Romanticism are par-ticularly indebted to this essay.

7. I should also note that all three of these terms have been applied to aspects of Warren's poetry by critics in the past, but this study is unique in that it explores the political and ideological assumptions contained within the broader aesthetic trends in Warren's poetic career.

8. "Modernism" certainly was not a monolithic literary movement; rather, as critics have shown again and again, there are numerous traditions within literary modernism. For instance, Cary Nelson in *Repression and Recovery* has argued for the inclusion of Harlem Renaissance and proletarian writers within the modern canon, while Marjorie Perloff, in works like *The Poetics of Indeterminacy*, has con-sistently emphasized the importance of the avant-garde traditions within modern poetry. While the early avant-garde modernism had proclaimed itself a revolution-ary break from orthodoxy, Warren aligned himself with the classically inclined, tra-dition-oriented modernism of the 1920s, of which Eliot was the leading proponent and practitioner. As Michael Levenson shows in *A Genealogy of Modernism*, this particular strain of modernism betrays a "suspicion of progress" and an "insistence on hierarchy and order" (210). Levenson traces the evolution of modernism from early avant-garde efforts up to the "institutionalization of the movement" in 1922 with the publication of *Ulysses* and *The Waste Land* and the founding of Eliot's *Criterion* (213). See in particular part 3 of Levenson's study, which discusses this "consolidation" (137–213). Other critical trends have further complicated the criti-cal map of modern poetry by blurring the boundaries between modernism and the periods that preceded and followed it. Albert Gelpi, as mentioned above, argues for greater continuity between modernism and Romanticism, while James Longenbach in *Modern Poetry after Modernism* argues for greater continuity between modern-ism and the post–World War II poetic landscape. In regard to this latter endeavor, also see Lynn Keller's *Re-Making It New*, which discusses four contemporary poets (Ashbery, Creeley, Merrill, and Bishop) in relation to their modern precursors (Stevens, Williams, Auden, and Moore). Keller's analysis highlights both important "continuities" and "divergences" between the periods.

9. My use of the terms "diagnostic" and "therapeutic" is based upon Warren's own use of the terms in *Democracy and Poetry*.

10. My use of the term "postmodern" is influenced by Lynn Keller's more gen-eral and incluive definition. In *Re-Making It New*, Keller is critical of the use of "postmodern" as a "narrow evaluative label applied ... to experimental works whose aggressive emphasis on textuality and on the web of society's semiotic codes may be linked to poststructuralist criticism" (8). As an alternative, she argues that "'post-modernism' may more usefully serve as a general period term encompassing a broad spectrum of work that both follows after and depends upon modernism" (8). Accord-

ing to the characteristics outlined by Keller, many aspects of Warren's later poetry may be characterized more generally as postmodern: his foregrounding of the self's flux and fluidity and of the self's inability to transcend the arbitrary nature of language, and his growing suspicion regarding all fictive ordering systems. In the conclusion, I will also discuss Warren's late views of language in relation to Jean-François Lyotard's influential work *The Postmodern Condition*.

Chapter 1. The Racialized Order of Warren's "Pondy Woods" Sequence (1929)

1. See, for example, "The American Race Problem as Reflected in American Literature" (47–67) and "Negro Character as Seen by White Authors" (149–83), both of which are reprinted in *A Son's Return,* edited by Mark A. Sanders. The collection also contains "A Romantic Defense" (281–83), Brown's review of *I'll Take My Stand*.

2. Sterling Brown's reply is quoted by Henry Louis Gates Jr. in *Figures in Black*, xix, 225, and in *"Race," Writing, and Difference*, 4.

3. The second half of Brown's poem (*Collected Poems* 40–41) reads:

Fred look up
When he hear dis trash,
Grin crack his mouth
An' de lightnin' flash,
Thoe back his head
An' de thunder crash:

"Whoever sent yuh
Tell him, say,
Fred leave frettin'
Fo' nother day;
Mister Bal'head Buzzard
Git Away!

"Doan give a damn
Ef de good things go,
Game rooster yit,
Still kin crow,
Somp'n in my heart here
Makes me so.

"In roas'n ear time
A man eats co'n,
Dough he knows in winter
Co'n's all gone,
Worry's no good
To whet teeth on.

"No need in frettin'
Case good times go,
Things as dey happen
Jes' is so;
Nothin' las' always
Farz I know. . . ."

4. Many critics have attempted to define the complex relationship between the subject of race and the formation of modernism, the New Criticism, and the the canon. See, for example, Cary Nelson, *Repression and Recovery*, and Michael North, *The Dialect of Modernism*. Also see Henry Louis Gates Jr.'s introduction to *"Race," Writing, and Difference*. Gates mentions Warren and the Agrarians very briefly as he describes the ways in which modernism and the New Criticism created a white canon (4). While I agree with his assessment of the group's role in the formation of the canon, what I find particularly interesting and compelling in Warren's case is that he did change politically, and these political changes also inform his poetry's altering aesthetic. Warren in 1966 actually claimed that both modernism and the New Criticism were dead.

5. According to critics such as Nielsen and Henry Louis Gates Jr., race is a function of ideology, and as a function of ideology it has no basis in the real conditions of existence. As Gates and others demonstrate in the essay collection *"Race," Writing, and Difference*, our concept of racial difference is an arbitrary, fictional construct which has developed over time to support and maintain an ever-evolving hierarchical power structure. Unlike the biological difference in the sexes, for instance, racial categories simply do not retain their boundaries when queried; nonetheless, as Gates explains, "we carelessly use language in such a way as to *will* this sense of *natural* [racial] difference into our formulations. To do so is to engage in a pernicious act of language, one which exacerbates the complex problem of cultural or ethnic difference, rather than to assuage or redress it" (5).

6. This in spite of the fact that the New Criticism Warren would help to establish (and which helped shape the canon) would promote the reading of poetic texts as self-contained objects, free from such political concerns. For a discussion of what Cary Nelson describes as the consequent "white-washing" of the canon, see *Repression and Recovery*, 244. I should also note that I generally agree with much of Nielsen's analysis of Warren's representations of race in his poetry, but while Nielsen limits his discussion to the poems that deal directly with race, I am attempting to draw a clearer connection between Warren's political transformation and the striking changes that occur in his overall aesthetic. For Nielsen's discussion of Warren, see *Reading Race*, 113–22.

7. Gray describes the time between the wars in the South as a "climate of fear." See chapter 4 of *Writing the South*, 122–64. For an exhaustive study of the cultural transitions that took place in the South, see Daniel Joseph Singal's *The War Within*.

8. See M. Thomas Inge, "The Fugitives and the Agrarians: A Clarification." John

Gould Fletcher also published in both the *Fugitive* and *I'll Take My Stand,* but he was not as closely involved in the Fugitive group as the other four, who were all at Vanderbilt when the *Fugitive* was launched.

9. See the foreword to the first issue of the *Fugitive* from 1922, which claims that the journal "flees from nothing faster than from the high-caste Brahmins of the Old South."

10. For overviews of this transition between the Fugitive and Agrarian groups, see Louise Cowan, *The Fugitive Group,* 222–57, and Richard Gray, *Writing the South,* 122–64.

11. See, for instance, *John Brown* 86, 102, 245–46, 391. For an excellent in-depth discussion of Warren's biography of Brown, see Jonathan S. Cullick, *Making History,* 28–50.

12. Quoted in Daniel Joseph Singal's *The War Within,* 348. Davidson's typescript letter, among the Robert Penn Warren Papers at Yale, contains an interesting strikeover here: he had first typed "animals" before crossing it out and replacing it with "folks." In his study, Singal suggests that Warren had no choice of subject because the issue of segregation was the only topic left when he signed on to the project; however, Ransom's comments in his letter of January 20, 1930, clearly gave Warren more freedom of choice. Donald Davidson's letter to Warren dated March 10, 1930, also shows that segregation was Warren's chosen subject (RPW Papers).

13. "Kentucky Mountain Farm" is listed in the manuscript's table of contents as a five-part poem; however, the Robert Penn Warren Papers do not include the third section, and no title is listed in the table of contents. It is quite likely that the third section at this time was "History among the Rocks" which had already been published in the *New Republic* in December of 1928. The other sections are: I. "Rebuke of the Rocks," II. "At the Hour of the Breaking of the Rocks," IV. "The Owl" (alternate version titled "The Moon"), and V. "The Return." See James A. Grimshaw Jr., *Robert Penn Warren: A Descriptive Bibliography,* 185–86, 265.

14. For my discussion of the "Pondy Woods" sequence, I will refer to the texts of the poems as they appear in *The Collected Poems.* Following the failure of Payson and Clarke, Warren apparently reused the original typescripts from some of these early poems in order to construct other, later proposed volumes; consequently, the "Pondy Woods and Other Poems" folder among the Robert Penn Warren Papers lacks a few of the poems listed in the table of contents. A collation of the texts of the existing typescript and *The Collected Poems* revealed only minor variations.

15. Critics have attempted to read Jim as a sort of everyman facing death, and according to this interpretation it seems that you would have to read "breed" as referring to the human race as a whole. But as I will show through my discussion of "Tryst on Vinegar Hill," when Warren uses "breed" in these poems, he is voicing an assumption about the black race specifically.

16. Also see Randy Hendricks's recent discussion of the poem in *Lonelier than God,* 107–10. Hendricks similarly argues that through the buzzards Warren is attacking the "Brahmin" class of the South; like many others, he argues that the racist

rhetoric in the poem is "objectionable ... only if readers take it as a direct statement from Warren and reduce Warren to a twentieth-century Confederate writing a metaphysical poem" (108). I obviously am taking a different approach to the poem.

17. Published the same year in which "Pondy Woods and Other Poems" was accepted for publication, Warren's *John Brown* likewise exhibits an unquestioning belief in such racial stereotypes as well as a willingness to invoke racist rhetoric (see, for instance, 61, 79, 308). Also, in response to Nielsen's and Raper's ironical interpretations of Warren's speaking buzzard, it seems possible—in light of the time of publication—that Warren has a buzzard address Jim simply because it is among the basest of creatures, thereby suggesting that Jim is on a similar level.

18. Sterling Brown comments on these stereotypes and others in "Negro Character As Seen by White Authors," first published in 1933. Reprinted in *A Son's Return*, edited by Mark A. Sanders, 149–83.

19. In this sequence of poems, a central narrative consciousness emerges and may be seen as the poetic figure surveying his cultural landscape and attempting to define his place within it. This becomes progressively clearer as the sequence moves toward its concluding poem, "The Last Metaphor."

20. It is also revealing to contrast the lovers in "Tryst on Vinegar Hill" with the lovers in Warren's metaphysical love poems published in *Eleven Poems on the Same Theme,* especially "Bearded Oaks," "Picnic Remembered," and "Love's Parable." The characters in those poems have much more in common with the narrator of "Tryst" than with the poem's young black couple.

21. From a typescript lecture dated 1934 and titled "Modern Poetry, or Modernism in Poetry" (RPW Papers).

Chapter 2. Rereading "The Briar Patch"

1. In a later introduction published in 1977, Rubin explains his earlier lack of commentary on the race issue thus: "It seemed to me that issues which by 1962 were highly controversial, seen by many southerners then in very different ways than in 1930, should not be permitted to distort the real importance of what the Agrarians had written" (xvii). In *Inventing Southern Literature,* Michael Kreyling provides an in-depth analysis of Rubin's role in defining the canon of Southern literature. According to Kreyling, Rubin's criticism illustrates "the process by which history was detoxified and recoupled with literary criticism as part of the conservative reaction against desegregation in society and theory in literary study" (xii–xiv).

2. Sanders's confusion here between Fugitives and Agrarians provides further evidence to support M. Thomas Inge's argument in "The Fugitives and the Agrarians."

3. A concise overview of these assumptions is provided by George M. Fredrickson in the concluding chapter of *The Black Image in the White Mind.* Fredrickson argues that the "basic white-supremacist propositions" dominating discourse on race in both the North and the South from the early nineteenth century to the beginning of

World War I were: "1. Blacks are physically, intellectually, and temperamentally *different* from whites. 2. Blacks are also *inferior* to whites in at least some of the fundamental qualities wherein the races differ, especially in intelligence and in the temperamental basis of enterprise or initiative. 3. Such differences and differentials are either permanent or subject to change only by a very slow process of development or evolution. 4. Because of these permanent or deep-seated differences, miscegenation, especially in the form of intermarriage, is to be discouraged. . . . 5. Racial prejudice or antipathy is a natural and inevitable white response to blacks when the latter are free from legalized subordination and aspiring to equal status. . . . 6. It follows from the above propositions that a biracial equalitarian (or "integrated") society is either completely impossible, now and forever, or can be achieved only in some remote and almost inconceivable future" (321).

4. I am reminded in particular of a heated debate at the annual Robert Penn Warren Conference in 1994, precipitated by a paper that Forrest G. Robinson delivered and later published as "A Combat with the Past." Also, I would like to emphasize that my present comments refer only to Warren's early career up to the mid-1930s. I will argue that later in his career Warren at times uses racist rhetoric in a self-conscious and self-deprecating fashion.

5. Again, as I mention in the introduction, my comments on the strategy of development are indebted to Clifford Siskin's *The Historicity of Romantic Discourse.*

6. I am not suggesting that Warren's early views were in any way identical to Davidson's; I am simply saying that Warren's shift to an integrationist position was not as inevitable as some have portrayed it.

7. See also Jancovich, *Cultural Politics,* 24–25; Justus, *Achievement,* 138–42; and Casper, *Robert Penn Warren,* 27–28. For contrasting analyses see Gray, *Writing the South,* 132–33, and Nielsen, *Reading Race,* 113–14.

8. In *But Now I See,* Fred Hobson points out that even white Southerners who were critical of segregation during its early days tended to approach the subject "less on moral than on social and economic grounds" (13).

9. Also see Watkins et al., *Talking with Robert Penn Warren,* 384, 392. In the interview with Marshall Walker, Warren explains that he began to question his views on segregation shortly after he returned to the South following his time spent at Oxford, but it is difficult to say when exactly he changed his position on segregation. Evidence of Warren's views on the Scottsboro case which I will discuss below suggests he was still a segregationist at least through 1933. Perhaps the first clear sign of his questioning of his own racial assumptions is his 1935 short story "Her Own People," which was later included in *The Circus in the Attic.* I'll discuss this story in chapter 4.

10. See chapter 5, "Deadly Amusements," in Hale's *Making Whiteness,* 199–239. Hale explains that with the advent of consumer culture in the South, "More people participated in, read about, saw pictures of, and collected souvenirs from lynchings even as fewer mob murders occurred" (201).

11. This revitalization of the Ku Klux Klan was a national movement not limited to the South. For a discussion of the lynching of Jesse Washington, see Hale, *Making Whiteness*, 215–22. Hale also argues for a causal connection between the emergence of the New Negro and the institution of segregation as the culture of the South: "Making and perpetuating the myth of absolute racial difference in this region, the division of the world into absolute blackness and whiteness, required the creation of racial segregation as the central metaphor of the new regional culture. In important respects, the 'New Negro,' the name some educated African Americans of the generation born into freedom chose for themselves, forced white southerners to create a 'New South'" (21–22).

Chapter 3. The Conservative Modernist Aesthetic of Warren's Early Poetry, 1923–1943

1. "Warren and Race Revisited," delivered by William Bedford Clark at the 1998 American Literature Association Convention in San Diego, California.

2. The letter, among the Allen Tate Papers in Princeton's Firestone Library, is merely dated November 1932. However, Warren's reference to the Vanderbilt-Tennessee football game, which took place on November 12 that year, allows us to narrow the date of composition. The Supreme Court handed down its decision in the Powell case on November 7 of that year.

3. The tenor and tone of Owsley's article show that he was already quite embittered, as do his comments on reconstruction in *I'll Take My Stand*. See "The Irrepressible Conflict," 61– 64.

4. Warren's criticism of this period reveals a consistent antipathy toward writers of the left. See, for instance, his comments in "Literature as a Symptom," "The Present State of Poetry: In the United States," and "The Situation in American Writing, Part II." In *American Fiction in the Cold War*, Thomas Hill Schaub describes how the radical writers and critics of the left were chastened by the rise of totalitarianism in the 1930s. Following World War II, these intellectuals refashioned their old, optimistic liberalism into a new, more skeptical liberalism that acknowledged human evil and fallibility. Significantly, Warren's new aesthetic of the 1950s would occupy similar ground.

5. Warren is referring to Cleveland B. Chase's *Sherwood Anderson* (New York: Robert M. McBride, 1927) and N. Bryllion Fagin's *The Phenomenon of Sherwood Anderson: A Study in American Life and Letters* (Baltimore: Rossi-Bryn, 1927).

6. Eliot's influential essay "Ulysses, Order and Myth" was first published in the *Dial* in November 1923.

7. I borrow the phrase from Fredric Jameson's *The Political Unconscious*. While I generally agree with Jameson's imperative "Always historicize" (9), I do not entirely subscribe to the Marxist agenda of his argument. For appraisals of the fascistic, authoritarian tendencies of modernism, see Jameson's own *Fables of Aggression*, chap. 4 ("The Modern Apocalypse"), and Frank Kermode's *Sense of an Ending*, 93–

124. Also see Karen O'Kane's discussion of the conservative political origins of the New Criticism in "Before the New Criticism."

8. See Louise Cowan, *The Fugitive Group*, 108–9.

9. For instance, see Justus, *Achievement*, 50–52, and Koppelman, *Warren's Modernist Spirituality*, 71.

10. Warren's essay "Literature as a Symptom" was published in *Who Owns America?* in 1936. For other evidence of Warren's growing wariness regarding the regionalist label, see his essay "Some Don'ts for Literary Regionalists," also published in 1936.

11. Warren makes essentially the same argument in "Literature as a Symptom," published the same year, where he points out that, unlike modern literature, the work of writers of the past was "defined, in its theme and essence, by a powerful and coherent culture" (265).

12. See Stewart, *The Burden of Time*, 463–66; Strandberg, *Poetic Vision*, 132; and Blotner, *Robert Penn Warren*, 199–200.

13. Warren explains this as a reference to "the 'death' of the chicken heart which Alexis Carrel had kept alive for a long time in his laboratory and which had for popular-science writers the promise of a mortal immortality. . . . the business about the chicken heart seemed to summarize a view current in our time—that science (as popularly conceived) will solve the problem of evil by reducing it merely to a matter of 'adjustment' in the physical, social, economic, and political spheres" ("Author's Note" 542).

14. See F. Cudworth Flint, "Five Poets." Victor Strandberg interprets Warren's reference to Flint as a sign that Warren felt "stung" by Flint's criticism. Strandberg argues that Warren's early governing myth is that of the Fall, and he also argues, I believe rightly, that the later poetry attempts to provide the very sort of "myth" Flint here desires; see *Poetic Vision*, 36–37.

Chapter 4. Racial Themes and Formal Transitions
in Warren's Early Fiction

1. See Miller, "Faith in Good Works," and Perkins, "Racism and the Personal Past."

2. The plots of *Night Rider* and *At Heaven's Gate* momentarily turn on the wrongful persecution of innocent black men, while in *World Enough and Time* Rachel Jordan faces a false charge of miscegenation.

3. The trend toward the personal confrontation with race in Warren's work of this period can also be considered as part of a larger literary phenomenon that was beginning in the South at the time. In *But Now I See*, Fred Hobson describes the "outburst of white southern autobiography driven by racial guilt" that occurred from the 1940s through the 1960s (15). Hobson calls this distinctly new form of autobiography in the South the "racial conversion narrative."

4. See Warren's comments in Watkins et al., *Talking with Robert Penn Warren*, 74, 180. Also see Blotner, *Robert Penn Warren*, 213.

Chapter 5. Confession and Complicity in *Brother to Dragons* (1953)

1. See Watkins et al., *Talking with Robert Penn Warren*, 162; also 130, 239.

2. Throughout *Robert Penn Warren and American Idealism*, John Burt argues that Warren is simultaneously attracted to and repulsed by Romantic idealism. Also see Strandberg, *Poetic Vision*, 31–32.

3. As shown in chapter 3, Warren's 1933 essay on Sidney Lanier harshly criticizes the very features of Romanticism—subjectivity and synthesis—that he now adopts in his own poetry. See "The Blind Poet," 44–45.

4. This oversight is understandable, for as Siskin explains in his study, development has been so thoroughly naturalized into an accepted "truth" that critics generally overlook its formal literary features. During this period, Warren similarly seems to embrace this view of the self and method of self-representation in an uncritical manner; however, his poetry of the late 1960s and early 1970s actually begins to interrogate this very strategy much in the way that Siskin does in his pioneering study of Romantic discourse. Development in Warren's poetry thus goes from being a relatively transparent method of self-representation to a subject of inquiry in itself.

5. See John Burt's *Robert Penn Warren and American Idealism*, particularly his chapter on *Night Rider* (127–40), for an interesting discussion of Warren's particular brand of naturalism in his early works. That the young Warren held a more deterministic view of the individual's place in history may be seen in early poems like "Terror," "Pursuit," and "The Ballad of Billie Potts" and early novels like *Night Rider* and *At Heaven's Gate*. By the 1950s, however, Warren dismisses such views, arguing in *Segregation* that we cannot simply view ourselves as "prisoners of history." By the 1950s, Warren had come to see the self as a more responsible, active agent, capable of engaging in and changing the moral landscape of contemporary culture and politics.

6. In "Racism and the Personal Past," James A. Perkins argues that Warren's conversion on the issue of race "allowed him to recover his childhood memories as a subject for poetry" (73). Also see Fred Hobson's brief discussion of Warren's *Segregation* and *Who Speaks for the Negro?* in *But Now I See*, 80–82. Warren's numerous textual engagements with race during this period—including *Brother to Dragons*—can certainly be read within the framework of what Hobson calls the "racial conversion narrative."

7. Much has been said of Warren's thematic inquiries into determinism and individual will and responsibility; certainly these issues formed something of an obsession for him throughout his career. Perhaps nowhere in his canon are the interrelated subjects of will and determinism more complex and fascinating than when he

considers his own evolving views on race and segregation. At times Warren seems somewhat willing to blame his environment and background for his early segregationist views; elsewhere he offers the counterargument that we cannot view ourselves simply as "prisoners of history." But this unresolved dilemma not only is relevant to his early positions, it also complicates the way we approach his later conversion to an integrationist position. While Warren's conversion suggests a deliberately willed self-examination and self-revision, we would also have to admit that this self-examination was to some extent prompted by environmental factors— by the changing landscape of racial politics in America and perhaps by the fact that he had not lived in the South since he left LSU in 1942.

8. It is also relevant to note that in the period before the United States entered the war, Warren was an isolationist. The true horror of the Nazi regime which came to light after the war may have offered a rebuke to his earlier position and, combined with other factors, may have prompted Warren's adoption of a more engaged aesthetic. As I will discuss below, the totalitarian regimes of Hitler and Mussolini are important contextual factors behind the writing of *Brother to Dragons*. See Blotner, *Robert Penn Warren*, 170. Also see Warren's comments on the war in "The Situation in American Writing," 112–13.

9. Ruppersburg, like most critics, discusses the 1979 version. I believe the 1953 version of *Brother to Dragons* presents a more important moment in Warren's career—serving as a breakthrough to his later aesthetic—in addition to being a more effective poem. While the 1953 version seems excessive in its rhetoric and tone, it is perfectly appropriate to the brutal subject matter.

10. One critic who does focus at length on race in the poem is Aldon Lynn Nielsen, but even Nielsen expresses a certain degree of puzzlement regarding R.P.W.'s inconsistent racial rhetoric. According to Nielsen, R.P.W. at times seems to "turn racial metaphors inside out," while at others he makes racist comments "which are not so evidently to be read as irony" (*Reading Race* 122).

11. Quoted in Richard Gray, *American Poetry*, 251. Jonathan Cullick's argument that over the course of his career Warren felt a growing need to personalize history in his work is especially relevant here; see *Making History*, 3–4.

12. See Thomas Hill Schaub's discussion of Niebuhr in *American Fiction in the Cold War*, 9–13. Schaub's study describes the emergence of a new, more skeptical form of liberalism following the rise of totalitarianism and in the wake of World War II. Niebuhr was a major proponent of this new liberalism which freely acknowledged the deep human capacity for evil.

13. In a 1977 interview with Peter Stitt, Warren provides some specific details about his creative process for *Brother to Dragons*. Stitt points out that *Brother to Dragons* is perhaps Warren's "most abstract and intellectual poem" and asks if he were "intentionally putting ideas first." Warren responds that for him "the process of writing . . . is to grope for the meaning of the thing, and exploration for the meaning rather than an execution of meanings already arrived at; see *The World's*

Hieroglyphic Beauty, 247. Warren's notes for the poem provide an interesting glimpse into the type of internal dialogue and debate Warren engaged in as he constructed the poem's meaning.

14. Warren's repeated use of this image—in *All the King's Men, Brother to Dragons,* and later poems—almost calls to mind Jacques Lacan's operational metaphor of "the gaze." But while the gaze for Lacan provides the subject with the ability to sense itself holistically as something more than its conscious self, the black gaze in Warren's poetry actually works to disrupt and undermine such a sense of the self. Hugh Ruppersburg also discusses these scenes in *Robert Penn Warren and the American Imagination,* 60–62.

15. W.E.B. Du Bois will also invoke this image of the veil more than a century later, making it a central metaphor in *The Souls of Black Folk.*

Chapter 6. *Segregation:* The Inner Conflict in Robert Penn Warren

1. See Blotner, *Robert Penn Warren,* 219, 232, 267, 284–85.

2. For representative appraisals of the novel, see Blotner, *Robert Penn Warren,* 298–300, and Justus, *Achievement,* 236. For an interesting discussion of *Band of Angels* which is particularly relevant to my line of inquiry in this study, I refer the reader to Lucy Ferriss's recent reappraisal and analysis of the novel in *Sleeping with the Boss.* Ferriss challenges thematic approaches to the novel by focusing on the subtleties of Manty Starr's subjectivity. Significantly, she also frames her discussion within the context of the slave narrative tradition and its unique narrative characteristics. This is a particularly important aspect of her discussion, for the Robert Penn Warren Papers at Yale show that Warren was reading extensively in this genre while preparing to write his novel.

3. John Jessup was the husband of Eunice Clark, Eleanor Clark's sister; see Blotner, *Robert Penn Warren,* 301–2.

4. In *Divided Minds,* Carol Polsgrove offers a revisionary history of the civil rights movement, one showing "that people designated as intellectuals often fail, not only in courage and compassion, but also in vision" (246). While there is much truth to her charge that the American media essentially silenced radical and progressive perspectives on the movement by seeking out more moderate voices, portions of her discussion seem unfair. Such is the case in her treatment of Robert Penn Warren, which is suspiciously selective. Despite the fact that Warren is presented in her introduction (and on the dust jacket) as a prominent figure in her narrative, he appears more as a straw man: she discusses only one of his texts, *Segregation,* in any detail, and that for a scant four pages (25–28). Moreover, she seems to stack the deck against Warren, pointing out that the word "nigger" falls "casually from the lips of characters in *All the King's Men* . . . and in *Brother to Dragons,* a long poem about Thomas Jefferson's nephews' murder of a slave" (25). Strangely enough, after pointing out the racial subject matter of *Brother to Dragons,* she immediately states: "Indeed, throughout his work Robert Penn Warren had circled the issue of race

without coming to land on it. From his first book *(John Brown)* to his latest novel *(Band of Angels)*, slavery and its legacy had preoccupied him. Yet there was something abstract about his approach to the subject, as if he could not quite get hold of it" (25). The manner in which these texts qualify as "abstract" is never explained.

5. Still, the majority of the text is devoted to dialogue, and many critics have commented on Warren's use of the dialogic method in both his prose and poetry. Most notably, Karen Ramsay Johnson has demonstrated that Warren's use of this method in *Segregation* and *Who Speaks for the Negro?* is evidence of his awareness that both personal and social change are contingent upon the flexibility of language; see "'Voices,'" 33–45.

6. See John Burt's in-depth analysis of *The Legacy of the Civil War* in *Warren and American Idealism*, 10–33. Burt shows that the text outlines America's central historical conflict between higher law and legalism, and affirms the need to stake out the neutral territory of pragmatism.

7. Also see Warren's comments in *Who Speaks for the Negro?*, 11–13.

8. This is not to say that the young Warren was incapable of looking at the past from an extremely critical vantage point. Consider, for example, his biography *John Brown*. Significantly, however, Warren's regional biases in that text do prevent him from looking either very critically or from a moral standpoint at the issue of slavery itself.

Chapter 7. The Consolidation of Warren's Romantic Aesthetic, 1955–1966

1. Warren in a number of interviews comments on his early reading of all of the poets named in the poem. See, for example, Watkins et al., *Talking with Robert Penn Warren*, 9–10, 29, 88, 360–61.

2. See Corrigan, *Poems of Pure Imagination*, 13–18, and Jancovich, *Cultural Politics*, 127; also see Homer Obed Brown, "The Art of Theology and the Theology of Art," and Jonathan Arac, "Repetition and Exclusion."

3. For example, see Jerome McGann, *The Romantic Ideology*, 40–49.

4. Lesa Carnes Corrigan directly links this essay to Romantic influences; see *Poems of Pure Imagination*, 17–19. Victor Strandberg also provides thorough discussions of this essay in "Warren's Osmosis" and in *Poetic Vision*, 190–254. Also see Burt, *Warren and American Idealism*, 47–49, and Koppelman, *Warren's Modernist Spirituality*, 10–11.

5. In some ways, one might say that the narrative of this book is likewise a developmental narrative as I trace Warren's changing politics and aesthetics. However, the changes I am attempting to describe were not inevitable; rather, they came about through personal conflicts involving self-criticism and self-revision. The problem for critics is that any developmental narrative we create as an act of interpretation runs the risk of erasing points of conflict and contradiction in order to achieve a sense of consistency and inevitability. An additional problem that presents itself in Warren's case is that his poetry of this period relies heavily on the Romantic dis-

course of development, and critics have generally overlooked the strategic aspects of such discourse. Moreover, as I will explain later, they also have overlooked the ways in which Warren later came to question and undermine these very strategies. Siskin persuasively demonstrates how and why the rhetoric of development infects not only creative texts but critical narratives as well; see especially chapters 2 and 3. Siskin in fact goes so far as to claim that "development is an all-encompassing formal strategy underpinning middle class culture itself: its characteristic way of representing and evaluating the individual as something that grows" (12).

6. See Mark Royden Winchell, "O Happy Sin!" Also see John Burt's discussion of transgression and recovery in *Warren and American Idealism*, 47–49.

7. See Strandberg, *Poetic Vision*, 261–67.

8. In fact, various critics have singled out every volume between 1943 and 1969 as being somehow "transitional." Perhaps any effort to divide and classify Warren's canon of poetry by only using prosodic indicators is moot, considering the breadth and variety of Warren's verse at each moment in his career.

9. This sense of interpenetration is succinctly conveyed in a remarkable passage from Warren's 1966 poem "Saul at Gilboa":

I am the past time, am old, but
Am, too, the time to come, for I,
In my knowledge, close my eyes, and am
The membrane between the past and the future, am thin, and
That thinness is the present time, the membrane
Is only my anguish, through which
The past seeps, penetrates, is absorbed into
The future, through which
The future bleeds into, becomes, the past even before
It ceases to be
The future. Am also

The knife edge that divides. (*CP* 211)

10. In my discussion of Warren's poems of this period, I will often refer to a particular poem's "narrator" or "speaker." It should be kept in mind, however, that in most of these poems Warren is drawing from his own personal experience, and so the gap between the narrator and the poet himself is diminished. The complications surrounding the autobiographical act become the subject of much of Warren's later poetry, as I'll discuss in later chapters. For an interesting discussion of the biographical backgrounds for many of these poems, see Floyd Watkins, *Then & Now*.

11. See Koppelman's comments on the narrator's acceptance of uncertainty, *Warren's Modernist Spirituality*, 44.

12. *William Wordsworth (The Oxford Authors)*, edited by Stephen Gill (Oxford: Oxford University Press, 1984), 464. Also see the comparison of Warren's poem

"Language Barrier" and this particular passage from Wordsworth's *Prelude* in Burt, *Warren and American Idealism*, 4–9.

13. See the discussion of this tendency in Warren's poetry by Strandberg in *Poetic Vision*, 205–11.

14. John Burt links the poem's acceptance of this failure not to Romanticism but to the elegiac form itself: "Elegy does not affirm meaning but the possibility of meaning which inheres in becoming. It is this possibility that is the final form of consolation" (75). Nonetheless, the emphasis on "becoming" may owe something to the rhetoric of Romanticism as well.

Chapter 8. Warren in Transition: *Who Speaks for the Negro?* and *A Plea in Mitigation*

1. Also see John Van Dyke's excellent discussion of *A Plea in Mitigation* in "Language at the End of Modernism." Van Dyke argues that, for Warren, "The death of the modern is marked by a sense of linguistic crisis. . . . there is a new awareness that language does not always perform the way we think it should. Sometimes it will give us adequate images, but at others it withdraws and holds itself in reserve" (240). I agree with Van Dyke's view that there is a "growing suspicion" regarding the nature of language over the course of Warren's career, but as I hope to show in this chapter, this suspicion—or awareness—can be linked to Warren's immersion in the racial politics of the early 1960s.

2. As mentioned in the previous chapter, locating discernible "transition" points in Warren's canon is a difficult task, for his poetry is always richly varied in style and form. This is why I have chosen to adopt his four volumes of selected poems as boundaries for my discussion. Certainly many of the poems in his 1966 *Selected Poems* are similar to those published in the period 1966–75 which I shall discuss in the following chapter; however, I believe that his decision to publish his 1966 *Selected Poems* so shortly after finishing *Who Speaks for the Negro?* is fascinating, for a midcareer volume of selected poems suggests both a sense of an ending and a new beginning. *A Plea in Mitigation* makes this abundantly clear; moreover, when this essay is examined alongside the text of *Who Speaks for the Negro?* it becomes apparent that this poetic transition is again closely linked to his contemplation of race in America.

3. The turmoil I have in mind is not the civil unrest and assassinations that occurred in the United States in 1968; I am referring to that year's strikes by students and workers in Paris, which are often linked with the emergence and consolidation of poststructuralist theory.

4. Contemporary theorists use the term "subject" rather than "self." The term "self" implies an autonomous being whose sense of itself is synonymous with consciousness, such as that evident in Descartes's dictum "I think, therefore I am." In contrast, the term "subject" implies that human reality is a culturally and histori-

cally specific linguistic construction, and that we are generally unconscious of this fact. I will argue that Warren comes to share some of the perspectives we associate with poststructuralism; however, I will continue to use the term "self," particularly since it is the term Warren employs. I will discuss below the distinction between self and identity.

5. It is nonetheless intriguing to note that Warren's final years at Yale coincided with the emergence of the "Yale school" of deconstruction: Paul de Man, Geoffrey Hartman, J. Hillis Miller, and Harold Bloom. Also, Warren and Harold Bloom developed a close relationship during the early 1970s, corresponding at great length on Warren's poetry and Bloom's developing psychopoetic theories of influence. Warren's relationship with Bloom marks one instance in which Warren *was* influenced by a critic, as seen in "Red-Tail Hawk and Pyre of Youth." Bloom's letters to Warren are among the Robert Penn Warren Papers at Yale's Beinecke Library.

6. In addition to Thiemann, also see Koppelman, *Warren's Modernist Spirituality*, Scott, *Visions of Presence*, and Cain, "Robert Penn Warren, Paul de Man, and the Fate of Criticism." Perhaps the most extensive study of the relationship between Warren and contemporary literary theory is to be found in Mark Jancovich's *The Cultural Politics of the New Criticism*.

7. The poststructuralists Thiemann mentions here are Derrida, Lacan, Kristeva, Foucault, and Barthes.

8. For an interesting example of Warren's response to the sit-ins and the often violent response to them, see his unfinished 1960 essay "Episode in a Dime Store," discovered by James Perkins among the Robert Penn Warren Papers.

9. In a 1998 Robert Penn Warren Conference panel discussion titled "Warren and Race," John Burt pointed out that when Warren published *Who Speaks for the Negro?* in 1965, Random House designed a rather unfortunate dust jacket for the book. Against a black background bold red letters ask the titular question, while immediately below in equally bold white letters appears the name of Robert Penn Warren. The result of the design is that Warren's name seems to be the answer to the title's question, an idea thaat clearly goes against his intentions in the book.

10. For other in-depth discussions of *Who Speaks for the Negro?*, see Clark, *American Vision*, 111–20; Johnson, "'Voices'"; and Ruppersburg, *American Imagination*, 139–50.

11. To this reason, the Reverend Wyatt Tee Walker responds that Warren is "very courageous" (*WSN* 232). Warren's response is noteworthy. He first feels "a cold flash of rage" and goes on to comment in his notebook: "*At the condescension—moral condescension. The Negro Movement is fueled by a sense of moral superiority. No wonder that some sloshes over on the white bystander as condescension. The only effective payment for all the other kinds of condescension visited on black men over the years. Antidote indicated: humor. And not only self-humor*" (*WSN* 232).

12. This seems to have been a particularly complex task for Warren, as the holo-

graph and typescript manuscripts among the Robert Penn Warren Papers show substantive revisions and deletions in these "confessional" passages.

13. Also see his interview with Ralph Ellison (*WSN* 334).

14. Warren also alters his view of Emerson in this passage (*WSN* 321).

15. John Burt provides an interesting discussion of three separate forms of identity in *Robert Penn Warren and American Idealism*; see 55–65 especially.

16. For an illustration of the way race can complicate this gap or misinterpretation between self and identity, see the opening chapter of Warren's novel *Flood*, in which Blad Tolliver and a black gas station attendant completely misread one another. Also see Warren's comments in *Who Speaks for the Negro?* on the "Sambo" stereotype of the cravenly servile slave (58–59).

17. Karen Ramsay Johnson effectively argues in "'Voices in My Own Blood'" that Warren's use of the dialogic method in *Who Speaks for the Negro?* and *Segregation* demonstrates his awareness that both personal and social change are contingent upon the flexibility of language.

18. This is particularly true of Warren's anecdote, repeated in *Who Speaks for the Negro?*, *Portrait of a Father*, and several interviews, regarding the way his father admonished him for using the word "nigger."

19. In his poetry of 1966–75, Warren continually investigates the more radical implications of this premise, concluding that the self is indeed a fictional construct created through language. In contrast to Fred Thiemann, I believe Warren's late poetry can be fruitfully examined in the light of some of the basic principles of Jacques Lacan's psychoanalytic theories, which effectively blended Freudian principles with structural linguistics. According to Lacan, the notion of the stable, autonomous ego is an illusion; instead, "the law of man" is "the law of language" (*Écrits* 61). Importantly, for Lacan, language does not transmit positive and concrete value; rather, it is a self-contained and self-referential system which is forever removed from reality, functioning primarily through difference and absence. And yet it is through words that we give the fleeting, transitory perceptions of consciousness a sense of permanence. Lacan states, "Through the word—already a presence made of absence—absence gives itself a name in that moment of origin," and from this play of presence and absence, "there is born the world of meaning of a particular language in which the world of things will come to be arranged." In other words, "It is the world of words that creates the world of things . . . by giving its concrete being to their essence, and its ubiquity to what has always been" (*Écrits* 65). Importantly, this process includes the way we conceive of the self (or "subject"); as a result, Lacan believes, we experience alienation even as we create ourselves and our reality through words.

20. In chapter 3, "The Big Brass," Warren counterpoints King with Malcolm X, and in chapter 4, "Leadership from the Periphery," he likewise counterpoints Baldwin's views with those of Ralph Ellison.

21. See Clark, *American Vision*, 118, and Ruppersburg, *American Imagination*, 140, 145.

Chapter 9. Reinterpreting the Personal Past: Race in Warren's Later Poetry

1. My comments on Warren and Heidegger are indebted to Richard Jackson's excellent article "The Generous Time: Robert Penn Warren and the Phenomenology of the Moment."

2. Consider, for instance, Floyd Watkins's *Then & Now*.

3. Aldon Nielsen and Fred Thiemann are the only critics who take into consideration the speaker's racist attitudes. It would seem, however, that Nielsen believes the poem is uncritically accepting of these racist assumptions. In very brief comments, Nielsen claims that the poem "doesn't so much seek out the human truth hidden by the term as it confirms . . . discourse agreements regarding the morality of blacks" (*Reading Race*, 117). Thiemann, on the other hand, echoing Ruppersburg's analysis, sees the speaker's racism as a symptom of the "dehumanization" rampant in modern society ("Politics and the Self," 87–88). For other analyses which do not consider the issue of racism in the poem, see Justus, *Achievement*, 86–87; Walker, *Robert Penn Warren*, 165–67; and Scott, *Visions of Presence*, 157–58.

4. The opening and concluding stanzas read:

Nigger, nigger, burning bright,
In the forests of the night,
Why does your mouth stretch so wide, thin, and round
So long before I can hear the scream's sound?
. . . .
Nigger, nigger, burning bright
In the forests of the night,
What immortal hand or eye
Could frame such Delphic ecstasy?

5. From a letter to Howard Moss dated May 16, 1975, in the Robert Penn Warren Papers.

6. In *Fictions in Autobiography*, Eakin provides an excellent overview and analysis of competing theories of autobiography, and my comments on the autobiographical in Warren's poetry are greatly influenced by his discussion. See chapter 4, "Self-Invention in Autobiography: The Moment of Language," especially 181–235.

Chapter 10. Toward the Self as Fiction: Language, Time, and Identity in Warren's Poetry, 1966–1975

1. See John Burt's well-reasoned discussion of the relationship between aesthetics and politics in *Warren and American Idealism*, 10–13. While Burt notes that it is difficult "to trace hard continuities between art and politics," he is correct in noting that the two "share a similar logic." Warren's extensive writings on race allow us to trace these continuities a bit more specifically than has been done so far.

2. See, for instance, Calvin Bedient's *In the Heart's Last Kingdom*, Lesa Carnes Corrigan's *Poems of Pure Imagination*, and Harold Bloom's foreword to Warren's *Collected Poems*.

3. See *Collected Poems*, 726.

4. While his poetry of the 1950s similarly often lacked a real sense of closure, Warren now is much more self-conscious regarding the provisional resolutions his poems offer; he often draws attention to the word's inability to apprehend reality.

5. This image of the unopened present also seems to accord with a statement of Lacan: "I identify myself in language, but only by losing myself in it like an object. What is realized in my history is not the past definite of what was, since it is no more, or even the present perfect of what has been in what I am, but the future anterior of what I shall have been for what I am in the process of becoming" (*Écrits*, 86).

6. The same may be said of the entire volume, for Warren's prefatory note describes the volume as "a single long poem composed of a number of shorter poems as sections or chapters" (*CP* 709).

7. For other in-depth readings of *Audubon*, see Bedient, *Heart's Last Kingdom*, 134–45; Burt, *Warren and American Idealism*, 92–111; Corrigan, *Poems of Pure Imagination*, 116–41; Ruppersburg, *American Imagination*, 79–111; and Hummer, "Robert Penn Warren: Audubon and the Moral Center."

8. Most notably, the long narrative that forms part 2 of the sequence has been the focus of much critical attention for its blatant departures from Audubon's own journals. See, for instance, Allen Shepherd, "Warren's *Audubon*."

9. The counterpointing I have in mind here occurs with the sequence's lyrical subsections focusing on nature scenes, all of which were added late in Warren's process of composition as a means of clarifying his themes. For a discussion of Warren's process of composing *Audubon*, see my article "Robert Penn Warren's *Audubon*: Vision and Revision," *Mississippi Quarterly* 47 (1994): 3–14. Also, regarding this theme of separateness, the reader may want to consider Warren's essay "Love and Separateness in Eudora Welty," which clearly informs section 7 of *Audubon*. Critics have discussed the poems's relationship to Welty's short story "A Still Moment." See, for instance, Nancy Cluck, "Audubon: Images of the Artist in Eudora Welty and Robert Penn Warren," and Max Webb, "*Audubon: A Vision*: Robert Penn Warren's Response to Eudora Welty's 'A Still Moment.'"

10. Hugh Ruppersburg discusses the poem's historical and cultural context in *Warren and the American Imagination*, 101.

Conclusion: Warren at the "Inevitable Frontier" of Postmodernism,
1975–1985

1. My comments on the "sublime sentiment" are indebted to Jean-François Lyotard's discussion of Kant in *The Postmodern Condition*, 77–78.

2. See Strandberg, *Poetic Vision*, 60; Bloom, "Sunset Hawk," 195–210; and Burt, *Warren and American Idealism*, 103–6.

3. The figure of a crow functions in a somewhat similar way in Warren's poem "Fog," from the final sequence of *Incarnations*; see *CP*, 248–49.

4. See, for example, "Language Barrier": "The world / Is the language we cannot utter. / Is it a language we can even hear?" (*CP* 421); "Code Book Lost": "Yes, message on message, like wind or water, in light or in dark, / The whole world pours at us. But the code book, somehow, is lost" (*CP* 360); "Truth": "Truth is what you cannot tell. / Truth is for the grave" (*CP* 415); and "What is the Voice that Speaks?": "What tongue knows the name of Truth? Or Truth to come? / All we can do is strive to learn the cost of experience" (*CP* 420).

5. As explained in note 10 to the introduction, my use of the term "postmodernism" is influenced by Lynn Keller's more inclusive definitions of the term in *Re-Making It New*.

6. Charlotte Beck, Victor Strandberg, and, most recently, John Van Dyke have all applied the postmodern label to various aspects of Warren's writing. Beck in "The Postmodernism of Robert Penn Warren" uses the term as an historical marker to designate trends in American poetry beginning in the 1950s and links features of Warren's "new" poetry to these "postmodern" trends—namely, his "frankly subjective I," "looser approach to poetic form," and "composition of poems in sequences" (212). In contrast to this designation of formal features associated with a historical moment in American poetry, Strandberg uses the term to describe more general philosophical assumptions underpinning various aspects of Warren's canon: "a conception of literature as an active agent for social change," "the concept of the self as a social construct that is unstable and non-unitary," and finally, a "willingness to erase the line between high art and popular culture" ("R.P.W. and T.S.E.," 35). John Van Dyke in "Language at the End of Modernism" links Warren with postmodernism through the poet's "growing suspicion about the problems of language" and referentiality (237) and reads *A Plea in Mitigation* in the light of Lyotard's *The Postmodern Condition*.

7. Warren borrows this label from Zbigniew Brzezinski; see page 99, note 20 of *Democracy and Poetry*. Also, it should be noted that by "poetry" Warren means any form of art, but his comments obviously resonate most specifically with his own literary efforts.

8. Warren's numerous comments in his late poetry on the deficiencies of language may perhaps best be understood if we first consider Lyotard's discussion of the Kantian sublime. As Lyotard explains in *The Postmodern Condition*, the sublime

is a "strong and equivocal emotion" that carryies with it "both pleasure and pain" since the sublime sentiment springs from a conflict between the subject's "faculty to conceive of something and the faculty to 'present' something" (77). In short, we experience the sublime sentiment when the capacity to conceive of something outruns our capacity to present it. Importantly, the capacity to *present* the *conceived of* is the basis of the human claim to universal truth and knowledge; the sublime sentiment essentially short-circuits this claim; see 77–79.

9. The contemporary poets Keller discusses are Ashbery, Bishop, Creeley, and Merrill; she compares each to a modern precursor—Stevens, Moore, Williams, and Auden, respectively—in order to define both the contunities and the divergences between the modern and the postmodern in twentieth-century American poetry.

10. It should also be noted that the subtitle of Kierkegaard's *Fear and Trembling* is *A Dialectical Lyric*—a phrase that could very well be used to describe Warren's own poetic practices in his last four collections. Many critics have noticed the dialectical and dialogical qualities of Warren's late poems. As Randolph Runyon has exhaustively demonstrated in *The Braided Dream*, Warren's last four collections may be read as a single continuous poem, with each individual poem connected to others by recurring words, images, phrases, or situations. In a sense, the poems modify one another in what Robert Koppelman describes in *Robert Penn Warren's Modernist Spirituality* as a "continuing dialectic."

11. Bloom mentions Warren's ambivalence toward Ashbery's poetry in a letter from late 1974. In the letter Bloom is discussing his forthcoming *A Map of Misreading*, which includes analyses of poems by Warren, Ashbery, and A. R. Ammons in its concluding chapter, 193–206.

12. Of the several "language-oriented" poets he discusses in his essay "A Genealogy of Postmodernism," Gelpi is most impressed by Susan Howe, Lyn Hejinian, David Bromige, Michael Palmer, and Fanny Howe, whose works "discover new and old possibilities for language to mediate a consciousness of a phenomenal world" (538). In contrast, he is harshly critical of works by Christopher Dewdney and Jackson MacLow, who "would not warrant attention except that they reduce the Postmodernist emphasis on the materiality of language and the anonymity of the speaker to absurdity" (529).

13. While Warren was certainly no Marxist revolutionary, his late work nonetheless stands in opposition to bourgeois complacency. The issue for a contemporary poet, as Vernon Shetley points out in *After the Death of Poetry*, is "whether content or form is the more appropriate locus for oppositional practices" (144). Shetley provides an interesting analysis of "difficulty" and accessibility in contemporary American poetry, offering excellent discussions of Bishop, Merrill, and Ashbery. Also see his criticisms of the Language poets, 135–52. Warren in both *A Plea in Mitigation* and *Democracy and Poetry* addresses at some length the issue of accessibility and the problems of elitism in the arts. For other interesting related discussion of issues of accessibility, audience, and the relationship between Southern po-

etry and major contemporary poetic movements, see Ernest Suarez, "Contemporary Southern Poetry and Critical Practice." Suarez also discusses the problems critics have had in placing Warren amid the landscape of contemporary American poetry.

14. See Blotner, *Robert Penn Warren*, 9; also see Warren, *Collected Poems*, 816.

15. See Warren's analysis of this very type of response in *Who Speaks for the Negro?*, 437.

16. In the poem's closing pages, Warren decided to delete all of the following lines, a decision that has always perplexed Warren scholars:

Fulfillment is only in the degree of recognition
Of the common lot of our kind. And that is the death of vanity,
And that is the beginning of virtue.

The recognition of complicity is the beginning of innocence.
The recognition of necessity is the beginning of freedom.
The recognition of the direction of fulfillment is the death of the self,
And the death of the self is the beginning of selfhood.
All else is surrogate of hope and destitution of spirit. (*BD* 214–15)

17. For example, consider Robert Peters's criticism of *Chief Joseph*. His assessment reflects a growing awareness among critics and scholars of the politics of literary authority and authenticity: "I can't imagine Simon Ortiz, Wendy Rose, Joy Harjo, or a host of other Native American writers will be pleased at seeing their magnificent history reduced to cardboard, to coloring-book history. I can see *Chief Joseph* adapted by some junior high school class, as a pageant; I can't see it inspiring many dedicated poetry readers" (4). A number of critics have attacked Warren's representations of Native Americans in the poem.

Bibliography

Arac, Jonathan. "Repetition and Exclusion: Coleridge and New Criticism Reconsidered." *Boundary 2* 8 (1979): 261–73.

Arendt, Hannah. *The Origins of Totalitarianism.* New York: Harcourt, Brace, 1951.

Beck, Charlotte. "The Postmodernism of Robert Penn Warren." In *To Love So Well the World: A Festschrift in Honor of Robert Penn Warren,* edited by Dennis L. Weeks, 211–21. New York: Peter Lang, 1992.

Bedient, Calvin. *In the Heart's Last Kingdom: Robert Penn Warren's Major Poetry.* Cambridge: Harvard University Press, 1984.

Bloom, Harold. *The Anxiety of Influence: A Theory of Poetry.* New York: Oxford University Press, 1973.

———. Foreword to *The Collected Poems of Robert Penn Warren,* edited by John Burt, xxiii–xxvi. Baton Rouge: Louisiana State University Press, 1998.

———. *A Map of Misreading.* New York: Oxford University Press, 1975.

———. "Sunset Hawk: Warren's Poetry and Tradition." In *Robert Penn Warren,* edited by Harold Bloom, 195–210. Modern Critical Views. New York: Chelsea House, 1986.

Blotner, Joseph. *Robert Penn Warren: A Biography.* New York: Random House, 1997.

Brown, Homer Obed. "The Art of Theology and the Theology of Art: Robert Penn Warren's Reading of Coleridge's *The Rime of the Ancient Mariner.*" *Boundary 2* 8 (1979): 237–60.

Brown, Sterling A. *The Collected Poems of Sterling A. Brown.* Selected by Michael S. Harper. Evanston, Ill.: TriQuarterly Books, 1996.

———. "A Romantic Defense." In *A Son's Return: Selected Essays of Sterling A. Brown,* edited by Mark A. Sanders, 281–83. Boston: Northeastern University Press, 1996.

Burt, John. *Robert Penn Warren and American Idealism.* New Haven: Yale University Press, 1988.

Cain, William E. "Robert Penn Warren, Paul de Man, and the Fate of Criticism." In *The New Criticism and Contemporary Literary Theory: Connections and Con-*

tinuities, edited by William J. Spurlin and Michael Fischer, 297–319. New York: Garland, 1995.

Casper, Leonard. *Robert Penn Warren: The Dark and Bloody Ground.* Seattle: University of Washington Press, 1960.

Clark, William Bedford. *The American Vision of Robert Penn Warren.* Lexington: University of Kentucky Press, 1991.

———. "'Canaan's Grander Counterfeit': Jefferson and America in *Brother to Dragons.*" In *Robert Penn Warren's Brother to Dragons: A Discussion,* edited by James A. Grimshaw Jr., 144–52. Baton Rouge: Louisiana State University Press, 1983.

———. "In the Shadow of His Smile: Warren's Quarrel with Emerson." *Sewanee Review* 102 (1994): 550–69.

Cluck, Nancy. "Audubon: Images of the Artist in Eudora Welty and Robert Penn Warren." *Southern Literary Journal* 17 (1985): 41–53.

Corrigan, Lesa Carnes. *Poems of Pure Imagination: Robert Penn Warren and the Romantic Tradition.* Baton Rouge: Louisiana State University Press, 1999.

Cowan, Louise. *The Fugitive Group: A Literary History.* Baton Rouge: Louisiana State University Press, 1959.

Cullick, Jonathan S. *Making History: The Biographical Narratives of Robert Penn Warren.* Baton Rouge: Louisiana State University Press, 2000.

de Man, Paul. "Autobiography as De-Facement." In *The Rhetoric of Romanticism,* 67–82. New York: Columbia University Press, 1984.

Dooley, Dennis. "The Persona R.P.W. in Warren's *Brother to Dragons.*" In *Robert Penn Warren's Brother to Dragons: A Discussion,* edited by James A. Grimshaw Jr., 101–11. Baton Rouge: Louisiana State University Press, 1983.

Du Bois, W.E.B. *The Souls of Black Folk.* 1903; New York: Bantam, 1989.

Eakin, Paul John. *Fictions in Autobiography: Studies in the Art of Self-Invention.* Princeton: Princeton University Press, 1985.

Eliot, T. S. "The Metaphysical Poets." In *Selected Essays,* 241–50. New York: Harcourt, Brace, 1964.

———. "Tradition and the Individual Talent." In *Selected Essays,* 3–11. New York: Harcourt, Brace, 1964.

———. "Ulysses, Order and Myth." *Dial* 75 (November 1923): 480–83.

Emerson, Ralph Waldo. *Essays: First and Second Series.* New York: Vintage: Library of America, 1990.

Ferriss, Lucy. *Sleeping with the Boss: Female Subjectivity and Narrative Pattern in Robert Penn Warren.* Baton Rouge: Louisiana State University Press, 1997.

Fiedler, Leslie. *Love and Death in the American Novel.* Rev. ed. New York: Stein and Day, 1966.

Flint, F. Cudworth. "Five Poets." *Southern Review* 1 (1936): 658–74.

Fredrickson, George M. *The Black Image in the White Mind: The Debate on Afro-American Character and Destiny, 1817–1914.* New York: Harper and Row, 1971.

Freedman, Carl. "Power, Sexuality, and Race in *All the King's Men.*" In *Southern*

Literature and Literary Theory, edited by Jefferson Humphries, 127–41. Athens: University of Georgia Press, 1990.

Gabbin, Joanne V. *Sterling A. Brown: Building the Black Aesthetic Tradition.* Westport, Conn.: Greenwood Press, 1985.

Gates, Henry Louis, Jr. *Figures in Black: Words, Signs, and the "Racial" Self.* New York and Oxford: Oxford University Press, 1987.

Gates, Henry Louis, Jr., ed. *"Race," Writing, and Difference.* Chicago: University of Chicago Press, 1986.

Gelpi, Albert. *A Coherent Splendor: The American Poetic Renaissance, 1910–1950.* Cambridge: Cambridge University Press, 1987.

———. "The Genealogy of Postmodernism: Contemporary American Poetry." *Southern Review* 26 (1990): 517–41.

Gossett, Thomas F. *Race: The History of an Idea in America.* Dallas: Southern Methodist University Press, 1963.

Grattan, C. Hartley. "New Voices: The Promise of Our Youngest Writers." *Forum and Century* 88 (1932): 284–88.

Gray, Richard. *American Poetry of the Twentieth Century.* London and New York: Longman, 1990.

———. *Writing the South: Ideas of an American Region.* Cambridge: Cambridge University Press, 1986.

Grimshaw, James A., Jr. *Robert Penn Warren: A Descriptive Bibliography 1922–79.* Charlottesville: University Press of Virginia, 1981.

Hale, Grace Elizabeth. *Making Whiteness: The Culture of Segregation in the South, 1890–1940.* New York: Pantheon, 1998.

Hendricks, Randy. *Lonelier than God: Robert Penn Warren and the Southern Exile.* Athens: University of Georgia Press, 2000.

Hobson, Fred. *But Now I See: The White Southern Racial Conversion Narrative.* Baton Rouge: Louisiana State University Press, 1999.

Hughes, Langston. "The Negro Artist and the Racial Mountain." In *The Heath Anthology of American Literature,* edited by Paul Lauter et al., 2d ed., 2:1630–33. Lexington, Mass.: D.C. Heath, 1994.

Hummer, T. R. "Robert Penn Warren: Audubon and the Moral Center." *Southern Review* 16 (1980): 803–10.

Inge, Thomas M. "The Fugitives and the Agrarians: A Clarification." *American Literature* 62 (1990): 486–93.

Jackson, Richard. "The Generous Time: Robert Penn Warren and the Phenomenology of the Moment." *Boundary 2* 9 (1981): 1–30.

Jameson, Fredric. *Fables of Aggression: Wyndham Lewis, the Modernist as Fascist.* Berkeley and Los Angeles: University of California Press, 1979.

———. *The Political Unconscious: Narrative as a Socially Symbolic Act.* Ithaca, N.Y.: Cornell University Press, 1981.

Jancovich, Mark. *The Cultural Politics of the New Criticism.* Cambridge: Cambridge University Press, 1993.

Jarrell, Randall. Review of *Brother to Dragons*, by Robert Penn Warren. In *Robert Penn Warren's Brother to Dragons: A Discussion*, edited by James A. Grimshaw Jr., 161–62. Baton Rouge: Louisiana State University Press, 1983.

Jefferson, Thomas. *Notes on the State of Virginia*. New York: Harper and Row, 1964.

Johnson, Karen Ramsay. "'Voices in My Own Blood':The Dialogic Impulse in Warren's Non-Fiction Writings about Race." *Mississippi Quarterly* 52 (1999): 33–45.

Justus, James. *The Achievement of Robert Penn Warren*. Baton Rouge: Louisiana State University Press, 1981.

Kauvar, Elaine M. "This Doubly Reflected Communication: Philip Roth's 'Autobiographies.'" *Contemporary Literature* 36 (1995): 412–46.

Keller, Lynn. *Re-Making It New: Contemporary American Poetry and the Modernist Tradition*. Cambridge: Cambridge University Press, 1987.

Kermode, Frank. *The Sense of an Ending: Studies in the Theory of Fiction*. New York: Oxford University Press, 1967.

Kierkegaard, Søren. *Fear and Trembling, and The Sickness Unto Death*. Translated by Walter Lowrie. Garden City, N.Y.: Doubleday, 1954.

Koppelman, Robert S. *Robert Penn Warren's Modernist Spirituality*. Columbia: University of Missouri Press, 1995.

Kreyling, Michael. *Inventing Southern Literature*. Jackson: University Press of Mississippi, 1998.

Lacan, Jacques. *Écrits: A Selection*. Translated by Alan Sheridan. New York: Norton, 1977.

———. *The Four Fundamental Concepts of Psycho-analysis*. Edited by Jacques-Alain Miller. Translated by Alan Sheridan. New York: Norton, 1981.

Levenson, Michael H. *A Genealogy of Modernism: A Study of English Literary Doctrine, 1908–1922*. Cambridge: Cambridge University Press, 1984.

Longenbach, James. *Modern Poetry After Modernism*. New York and Oxford: Oxford University Press, 1997.

Lyotard, Jean-François. *The Postmodern Condition: A Report on Knowledge*. Translated by Geoff Bennington and Brian Massumi. Minneapolis: University of Minnesota Press, 1984

McGann, Jerome J. *The Romantic Ideology: A Critical Investigation*. Chicago: University of Chicago Press, 1983.

Miller, Mark D. "Faith in Good Works: The Salvation of Robert Penn Warren." *Mississippi Quarterly* 48 (1995): 57–72.

Morrison, Toni. *Playing in the Dark: Whiteness and the Literary Imagination*. Cambridge: Harvard University Press, 1992.

Nelson, Cary. *Repression and Recovery: Modern American Poetry and the Politics of Cultural Memory, 1910–1945*. Madison: University of Wisconsin Press, 1989.

Niebuhr, Reinhold. *The Nature and Destiny of Man*. New York: Scribner's, 1949.

Nielsen, Aldon Lynn. *Reading Race: White American Poets and the Racial Discourse in the Twentieth Century*. Athens: University of Georgia Press, 1988.

North, Michael. *The Dialect of Modernism: Race, Language, and Twentieth-Century Literature.* New York and Oxford: Oxford University Press, 1994.

O'Connor, Flannery. "A Good Man Is Hard to Find." In *A Good Man Is Hard to Find, and Other Stories,* 9–29. New York: Harcourt, Brace and World, 1955.

O'Kane, Karen. "Before the New Criticism: Modernism and the Nashville Group." *Mississippi Quarterly* 51 (1998): 683–97.

Owsley, Frank Lawrence. "The Irrepressible Conflict." In *I'll Take My Stand: The South and the Agrarian Tradition,* by Twelve Southerners, 61–91. New York: Harper and Brothers, 1930; Baton Rouge: Louisiana State University Press, 1977.

———. "Scottsboro, the Third Crusade: The Sequel to Abolition and Reconstruction." *American Review* 1 (June 1933): 257–85.

Perkins, James A. "Racism and the Personal Past in Robert Penn Warren's Poetry." *Mississippi Quarterly* 48 (1995): 73–82.

Perloff, Marjorie. *The Poetics of Indeterminacy: Rimbaud to Cage.* Princeton: Princeton University Press, 1981.

Peters, Robert. Review of *Chief Joseph of the Nez Perce,* by Robert Penn Warren. *American Book Review* 6 (November–December 1983): 3–4.

Polsgrove, Carol. *Divided Minds: Intellectuals and the Civil Rights Movement.* New York: W. W. Norton, 2001.

Ransom, John Crowe. *Selected Letters of John Crowe Ransom.* Edited by Thomas Daniel Young and George Core. Baton Rouge: Louisiana State University Press, 1985.

Raper, Porter G. "Southern Identity and Myth in 'Pondy Woods.'" *Southern Quarterly* 30 (1991): 19–23.

Robinson, Forrest G. "A Combat with the Past: Robert Penn Warren on Race and Slavery." *American Literature* 67 (1995): 511–30.

Rubin, Louis D., Jr. Introduction to *I'll Take My Stand: The South and the Agrarian Tradition,* by Twelve Southerners, xi–xxxv. Baton Rouge: Louisiana State University Press, 1977.

Runyon, Randolph Paul. *The Braided Dream: Robert Penn Warren's Late Poetry.* Lexington: University Press of Kentucky, 1991.

Ruppersburg, Hugh. *Robert Penn Warren and the American Imagination.* Athens: University of Georgia Press, 1990.

Sanders, Mark A., ed. *A Son's Return: Selected Essays of Sterling A. Brown.* Boston: Northeastern University Press, 1996.

Sarcone, Elizabeth, and Thomas Daniel Young, eds. *The Lytle-Tate Letters: The Correspondence of Andrew Lytle and Allen Tate.* Jackson: University Press of Mississippi, 1987.

Schaub, Thomas Hill. *American Fiction in the Cold War.* Madison: University of Wisconsin Press, 1991.

Scott, Nathan A., Jr. *Visions of Presence in Modern American Poetry.* Baltimore: Johns Hopkins University Press, 1993.

Shepherd, Allen. "Warren's *Audubon*: 'Issues in Purer Form' and 'The Ground Rules of Fact.'" *Mississippi Quarterly* 24 (1971): 47–56.

Shetley, Vernon. *After the Death of Poetry: Poet and Audience in Contemporary America*. Durham: Duke University Press, 1993.

"Sin Rediscovered." Review of *The Nature and Destiny of Man*, by Reinhold Niebuhr. *Time*, March 24, 1941, p. 38.

Singal, Daniel Joseph. *The War Within: From Victorian to Modernist Thought in the South, 1919–1945*. Chapel Hill: University of North Carolina Press, 1982.

Siskin, Clifford. *The Historicity of Romantic Discourse*. New York and Oxford: Oxford University Press, 1988.

Stewart, John L. *The Burden of Time: The Fugitives and Agrarians*. Princeton: Princeton University Press, 1965.

Stitt, Peter. *The World's Hieroglyphic Beauty: Five American Poets*. Athens: University of Georgia Press, 1985.

Strandberg, Victor. *The Poetic Vision of Robert Penn Warren*. Lexington: University Press of Kentucky, 1977.

———. "R.P.W. and T.S.E.: In the Steps of the (Post)Modern Master." In *To Love So Well the World: A Festschrift in Honor of Robert Penn Warren*, edited by Dennis L. Weeks, 29–43. New York: Peter Lang, 1992.

———. "Warren's Osmosis." In *Critical Essays on Robert Penn Warren*, edited by William Bedford Clark, 122–36. Boston: G. K. Hall, 1981.

Suarez, Ernest. "Contemporary Southern Poetry and Critical Practice." *Southern Review* 30 (1994): 674–88.

Thiemann, Fred R. "Politics and the Self in Robert Penn Warren's Poetry." *South Atlantic Review* 64 (1996): 83–96.

Van Dyke, John. "Language at the End of Modernism: Robert Penn Warren's *A Plea in Mitigation*." *Mississippi Quarterly* 53 (2000): 237–50.

Walker, Marshall. *Robert Penn Warren: A Vision Earned*. New York: Barnes and Noble, 1979.

Warren, Robert Penn. *All the King's Men*. New York: Harcourt, Brace and World, 1946; reprint, San Diego: Harcourt Brace Jovanovich, 1982.

———. Author's note in *Modern Poetry: American and British*, edited by Kimon Friar and John Malcolm Brinnin, 541–43. New York: Appleton-Century-Crofts, 1951.

———. *Band of Angels*. New York: Random House, 1955.

———. "Blackberry Winter." In *The Circus in the Attic, and Other Stories*, 163–87. New York: Harcourt, Brace, 1947.

———. "'Blackberry Winter': A Recollection." In *Understanding Fiction*, edited by Cleanth Brooks and Robert Penn Warren, 2d ed., 638–43. New York: Appleton-Century-Crofts, 1959.

———. "The Blind Poet: Sidney Lanier." *American Review* 2 (November 1933): 27–45.

———. "The Briar Patch." In *I'll Take My Stand: The South and the Agrarian Tra-

dition, by Twelve Southerners, 246–64. New York: Harper and Brothers, 1930;
Baton Rouge: Louisiana State University Press, 1977.

———. *Brother to Dragons: A Tale in Verse and Voices.* New York: Random House,
1953.

———. *Brother to Dragons: A New Version.* New York: Random House, 1979.

———. *The Collected Poems of Robert Penn Warren.* Edited by John Burt. Foreword
by Harold Bloom. Baton Rouge: Louisiana State University Press, 1998.

———. *Democracy and Poetry.* Cambridge: Harvard University Press, 1975.

———. "Episode in the Dime Store." *Southern Review* 30 (1994): 654–57.

———. *Flood: A Romance of Our Time.* New York: Random House, 1964.

———. "Hawthorne, Anderson and Frost." *New Republic* 54 (May 16, 1928): 399–
401.

———. "Her Own People." In *The Circus in the Attic, and Other Stories,* 175–89.
New York: Harcourt, Brace, 1947.

———. *John Brown: The Making of a Martyr.* New York: Payson and Clarke, 1929.

———. "John Crowe Ransom: A Study in Irony." *Virginia Quarterly Review* 11
(1935): 93–112.

———. "Knowledge and the Image of Man." *Sewanee Review* 63 (1955): 182–92.

———. *The Legacy of the Civil War: Meditations on the Centennial.* New York:
Random House, 1961.

———. "Literature as a Symptom." In *Who Owns America? A New Declaration of
Independence,* edited by Herbert Agar and Allen Tate, 264–79. Boston: Houghton
Mifflin, 1936.

———. "Love and Separateness in Eudora Welty." In *Selected Essays,* 156–69. New
York: Random House, 1958.

———. Papers. Yale Collection of American Literature. Beinecke Rare Book and
Manuscript Library, Yale University.

———. *A Plea in Mitigation: Modern Poetry and the End of an Era.* Macon, Ga.:
Wesleyan College, 1966.

———. "A Poem of Pure Imagination: An Experiment in Reading." In *New and
Selected Essays,* 335–423. New York: Random House, 1989.

———. "The Present State of Poetry: In the United States." *Kenyon Review* 1
(1939): 384–98.

———. "The Romantic Strain." *New Republic* 53 (November 23, 1927): 23–24.

———. *Segregation: The Inner Conflict in the South.* New York: Random House,
1956.

———. *Selected Letters of Robert Penn Warren.* Vol. 1, *The Apprentice Years, 1924–
1934.* Edited by William Bedford Clark. Baton Rouge: Louisiana State University
Press, 2000.

———. "The Situation in American Writing Part II." *Partisan Review* 6 (fall 1939):
112–13.

———. "Some Don'ts for Literary Regionalists." *American Review* 8 (December
1936): 142–50.

————. "Straws in the Wind." *Poetry* 48 (June 1936): 172–75.

————. "The Use of the Past." In *New and Selected Essays*, 29–53. New York: Random House, 1989.

————. *Who Speaks for the Negro?* New York: Random House, 1965.

Watkins, Floyd C., John T. Hiers, and Mary Louise Weaks, eds. *Talking with Robert Penn Warren*. Athens: University of Georgia Press, 1990.

Watkins, Floyd C. *Then & Now: The Personal Past in the Poetry of Robert Penn Warren*. Lexington: University Press of Kentucky, 1982.

Webb, Max. "*Audubon: A Vision:* Robert Penn Warren's Response to Eudora Welty's 'A Still Moment.'" *Mississippi Quarterly* 34 (1981): 445–55.

Williams, Raymond. *The Politics of Modernism: Against the New Conformists*. London: Verso, 1989.

Winchell, Mark Royden. "O Happy Sin!: *Felix Culpa* in *All the King's Men*." *Mississippi Quarterly* 31 (1978): 570–85.

Index

Abraham (Genesis), 206

"Afterthought" (*Being Here*), 171

"Aged Man Surveys the Past Time," 47

Agrarianism, 1, 5, 6, 12–13, 26–27, 29, 32, 39, 42, 106–8, 220n.4. *See also* Warren, Robert Penn, and Agrarianism

"Alf Burt: Tenant Farmer," 15, 23–24

All the King's Men, 57, 58, 61–66, 67, 79, 83

"Altitudes and Extensions," 206

"America and the Diminished Self," 204

Anderson, Sherwood, 43–44

"Anniversary, The" (Donne), 52

"Antique Harvesters" (Ransom), 24

Anti-Semitism, 81–82, 86

Arendt, Hannah, 86–87

Ashbery, John, 208–9

At Heaven's Gate, 57, 58, 65

"At the Hour of the Breaking of the Rocks," 22, 221n.13

"Aubade for Hope," 47

Audubon, John James, 191, 194

Audubon: A Vision, 173, 189–98, 209

Augustine, Saint, 205

"August Revival: Crosby Junction," 15, 23–24

Baldwin, James, 142, 149–51, 216

"Ballad of Billie Potts, The," 55

"Ballad of a Sweet Dream of Peace," 126–27

"Ballad of Mister Dutcher and the Last Lynching in Gupton," 153–54, 180

Band of Angels, 58, 73, 98–100

"Bearded Oaks," 52

Bedient, Calvin, 112, 173, 177

Being Here, 155, 206

Bernstein, Charles, 209

Bilbo, Theodore, 147

Birds of America (Audubon), 194

Birmingham Church Bombing, 141

"Blackberry Winter," 61, 66–71, 127

"Blackberry Winter: A Recollection," 66–67, 70

Blake, William, 158

"Blind Poet, The," 50

Bloom, Harold, 7, 59, 111–13, 201, 209

Blotner, Joseph, 2

Boers, 86–87

"Briar Patch, The," 2, 16, 42, 47, 58–59, 77, 102; argument of, 33–34; on black economic opportunity, 34–35; on black radicalism, 35–38; compared with later works, 143, 144, 148, 155, 162; contradictions within, 34; critics' responses to, 26–33; origins of, 14–15; paternalism and, 38

"Brotherhood in Pain," 140, 175, 177–78

Brother to Dragons, 98, 109, 118, 132, 140, 159, 177, 188; Aunt Cat in, 94–96; as breakthrough for Warren, 4–5, 57, 58, 72, 77–78, 111; composition process of, 227n.13; and determinism, 92–93; and "development" (Romantic), 79–80, 117; form of, 87–88; influences on, 85–87; and racism, 88–92; revised version of, 215, 227n.9, 238n.16; Romantic resolution of, 96–97; and R.P.W., 83–85

Brown, John, 13–14, 145

Brown, Sterling, 8–11, 26–27, 219n.3

Brown v. Board of Education, 80, 82, 100
Burt, John, 4, 62, 64, 122, 132, 167, 191, 194, 201

"Canonization, The," (Donne), 52
Carr, Geraldine, 212
Carrel, Alexis, 53–54
"Chain Saw at Dawn in Vermont in Time of Drouth," 180–81
Chief Joseph of the Nez Perce, 238n.17
Child, Lydia Maria, 13
Circus in the Attic and Other Stories, The, 57
Civil Rights Act, 141
Civil rights movement, 135, 141–42, 153
Civil War, 68, 104
Clark, Eleanor, 81
Clark, Felton, 146
Clark, William Bedford, 30–32, 40, 59, 83, 117–18
"Code Book Lost," 236n.4
"Colder Fire," 120, 123, 124–25
Coleridge, Samuel Taylor, 63–64, 67, 73, 75, 111–13
Collected Poems of Robert Penn Warren, 4
Collins, Seward, 40
Communism, 42
"Conflict of Convictions, The" (Melville), 68
Congress of Racial Equality, 141
Corrigan, Lesa Carnes, 5, 72–73, 76, 81
Creeley, Robert, 209
Criterion, 45
"Croesus in Autumn," 15, 23
Cullick, Jonathan, 62, 77, 79

"Dark Night of," 127–29
Davidson, Donald, 12, 14, 29, 30, 31, 32, 65, 221n.12
"Debate: Question, Quarry, Dream," 130, 132
de Man, Paul, 138, 154, 155, 169–71, 195
Democracy and Poetry, 54–55, 119, 174, 204–6, 211
Derrida, Jacques, 17, 138, 181
"Divided South Searches Its Soul," 100
Dixiecrats, 82

Donne, John, 48
Dooley, Dennis, 83, 84
DuBois, W.E.B., 10, 11, 33, 35–36, 37

Eakin, Paul John, 154, 170
"Easter Morning: Crosby Junction," 15, 23
"Eidolon," 47
Eleven Poems on the Same Theme, 52–53
Eliot, T. S., 1, 4, 6, 12, 25, 55, 134. *See also* Warren, Robert Penn, Eliot's influence on
Ellison, Ralph, 78, 142, 149, 151
Emerson, Ralph Waldo, 13, 113, 117–18, 127, 128, 192
Evers, Charles, 147–48
Evers, Medgar, 141, 147–48

Fascism, 44, 53–54, 136
Faulkner, William, 61, 129, 150, 217n.1
Fear and Trembling (Kierkegaard), 206–7
"Fear and Trembling," 206–9
Fiedler, Leslie, 98
Flint, F. Cudworth, 55–56
Flood, 73, 233n.16
"Flower, The," 122–24
"Forever O'Clock," 155–56, 161–65, 213
Freedman, Carl, 62
Fugitive poets, 27, 39, 42. *See also* Warren, Robert Penn, and Fugitive poets

Gabbin, Joanne V., 9
"Garden, The," 50–52
"Garden Waters," 15, 23
Garrison, William Lloyd, 13
Gates, Henry Louis, Jr., 27
Gelpi, Albert, 6, 209
"Good Man Is Hard to Find, A" (O'Connor), 162
Gordon, Caroline, 39, 42
Gossett, Thomas F., 81–82
Grattan, C. Hartley, 39–40, 41–44, 47
Gray, Richard, 12

Hale, Grace Elizabeth, 21, 36–37
Harlem Renaissance, 37
"Hawthorne, Anderson and Frost," 43–44
Heidegger, Martin, 156, 181, 182–83, 185, 190

Hendricks, Randy, 66, 76
"Her Own People," 58–61, 68
"Homage to Emerson," 132
Howe, Susan, 209
Hughes, Langston, 59–60

"I Am Dreaming of a White Christmas: The Natural History of a Vision," 156, 183, 184–88, 193
I'll Take My Stand, 12–13, 14–15, 25, 26–27, 28, 29, 33
"In a Station of the Metro" (Pound), 19
Incarnations, 155, 173
"Inevitable Frontier," 202, 210–11
Inge, M. Thomas, 13
"In Moonlight, Somewhere, They Are Singing," 129
"Interim, The," 130–32
"Interjection #1: The Need for Re-evaluation," 180, 183
"Interjection #2: Caveat," 183, 188
"Internal Injuries," 155, 156–61
International Labor Defense, 40

Jackson, Richard, 180–81, 182–83, 184, 190
Jancovich, Mark, 73
Jefferson, Thomas, 83, 84, 86, 87, 90–91, 92
Jessup, Jack, 100
John Brown, 13–14, 15, 145, 222n.17
"John Crowe Ransom: A Study in Irony," 46–47
Johnson, Karen Ramsay, 197
Joyce, James, 43–44
Jung, Carl, 164
Justus, James, 102, 145

Kauvar, Elaine M., 154
Keats, John, 177
Keller, Lynn, 206
Kennedy, Robert, 197
"Kentucky Mountain Farm," 15, 21–23, 24, 221n.13
Kierkegaard, Søren, 205, 206–7
King, Martin Luther, Jr. 141, 147–48, 149, 197
"Knowledge and the Image of Man," 73, 135, 144, 150; and "osmosis of being," 63,

75–76, 97, 113–14, 129, 188; and personal voice, 77; Romantic premises of, 78, 79, 114–19; and self-division, 106
Koppelman, Robert S., 28, 31, 76, 120–21, 202
Ku Klux Klan, 12, 37

Lacan, Jacques, 138, 194
"Language Barrier," 231n.12, 236n.4
Language poets, 208–9
"Last Meeting," 212–13
"Last Metaphor, The," 15, 24
"Last Night Train," 212, 213–15
Legacy of the Civil War, 73, 76, 104
"Letter From a Coward to a Hero," 47
"Letter to a Friend," 47
Levenson, Michael, 45, 48
Lewis, Wyndham, 44
"Literature as Symptom," 50
"Love and Knowledge," 194–95
"Love Song of J. Alfred Prufrock, The" (Eliot), 48
"Love's Parable," 52–53
Lowe, Robert Liddell, 48
Lowell, Robert, 85, 209
"Lullaby: A Motion Like Sleep," 125–26
Lynching, 33, 36–37
Lyotard, Jean-François, 203–4, 205, 206, 208–9
Lytle, Andrew, 14

Mabry, Thomas, 40
Malcolm X, 141, 149
Map of Misreading, A (Bloom), 209
Marshall, Thurgood, 34
Marvell, Andrew, 48, 50–51
Melville, Herman, 59, 67, 68
"Metaphysical Poets, The," (Eliot), 46
Miller, Mark D., 57, 81
Miscegenation, 19–20, 98, 108, 223n.3
Mitchell, Margaret, 98
Modernism, 1, 4, 6–7, 44–45, 134–35, 136–37, 217n.3, 218n.8, 220n.4. *See also* Warren, Robert Penn, and modernism
"Modern Poetry, or Modernism in Poetry," 48–49
"Monologue at Midnight," 52

Montgomery bus boycott, 141
"Moon, The" 221n.13
Morrison, Toni, 2–3
"Mortmain," 130
Moss, Howard, 164–65, 169, 197
"Mountain Plateau," 199–201, 206

NAACP, 33, 36–37, 40, 141, 147
Nature and Destiny of Man, The (Niebuhr),
    85–86
"Nature of a Mirror, The" 179–80
Nazism, 53–54, 81–82, 87
"Negro Artist and the Racial Mountain,
    The," 59–60
New and Selected Poems: 1923–1985, 206
New Criticism, 134, 137, 138–39, 220n.4,
    220n.6. *See also* Warren, Robert Penn,
    and New Criticism
"News Photo,"153–54
"New Voices: The Promise of Our Youngest
    Writers" (Grattan), 39–40, 41–44
New Yorker, The, 164, 169
Niebuhr, Reinhold, 85–86
Nielsen, Aldon Lynn, 10, 11, 17, 93, 96, 103
"Nigger, Nigger, Burning Bright" (unpub-
    lished poem), 158, 234n.4
Night Rider, 58, 65
Notes on the State of Virginia (Jefferson),
    90–91
Now and Then, 199, 206

O'Connor, Flannery, 162
"Ode on a Grecian Urn" (Keats), 177
"Ode to the Confederate Dead" (Tate), 24
"Old Man Buzzard" (Brown), 9–10, 219n.3
"Old Mansion" (Ransom), 24
"Old Nigger on One-Mule Cart Encoun-
    tered Late at Night When Driving Home
    from Party in the Back Country," 155–
    56, 165–71, 177, 213, 214, 215
Olney, James, 154
Onan (Genesis), 53–54
Or Else, 155, 179–80, 183, 188, 189, 209
Origins of Totalitarianism, The (Arendt),
    86–87
"Owl, The," 221n.13
Owsley, Frank Lawrence, 41

Peale, Norman Vincent, 85–86
Penhally (Gordon), 39, 42
Perkins, James A., 57
Perloff, Marjorie, 209
Phillips, Wendell, 13
"Picnic Remembered," 52
Playing in the Dark (Morrison), 2–3
Plea in Mitigation, A, 134–38, 148
Poem of Pure Imagination, A, 73
Poems About God (Ransom), 47
"Poet, The" (Emerson), 117–18
"Poetry and Selfhood," 204
"Pondy Woods" (poem), 8–10, 15, 16–18,
    19, 20–21, 23, 96, 144, 153
"Pondy Woods" (poetic sequence), 15–25,
    32, 42, 47
"Pondy Woods and Other Poems" (unpub-
    lished collection), 15, 221n.14
Postmodern Condition, The (Lyotard),
    203–4
Postmodernism, 1, 5, 6–7, 136, 203–4, 208–
    9, 218n.10. *See also* Warren, Robert
    Penn, and postmodernism
Poststructuralism, 137–38
Powell v. Alabama, 40
Power of Positive Thinking, The (Peale),
    85–86
Pound, Ezra, 1, 4, 19, 44, 48, 134
Prelude, The (Wordsworth), 125
"Present State of Poetry, The" 55–56, 81
President's Committee on Civil Rights, 82
Promises, 110, 119, 120, 125, 127
Proud Flesh, 65
"Pursuit," 53

Race: and identity, 59–61, 98–99, 146, 174,
    220n.4, 220n.5, 233n.16; and racial dis-
    course, 9–11, 37, 220n.5, 222n.3. *See also*
    Warren, Robert Penn: and "black gaze";
    racial representations in writings of; and
    racism
Ransom, John Crowe, 12, 14, 24, 39, 42, 45,
    52
Raper, Porter G., 17
"Reading Late at Night, Thermometer Fall-
    ing," 185
"Rebuke of the Rocks," 21–22, 221n.13

"Red-Tail Hawk and Pyre of Youth," 111–13

"Return, The," 22–23, 221n.13

"Return: An Elegy, The," 47, 132

Rime of the Ancient Mariner (Coleridge), 64, 73, 111–13

Robinson, Forrest, 99

Robinson, Jackie, 82

Romanticism, 1, 6–7, 49–50, 129–30, 217n.3, 218n.8. *See also* Warren, Robert Penn, and Romanticism

"Romantic Strain, The," 43

Rubin, Louis D., Jr., 26, 32

Rumor Verified, 206

Ruppersburg, Hugh, 11, 17, 20–21, 30–31, 33, 84, 157

Russell, Bertrand, 205

Sanders, Mark A., 27

"Saul at Gilboa," 230n.9

Scopes trial, 12, 13, 37

Scottsboro case, 12, 33, 40–41, 143

"Scottsboro, the Third Crusade" (Owsley), 41

Segregation: The Inner Conflict in the South, 3, 133, 153; and critical response to "The Briar Patch," 28, 31, 32; origins of, 100; and personal voice, 101–2, 108–10; and self-division, 106–8; and sense of guilt, 102–3; and Warren's changing views of history, 104–6; and Warren's poetic breakthrough, 57, 58, 73, 76, 77–78, 79–80, 82; and *Who Speaks for the Negro?*, 142, 143

Selected Poems: 1923–1943, 5, 57

Selected Poems: 1923–1975, 155, 175

Selected Poems: New and Old, 1923–1966, 110, 119, 134

Shakespeare, William, 53–54

Shelley, Percy Bysshe, 122

Silliman, Ron, 209

Singal, Daniel Joseph, 29, 31

Siskin, Clifford, 78, 114, 171

Sitwell, Edith, 43

"So Frost Astounds," 47

"Some Quiet, Plain Poems," 129–30

Souls of Black Folk, The (DuBois), 35

South, The: Agrarian myth of, 106–7, 171; and *Brown v. Board of Education* decision, 82, 100, 101–2, 104–7, 141; and civil rights movement, 141–42; and legacy of slavery, 62, 63–64, 85; resistance to change in, 143–44; segregationist culture of, 21; social changes in 1920s, 12–13

Southern Christian Leadership Council, 141

Southern Review, The, 55

Spanish Civil War, 53

Stein, Gertrude, 209

Stevens, Wallace, 155, 209

Stewart, John L., 29, 31

Stitt, Peter, 3

Stowe, Harriet Beecher, 13

Strandberg, Victor, 4, 50, 119, 126, 127, 129, 159, 187, 201

"Straws in the Wind," 48

Student Nonviolent Coordinating Committee, 141

"Tale of Time," 130–33, 148

Tale of Time, 119

Tate, Allen, 12, 14, 24, 33, 39, 42, 45, 66, 143

"Tell Me a Story," 196

Tender Buttons (Stein), 209

"Terror," 53–54, 55

"There's a Grandfather's Clock in the Hall," 181–82

Thiemann, Fred, 139, 140

Thirty-Six Poems, 25, 47, 50, 55

Thoreau, Henry David, 13

Thurmond, Strom, 82

"To a Face in the Crowd," 55

"To a Little Girl, One Year Old, in a Ruined Fortress," 120–21, 122–25

"Tradition and the Individual Talent" (Eliot), 25, 49–50

Truman, Harry, 82

"Truth," 236n.4

"Trying to Tell You Something," 175–77, 189

"Tryst on Vinegar Hill," 15, 17–20, 21, 23, 96, 143, 144, 153, 214

Twain, Mark, 98

"Tyger, The" (Blake), 158

Ulysses (Joyce), 43–44, 45

"Unless," 203

"Use of the Past, The" 180

"Valediction: Forbidding Mourning, A"
   (Donne), 52
Vico, Giovanni Battista, 205
Voting Rights Act, 141

Walker, Marshall, 299–30, 36, 111
Walker, Wyatt Tee, 149
Warren, Robert Penn: aesthetic changes of,
   1–2, 4–6, 61–62, 70–71, 72–81, 119–20,
   135, 173–75; and Agrarianism, 1, 5, 6,
   12–13, 47, 80–81, 91, 106–8, 161, 204–5;
   and autobiographical voice, 50, 58, 61,
   65–67, 70–71, 74–75, 77–78, 83–84, 87–
   88, 108–9, 140–41, 148, 151, 154–55,
   156–57, 169–71; and "black gaze," 64,
   88–92, 159, 228n.14; and black radicalism,
   35–38, 142; and changing views on race,
   1–3, 58, 100–104, 106–7; and commu-
   nism, 39; conflicting poetic theories of,
   4–5, 111–13, 135; and determinism, 46,
   55, 62, 65, 74, 78, 79–80, 92–93, 99, 100,
   104–5, 108, 114–15, 146, 226n.5, 226n.7;
   and "development" (Romantic discourse
   of), 75, 78–79, 114–17, 118, 121–22, 133,
   135, 144, 155, 159–60; developmental
   views of his canon, 4, 28–29, 30–32,
   229n.5; and "diagnostic" poetry, 6, 54–55;
   and early bias against Romanticism, 49–
   50; Eliot's influence on, 44–48; and "felix
   culpa," 79, 116–17, 144; and first mar-
   riage, 52, 81; on first-person narratives,
   65–66; as formalist, 47–48, 51, 113, 118–
   19; and Fugitive poets, 5, 12–13, 80; and
   history (changing views of), 104–8; and
   imitation, 48–49; on identity (see War-
   ren, Robert Penn, on selfhood and iden-
   tity); on the individual (see Warren,
   Robert Penn, on selfhood and identity);
   integrationist views of, 29, 30, 32, 73, 76–
   77, 100, 103–4, 106–8, 153; and integra-
   tion (as trope in works), 7, 76–77; and
   Jack Burden, 65, 74, 79; and language, 7,
   136, 137–40, 147–48, 152, 170–71, 174–
   76, 178–79, 180, 189, 192–93, 197, 199–
   208, 210–12; and modernism, 1, 4, 6–7,
   25, 44–56, 74, 76, 108, 113, 134–35, 136–
   37; and naturalism (see determinism);
   and New Criticism, 1, 73, 74, 134, 137,
   138–39; and "osmosis of being" (see
   "Knowledge and the Image of Man," and
   "osmosis of being"); and postmodernism,
   1, 5, 6–7, 133, 203–6, 208–12, 236n.6; ra-
   cial representations in writings of, 11–12,
   17–21, 59–61, 64, 67–70, 84, 88–92, 94–
   96, 102–3, 130–32, 141–42, 156–59, 162,
   166–68, 212–16; and racism, 27–28, 91–
   92, 93–94, 156–58, 233n.18; regional bias
   of, 12–15, 145; and relationship between
   his politics and aesthetics, 2, 4–6, 41–47,
   58, 72–82, 100, 108–10, 117, 135–36,
   165–66, 173–74, 196–97; on relationship
   of poetry to fiction, 3, 61; and romance in
   fiction, 58, 62; and Romanticism, 1, 4–5,
   6–7, 58, 72–73, 75, 76, 78–79, 96–97,
   111–22, 125, 132–33, 171–72, 214–15; on
   Scottsboro case, 40–41; and second mar-
   riage, 81; on segregation and slavery as
   moral issues, 13–14, 103–4, 106; on seg-
   regation as an economic issue, 38; segre-
   gationist views of, 1, 25, 29, 30, 32–38;
   on selfhood and identity, 5, 6–7, 55, 74,
   98–99, 106, 119, 135, 137–41, 145–51,
   154–56, 164–65, 171, 174–75, 179–93,
   233n.19; and sequencing of poems, 15–
   16, 209, 235n.9, 237n.10; and ten-year
   poetic impasse, 4–5, 57–58, 72, 81; and
   "therapeutic" poetry, 7, 54–55, 77, 114,
   119, 204–6; and time, 121–22, 164–65,
   174–75, 178–90; and tradition, 9, 25, 44–
   45, 47, 48–49, 78, 100, 105, 145, 204. See
   also titles of individual works
Warren, Rosanna, 120, 122
"Wart, The" 132
Washington, Booker T., 33, 35, 103
Waste Land, The (Eliot), 25, 45
Watts riots, 142
"What is the Voice that Speaks," 236n.4
Whitman, Walt, 113, 117–18, 127
"Whole Question, The" 201–2
Who Owns America?, 47

Who Speaks for the Negro?, 3, 5, 109, 133, 135, 136, 153, 197; and critical response to "The Briar Patch," 28, 31, 32; and "felix culpa," 79; origins of, 141, and personal voice, 77, 109, 141–42; as testing ground for Warren, 73, 76; and Warren's altering views of selfhood, 146–52; and Warren's confrontation with his past, 142–46

Wilderness, 73, 132
Williams, Raymond, 48
Winesburg, Ohio (Anderson), 43
Wordsworth, William, 113, 125, 127
World Enough and Time, 57, 58
World War II, 80–82, 85, 108

Yeats, William Butler, 112, 134
You, Emperors, and Others, 119, 129

Anthony Szczesiul is assistant professor of English at the University of Massachusetts, Lowell, where he teaches courses in American literature, modern poetry, Southern literature, and film.